Dear Bill —

Trains may come or go, but OLD Pepper sass (pg. 73) there was an engine if there ever was one —

Best

James

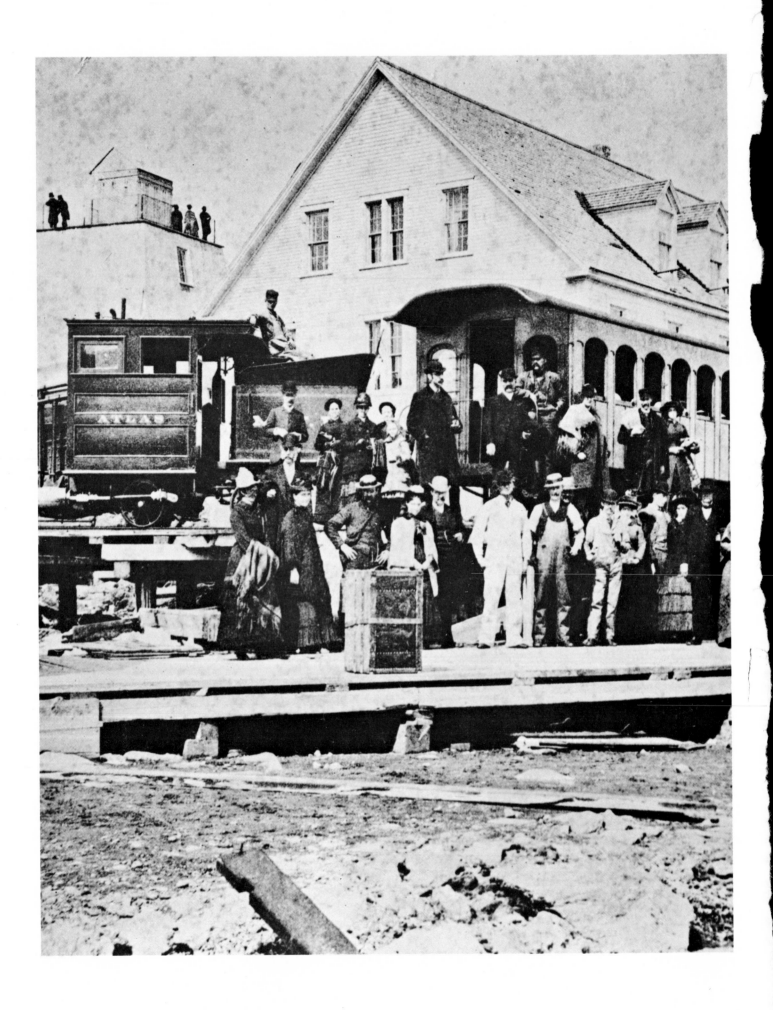

YANKEES UNDER STEAM

Edited by

Austin N. Stevens

Foreword by

Lynwood Bryant

*An anthology of the best stories
on the world of steam
published in Yankee Magazine
since 1935*

༺✦༻

Art Editor

Margo Letourneau

PUBLISHED BY YANKEE, INC., DUBLIN, NEW HAMPSHIRE

YANKEE, INC.

Publishers of *Yankee Magazine,
The Old Farmer's Almanac(k)*, *The Cape Cod Compass*,
and various books.

PRESIDENT
C. Robertson Trowbridge

VICE PRESIDENTS
Judson D. Hale
Trix T. Sagendorph

Yankee, Incorporated
Dublin, New Hampshire, 03444 U.S.A.

First Edition

Library of Congress Catalog
Card Number 71–141043

Manufactured in the United States of America

FOREWORD

The heart of the Age of Steam was a piston engine, with rods and cranks that you could see working, driving visible wheels—great locomotive wheels, taller than a man, or paddle wheels as big as a house. Nearby was a boiler, with dials to watch and intense heat to feel, if you were lucky enough to be close. It was fed by a sweating fireman who sometimes, I remember, was kind enough to let small boys shovel coal for him. And presiding over this marvelous concentration of power was the hero of generations of American boys, the engineer.

This type of engine, which dominated the American experience for a full century, has now disappeared, quite suddenly it seems to me. Most young people have never seen one working. Already a generation has grown up without hearing a whistle for the crossing. I do not mean that coarse diesel blast, which I privately regard as one cause for the social unrest that troubles us. I mean the voice of the real steam locomotive, that distant, prolonged yearning echoing up the valley, which was the only tranquilizer my grandfather ever needed. Only 25 years ago, 40,000 genuine steam locomotives were whistling for crossings in this country; now not a single one whistles in earnest. Steam still pushes tourists up Mt. Washington, just as it did a hundred years ago, and you can find a few amusement parks advertised in YANKEE where you can still hear and smell live steam, and even get a cinder in your eye, but you may have to drive your internal combustion engine a considerable distance to get there.

Steam was serious and exciting business in the last century, central to our economy. The steam railroad made Americans mobile, transformed their lives in a single generation, and taught them how to run a big business. It quickened the pulse of American towns every day at countless railroad stations. For fifty years an American railroad network of 250,000 miles was able to make money hauling freight for one cent per ton-mile.

The western steamboat, a beautiful American original, created a river culture, and turned the Mississippi and its tributaries into another transportation system that was able to offer even lower rates because the roadbed was free. In the west, where life tended to be fast and informal, a steamboat didn't last very long—four or five years on an average—and it often met a violent end by snag, fire, or explosion. On eastern bays and rivers steamboats ran under lower pressure and more conservative management, but they also gave Currier and Ives an occasional lurid accident to illustrate. Some New Englanders over forty recall those luxurious overnight cruises as the most memorable part of a trip to New York. No better way of going to New York has yet been discovered.

The railroad and the steamboat were only the most glamorous applications of steam power. But steam meant much more to our fathers. It meant an engine for the local factory when it outgrew its waterfall. It meant the local powerhouse where the same engine drove the same dynamo for forty years. It meant the steam roller and the steam shovel that fascinated casual observers of construction jobs right up to 1940. Steam even enriched the lives of farm boys. The story of portable steam engines on farms is now almost completely forgotten, but at one time 75,000 of them were doing the heavy work on large American farms. It was such a traction engine that gave Henry Ford his first vision of a self-propelled vehicle to liberate the American farmer.

Steam was also fascinating because it was mysterious and dangerous. Steam technology was well developed and widely used without much theoretical understanding of the conversion of heat energy into work. People did not know what was going on inside

4

boilers, but they learned from experience that these great reservoirs of energy could explode, which they did in quite large numbers, in factories and on farms, as well as on steamboats. A boiler explosion was a fearful thing, as unpredictable and uncontrollable as a bolt of lightning; and it could be very destructive, especially on steamboats where very large boilers were surrounded by people. Not even professors really understood the phenomenon in the early days.

It was steam that taught us, or began to teach us, how to cope with the social problems and the hazards to public health that come with technical progress. It took our ancestors about 75 years to develop effective ways of dealing with the boiler hazard, which was much like the current problem of automobile crashes—hard to understand, hard to control. Both generations have also confronted the pollution caused by their favorite machines, which raises even tougher problems. It was the steam engine that blackened the cities and created the first lethal smog a century ago. The internal combustion engine looked like the solution for a while. Now its exhaust seems so noxious that some people would like to go back to the smokestack.

But we cannot turn back. The old steam engine has gone, and gone forever, I am afraid. We still get most of our energy through steam, but the steam is invisible, it drives an invisible turbine, and the energy reaches us over unromantic wires. Railroads haul more ton-miles than they ever did in the age of steam, but they can no longer afford to do it with steam. The diesel has taken over all heavy transportation on land and water, except for the very largest ships. And that digging machine is a steam shovel in name only: it's really another diesel.

We hear talk about reviving the steam engine for road vehicles. For 200 years people have been talking about steam cars, and a good many were built in the old days, especially in the first few years of this century when as many as twenty firms were making steam cars in New England alone. For a time it looked as if steam could give the gasoline engine a run for its money, and some people like to think it still could. Recently, steam buffs have found new hope in the rising concern over the pollution caused by automobiles. They sometimes forget that the steam car also burns fuel, and more of it than a gasoline car. Any car, even an electric, has to get its energy from combustion somewhere, unless it comes from water power or atomic power. Combustion for a steam engine can probably be made cleaner than the rapid-fire bursts of an internal combustion engine because it is continuous and can be more carefully controlled, but if you want to be rational, I cannot recommend steam car projects as an investment for hard-earned money.

The trouble with steam power is that it is too heavy for a vehicle. An engine that has to carry itself around has to be light. That boiler that the steam engine always has to have may be fascinating, but it turns out to be heavy and costly if you have to take it everywhere with you. Steam is also difficult to control and not economical in small sizes. Rationally, steam can no longer compete with internal combustion for light road vehicles.

But who needs to be rational about steam engines? They were great machines, those antique reciprocating piston engines. They stirred the blood of our fathers and added a dimension to their experience, just as the jet engine and the space craft have done for us. If it is important to understand the experience of past generations, and I think it is, then we need a collection of memories like this one to tell us what it was like to live in the Age of Steam.

Lynwood Bryant

Professor of History
Massachusetts Institute of Technology

TABLE
OF
CONTENTS

SECTION IV—WHEN STEAM CHANGED HISTORY

SECTION V—GREAT YANKEE LINES

SECTION VI—PURE NOSTALGIA

SECTION VII—STEAM ANTIQUES

The new engine powered everything. In Section I trains, sidewheelers, bicycles, and racing cars . . .

. . . help create A VARIED WORLD OF STEAM for Yankees.

"Grand staircases of mahogany swept up to their 300-foot saloons. . . ."

SIDEWHEELERS OF THE SOUND

The steamboat was America's first invention of world-wide significance and the best of these plied the Sound, linking New England with New York and the world. They were the Sound Steamers, and, as a class, were known as one of the wonders of America in an era best described as "adventurous and glorious."

by Kevin J. Aylmer

History and historians have fostered many legends. From innumerable history textbooks, generations of American school children dutifully learned, for instance, that a young Virginian named George Washington once threw a silver dollar across the Potomac; that Henry Hudson discovered the Hudson River; James Watt invented the steam engine and Robert Fulton the steamboat. In reality, however, George Washington's biographer, a Parson Weems, conjured up the myth of the silver dollar caper; an Italian adventurer, Giovanni Verrazano (for whom the New York City bridge was named), found the majestic "Hudson" some eight years before the English explorer; and numerous other colonials had invented workable "steam engines" long before Watt's time. Of Robert Fulton, only the date of his "trek up the Hudson" is accurate. A Connecticut-born Puritan named Morey invented the first steamboat and ran it on the Connecticut River; Fulton's steamship, the *North River,* was given the name *Clermont* by another self-styled "authentic biographer" a few years after Fulton's death.

In much the same falsified manner, history and time have blurred the image of the American steamboat. To many, the true image of a steamboat is to be found in Edna Ferber's classic, *Showboat,* or as part and parcel of Samuel Clemens' boyhood adventures on the Mississippi. Once again, the mists of time and romanticism have blurred our vision. The American steamboat was neither born in the West of Ferber's imagination, nor dead by the close of the Civil War. In addition, the steamboat is not a minor chapter of the American saga, curiously brought to life in history books by courtesy of Currier & Ives, lithographers to the world.

The truth of the matter is that the steamboat was America's first invention of world-wide significance. In the first five decades of its existence, it provided a sorely needed means of conveyance that would propel American Manifest Destiny to the Rockies long before the Civil War. In short, the steamboat era in America was strategic, adventurous, and glorious.

Save for the serpentine Mississippi, upon which the river steamboats ferried the wandering home-seekers who wrested the West from the Indians, the steamboat probably did more for New England than for any region of the United States. *The accepted travel routes from New England to New York before the Civil War and long after the "irrepressible conflict" were by Long Island Sound. A little-known aspect of the American drama, the Sound Steamers, as a class, were known as one of the wonders of America. They rivaled the ocean liners of the 19th century in bulk and magnificence. *Hunt's Merchants Magazine,* a popular newsweekly of the last century, in 1857 wrote of them with unalloyed pride: "The steamers which ply between New York and Boston by way of Fall River and Stonington are unsurpassed for comfort, safety or speed on any similar route in the world."

The now-yellowed diaries of many famous New Englanders are replete with references to the glory of the Sound steamers and the convenience of the Sound route. Henry Wadsworth Longfellow, one February day in 1840, wrote of his great disappointment in finding the Sound frozen, preventing steamboat service from New York when he was ready to return to New England. The mail stage on which he was forced to take passage made the homeward journey almost an ordeal. Passengers, freight, communication to and from New England went willingly, regularly, for decades over that body of water Daniel Webster called "The

Mediterranean of the Western Hemisphere.

Even the rich and the famous personages of colonial America found overland travel uncomfortably boring. Speed was only a word in the dictionary, a word with a fantastic, supernatural connotation. Paul Revere's horse was almost a symbol for celerity. No casual or carefree jaunt was the overland stage trip between New York and Boston. The stages bounced and lurched unmercifully. The roads were frequently impassable and travelers were forced to alight and "work their passage" by pushing the coach out of the rutted mire. Usually a week was consumed in making the little more than 200-mile journey. The water routes were preferred but there was one drawback. Since the mode of travel was exclusively by sailing vessels, the length of the voyage depended upon the wind. And the wind was one thing the stern Puritans could not regulate!

Little wonder then that Sam Morey, Elijah Ormsbee, and John Fitch, together with Robert Fulton, Nicholas Roosevelt, and several others decided to defy both God and Nature with experiments designed to find a means of locomotion without wind.

Thus, just before the convening of the Constitutional Convention in 1787, Yankeedom produced two individuals who were to revolutionize travel and inaugurate the Sound's "Age of Sidewheelers." To begin the epoch, Capt. Samuel Morey voyaged down the Connecticut River out into the Sound from Hartford to New York in a "little boat just large enough to contain himself, rude machinery connected with a steam boiler and a handful of wood for the fire." Elijah Ormsbee, the second member of Yankeedom's Dynamic Duo, set Rhode Islanders gaping in 1792 by cruising about

Providence harbor in "a canoe with a tea kettle in her."

Morey's voyage (13 years before Fulton's *North River* venture) was at the exhilarating rate of five miles an hour. Fifty years later the steamboat was reeling off 20 miles an hour with ease and dispatch, albeit much smoke and clatter. The pounding paddles of the steamboats introduced America to speed and made every decently deep stream a busy highway.

From Fulton's widely publicized successes with the *North River* came a compelling desire to test his "fire canoe" on the Sound. At dawn, on a cold March morning in the year 1815, "Tricky Bob" (as he was commonly called) left New York to make the hazardous 75-mile voyage to New Haven. Eleven hours later, the familiar figurehead and black hull of the *North River* were sighted off New Haven Harbor. Fulton's engineer blamed the delay on a combination of adverse natural elements and the fact that "New York City's wood did not make good steam." That voyage, however, despite the lukewarm attitude of the press, was epoch making; from its success came the great Sound Steamers which really built New England. Steam was on the Sound to stay.

The steamer *Connecticut* came out the next year. She was a beauty —all white with vivid green trimmings. It is said she was built to go to St. Petersburg and was to have been named *Emperor Alexander,* but the capitalists got involved in money matters and she never went to Russia. Instead, she and another daring Connecticut Yankee named Elihu Bunker made history on Long Island Sound. The *Connecticut* was 150 feet long and cost $80,000. Like the *Fulton,* she had no upper saloon or staterooms. She burned wood, of course, in great shiny copper boilers, as striking as a volunteer fireman's red shirt on parade

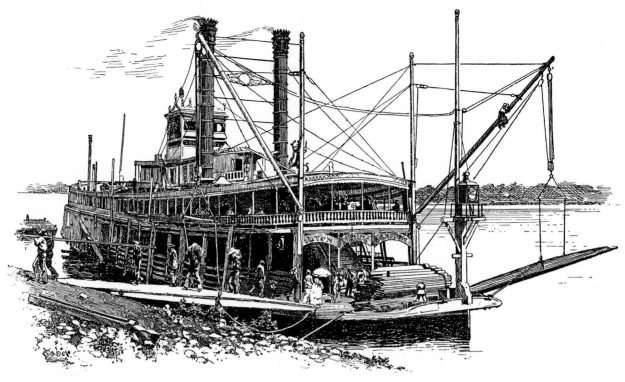

Western River Boat

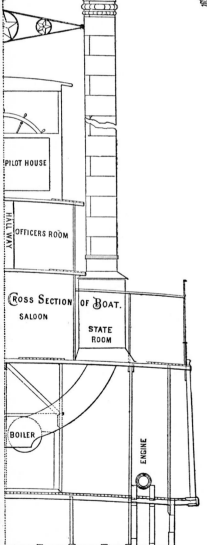

A cross section of a Western River Boat

day. She could carry little or no freight, every inch of space not utilized by the passengers being necessary for the piles of pine wood which were heaped on deck, fore and aft, and even on the guards. But for her time, the *Connecticut* was queen, and it was both fitting and proper that Elihu should leave "Tricky Bob's" *Fulton* (sister ship to the *North River*) and become master of this new, wondrous marine triumph.

When you linked the skill of Bunker with the strength of the *Connecticut,* you had something for the legend-makers. Hell Gate, so wild and so dangerous that the early Dutch settlers of New Amsterdam could think of no other name than of the infernal region to describe its fury, engaged the redoubtable twain in a death tussle and lost. That was news in 1816—big news. With the new *Connecticut,* Bunker determined to make the "novel and interesting experiment" of steaming through the Gate *against the full force of the tide.* Fortunately, a passenger aboard the *Connecticut* at the time of the exciting three-round battle took quill in hand. Since there were a "number of respectable passengers who witnessed the performance," his narrative leaves no room for doubt as to authenticity or accuracy.

The *Connecticut,* he tells us, was "built with all the strength to be obtained and careful workmanship." The predicted test was of such importance that the builder of the engine, one Robert McQueen, went aboard to witness at close range the exacting test of his handiwork. The *Connecticut*'s throttle was opened at floodtide. Plowing into the current, she slowed gradually until she was moving only by inches, and then she yielded. For the moment Bunker gave in, guiding her into an eddy so that the engineers could take measures to increase the steam. "With renovated power," wrote the spectator, "the effort was repeated, every

Albany Day Boat New York *built in 1887.*

man fixed immovable at his post . . . the engineers employing their utmost diligence to force the passage." Wracked and strained from the effort, she yielded again and Bunker returned her for a second rest. However, captain and engineer were still so determined that they thrust the *Connecticut* into a third assault. A weaker vessel would have been torn into pieces but the lumbering *Connecticut* shivered forward foot by foot. After a few moments of breathless anxiety on the part of the passengers, "the headstrong current yielded to the giant power of steam, and the triumph of art over nature was effected."

Strange to relate, the next forward step in Sound steamboat transportation was not pioneered by the high-spirited Bunker. A man named Smith has the accolade of history. Captain Smith first took a steamboat around Point Judith, that sandy heel of Rhode Island where the waters of the Atlantic, Block Island Sound, and Narragansett Bay crash

together in "a mad, nautical merry-go-round." Smith rounded the dangerous Point in the 100-foot *Firefly*, built by Fulton for the Hudson. On Monday, May 26, 1817, 28 hours after leaving New York, the *Firefly* burst into Newport harbor. Despite a strong southwest breeze and heavy sea, the diminutive *Firefly* "rode the waves like a bottle."

Sad to relate, the *Firefly* was not a commercial success. Before she was run off in her competition with sail, however, she made several memorable voyages. In June she carried President James Monroe from Bristol to Providence. In the matter of making precedents Elihu Bunker just could not be kept in the background. He, the first of the steamboat masters, transported the first President to set foot on a Sound steamer.

Elihu Bunker next bobs up as a connoisseur of literature. The New Haven steamboats *Connecticut* and *Fulton* were the first to install libraries for the education and entertain-

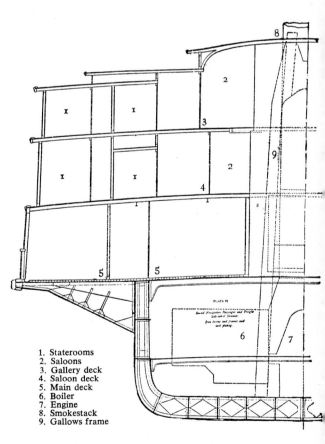

1. Staterooms
2. Saloons
3. Gallery deck
4. Saloon deck
5. Main deck
6. Boiler
7. Engine
8. Smokestack
9. Gallows frame

A cross section of a Sound Steamer

A Fall River Line favorite, the Priscilla was in service 44 years. Costing $1,500,000 in 1893, she had 361 staterooms and enough free bunk space to sleep 1,500 persons.

A newel in the form of a Dolphin.

ment of marine travelers. The *New York Post* of July 3, 1821, chronicled: "The *Connecticut* and the *Fulton* of the New Haven route have on board well-chosen libraries of 500 publications for the use of passengers. We learn that the Hudson steamboats intend to follow the example."

Before long, the increasingly stronger and larger steamboats were regularly sailing between New York and Providence, completing the voyage in less than 12 hours. In times past, a similar trip via stagecoach consumed almost a week in time and about $100 of the hapless voyager's purse.

There is a rich legacy of contemporary descriptions of steamboat traveling written by foreigners. Most were filled with awe and admiration, like that of the Frenchman de Crèvecoeur. Some were less than awed. Dickens, with characteristic English reserve, described his trip from Hartford to New York in this way:

It certainly was not called a steamboat without reason: I omitted to ask the question, but I should think it must have been half a pony power. Mr. Paap, the celebrated dwarf, might have lived and died happily in the cabin, which was fitted with common sash windows, like an ordinary dwelling house. The windows had bright red curtains, too, hung on slack strings across the lower panels; so that it looked like the parlor of a Lilliputian public house, which had got afloat in a flood or some other water accident and was drifting nobody knew where. But even in this chamber there was a rocking chair.

I am afraid to tell how many feet short this vessel was, or how many feet narrow; to apply the words length and width to such measurements would be a contradiction in terms. But I may state we all kept the middle of the deck, lest the boat should unexpectedly tip over, and that the machinery, by some surprising process of condensation

worked between it and the keel; the whole forming a warm sandwich, about three feet thick.

Price wars, if not elegant travel, were a common feature of the early steamboat routes. Monopolistic interests would inaugurate service for a grandiose sum of seven dollars, only to have the price invariably grow smaller, due to the influx of more high-pressure boatmen. First seven dollars, then five, three, a dollar fifty, a dollar, fifty cents, two bits, then nothing. As the steamship lines gradually regained normalcy, the price was established at about a dollar fifty for a trip between New York and Providence. Even at that low sum there was 100% profit. Some lines boasted annual profits of 70 per cent; stockholders on one line enjoyed a dividend of six per cent *a month*.

The boats that plied the Sound in the 1840s and the 1850s were in the vanguard of the great "floating palaces" of the post-Civil War period. The broadsides of the day announced in lofty terms the grand means of conveyance and comfort at every port. It was in this era that the steam calliope added a musical note of festivity and exoticism to the riverboats. Their notes of frivolity could sometimes be heard as much as eight miles downriver, if the wind was right. One newspaper account recalls:

There have been nights on the Sound when the fun was fast and furious; when songs floated out over the foaming water, and mirth and laughter kept company with the hours. The meals were not all public. There used to be private suppers which the stars watched all night long. And so amid the blaze of lights, the clink of glasses and the soft gurgle of rich wine, the feast became a flow of wit and story and the flash of repartee grew quicker, until grey streaks of dawn, paling the lustre of the lamps and creeping white and cold across the inky water, warned the gay revelers to seek an hour or two of sleep.

Gaiety, manners, imagination, ambition were all present on the riverboats. The hold of a steamer carried cotton, lumber, sugar, cattle, or manufactured goods. The deck above the hold was occupied by the engines, the boilers, and the kitchen. Deck passengers, consorting in the pillared open space around the sides, sometimes were crowded by an overflow of freight from the hold. Forward, a flight of stairs mounted to the level above—the location of the office, the barroom, and the long central cabin. A promenade stretched outside the staterooms on either side. And another stair led to the roof of the cabin, the hurricane deck, where officers' quarters were grouped in the texas house. On top of the texas roosted the pilot house, three flights up from the boiler deck. From his station there, the pilot gazed through glass on all sides of him upon the bustling decks below and upon the water he traveled.

The engines of such craft were twins, one to power each of the immense paddle wheels. A word through the pilot's speaking tube or a tug at the knob of a signal bell stopped a wheel to starboard or larboard, while the other wheel still whirled its paddle buckets and drove the boat into a turn so sharp as to bewilder, sometimes to frighten, passengers aboard and watchers on shore. Completely responsive to the men who guided them, the steamers slid through narrow channels, skimmed snugly around reefs and islands and snags, negotiated cramping chutes and abrupt ox-bow turns with barely a slackening of speed.

Steam was the life breath of the engines and was generated in a battery of cylindrical boilers, numbering from two to eight. These lay horizontally, side by side, like a clip of giant cartridges. Enclosing the boiler was the furnace, built of massive brick or tile, solid and tight as the foundation of a house, with heavy iron fire doors. Opposite the furnace lay stacks of fuel. The bottom of the furnace rose clear of the deck planking to allow the insertion of another iron cylinder, the mud drum, connected by broad pipes to the boiler above. Into this settled the silt and trash from the river water brought by the powerful "doctor" pump into the boilers. As the flames of the furnace raised the temperature of the boilers, the heat vapors coursed along the open flues that pierced the boilers from foot to head, adding heat to the water, and finally gushed out at the smokestacks above. The water, thus heated, expanded into steam, as indicated by gauges and valves.

Prized attributes of the river packets were size and capacity, shallowness of draft, grace of line, bounty of table, luxury of quarters for the cabin passengers, and, above all else, swiftness.

From 1850 on, riverboats raced often and fiercely on the Sound. Practical considerations underlay the rashness of such contests, for the first boat to reach a landing could claim the choicest rewards in freight and passenger loads. In the era just before the Civil War, boats scurried along in a safety-last spirit, water pumps shut off to heighten the pressure of steam in the boilers, escape valves weighted down with the carpenter's hammers and the laundress' flatirons. Sweating firemen fed their furnaces to almost incandescent heat with pitch pine and sides of rancid bacon. Then, sometimes, the water level in a boiler sagged below the danger point and the intolerable compression of steam drove out a rust-weakened patch of iron shell or a loose rivet with a sudden explosion like that of dynamite. The other wracked boilers exploded in turn, sundering the timbers of the hull in one grand panoply of death. Again and again, at the very moment of victory, a winner blew up and foundered, scalding and drowning both crew and passengers.

Such dramatic catastrophes filled the newspapers, excited the politicians, and at last impelled the United States Government to provide for the inspection and sealing of the valves of a steamer's boilers before departure on a trip, seeking to make sure that the steam poundage would not exceed a sane maximum. But the racing went on, amid hurricanes of dispute, torrents of wagered dollars.

It was a blue-eyed Dutchman who brought racing to the Sound. Vanderbilt by name, Robber Baron by trade, this American entrepreneur claimed ownership of "The Fastest Boat in the World," a claim promptly disputed by the captain of another Sound steamer, the *Richmond*. After the interminable bragging, boasting, and betting subsided, the race finally took place, commencing at Stonington, Connecticut, and before its termination becoming as much a part of the folklore of the Sound as that of the *Robert E. Lee* and *Natchez* race on the Mississippi.

For ten or a dozen miles down the Sound (observed a contemporary) there was no perceptible change in the relative position of the boats. Then dense clouds of smoke poured from the Lexington (Vanderbilt's craft), a sheet of flame shot up from her stack, her wheels turned swifter, and a cheer burst from the passengers as they realized the gap between them and the Richmond *was closing. It was an anxious moment on board the* Richmond *for the* Lexington *was gaining fast. Where was Captain Townsend? There was no reply. He was not to be found. But the movements on board* Lexington *had not escaped his eye. The moment that the boat left Stonington men had been set picking out the most resinous wood and piling it for immediate use. The engineer had been tightening bolts and screws, and* Richmond *was ready for the race.*

At the first puffs of black smoke from Lexington, *Captain Townsend had rushed to the engine room and was consulting the engineer. "Oh, she can stand considerably more," said that functionary; and the Captain answered, "Well, put in the fat wood and let her go." She did go. Volumes of smoke poured from her funnel, and the roar of her fires could be heard all over the boat. A column of flame stood a pillar of fire above her. She trembled at every revolution of her wheels. The water seethed and boiled beneath her, fire and smoke were round about her overhead. She advanced like the rush of an avalanche—she was a moving volcano. Slowly, steadily, she moved away from the* Lexington; *wider and wider grew the interval between them, until at last* Richmond *dashed between the rocks at Hell Gate and* Lexington *was seen no more until she came by an hour after the* Richmond *had made fast at her pier.*

The Commodore (Vanderbilt) sold the *Lexington* and although his brother Jake remained as skipper he was fortunate enough to be ill at home on January 13, 1840, the day of the *Lexington*'s destruction. (See YANKEE, Jan. 1966). Bound east on the Sound with over 120 passengers and crew, she was headed for Stonington, Connecticut, when flames shot up around the boiler and spread so rapidly that passengers could not even get from one end of the boat to the other. The captain seized the wheel and steered for land but the tiller ropes burned off. As the boat plunged aimlessly ahead he called down to stop the engine, but the engineer had been driven away from the controls. Soon there was no refuge anywhere from this wall of flame driving through the night. At least 119 were burned, drowned, or frozen on the timbers or bales of cotton with which they had taken to the water. Three lived to tell the story, one of them a fireman who floated two days and two nights on a bale of cotton. Half of the passen-

gers and crew might have been rescued had it not been for the disgracefully callous William Tirrell, master of the sloop *Improvement*, only five miles from the wreck. At the inquest Tirrell said he had not gone to the *Lexington* because he thought all the passengers had been safely transferred to her lifeboats. History has not blurred another eyewitness statement: fear that Captain Tirrell would lose a tide at the bar of the harbor was his excuse for his nefarious neglect of a *rival* craft.

Mark Twain's glamorous descriptions of the Mississippi steamboats were a curious assortment of myths, exaggerations, and half truths. Many people equate the phrase "floating palace" with the high, squarish, gleaming-white, twin-stacked Mississippi riverboat. Actually there was never a boat on western waters that compared with the later Hudson River and, particularly, Long Island Sound boats. The most pretentious Mississippi boat cost less than $400,000 to build; its eastern counterpart cost over $2 million.

The era of the true floating palace, East or West, started after the Civil War when Robber Barons were fashionable birds of prey. In 1869, the Boston, Newport and New York Steamboat Company, which owned the Fall River Line, was taken over by their rival, the Narragansett Steamship Company, whose president was now one James Fisk, Jr. The Vermont peddler in his shrewd way had come to control a line that had operated some of the finest sidewheelers in America, including the *Bay State, Empire State, Metropolis, Old Colony, Newport, Bristol,* and *Providence,* justifying a

Right: "The Departure"

18

The cabin of the ferryboat Bergen

remark that a short time before would have seemed like wistful thinking: "If Vanderbilt's a Commodore, I guess I ought to rank as an Admiral." Since the pioneer days of such superior vessels as Vanderbilt's *Lexington,* Sound steamers had become famous for their size and appointments.

The new steamboat tycoon now controlled seven vessels and promptly selected two of them, the *Bristol* and *Providence,* for conversion to floating palaces. Their paddle boxes were painted lavender and their smokestacks deep yellow, and their outside decks were replaced with alternating strips of black walnut and yellow pine. Grand staircases of mahogany swept up to their 300-foot saloons, from which rosewood doors opened into staterooms. Brilliant light from gas chandeliers flooded the white and gold trimmings and the acres of velvet-pile carpeting. A concert orchestra played on each vessel, joined by the trilling of 200 canaries in gold cages, each bird personally named by Fisk. Life-sized portraits of Fisk and his partner, Jay Gould, flanked the mirror at the turn of the staircase of one of the boats, a decoration that caused one wit to quip: "I see the two thieves, all right, but where is Jesus Christ?"

An interesting story is told of how another Fall River Line steamer owned by Fisk collaborated with President Grant to make history. The Chief Executive signed a proclamation recognizing Cuban belligerency in August, 1869. On the afternoon of the 19th, Grant arrived in New York and was driven directly "to the Newport boat" where he was met by Secretary of State Fish. The two statesmen entered the bridal suite where they conferred until the steamer sailed. Fish discreetly placed the proclamation in his pocket. Its promulgation might have precipitated the Spanish-American War then and there, say authoritative historians. Grant was grateful later that it had not been issued.

The era that Jim Fisk started was "the Gilded Age" of steamboating in the East. The postwar decades were affluent years for a mushrooming privileged class. Travel on the floating palaces was something of a status symbol, and on the Long Island Sound vessels, social climbers might rub shoulders with the true elite, as the Vanderbilts, Astors, Belmonts, and Rockefellers used the palatial boats regularly to journey to their estates in Newport.

One of the competing companies in the 1870s was the Stonington Line, which promoted its accident-free record by calling itself "the Old Reliable Line." No sooner did it adopt this slogan, after a long accident-free operation, than two of its vessels, the *Massachusetts* and

Sweating firemen fed their furnaces to almost incandescent heat with pitch pine and sides of rancid bacon

the *Rhode Island,* ran aground in close succession. Shortly after, Old Reliable's *Stonington* and *Narragansett* were proceeding in opposite directions in a fog at full speed, to maintain their schedule and "lick" the rival Fall River Line boats, when they crashed headon. (See YANKEE, June, 1968.) The *Narragansett* caught fire and sank as the wounded *Stonington* probed the fog for survivors. At least 30 lives were lost, and the press lashed out at the evil steamboat barons who wantonly risked the lives of travelers in their lust for profits. In Jersey City a minister preached a sermon on the subject in a service attended by the captain of the *Narragansett.* When the reverend branded the officers of that vessel as "the biggest set of cowards in existence," the captain

rose in his pew and shouted, "Sir, you're a liar." His trial for breach of the peace brought about an interesting judicial decision. The judge ruled that, since those who agreed with the preacher traditionally shouted "amen," the captain of the *Narragansett* had the right to express his disagreement vocally.

In the decade starting in 1883 the Fall River Line produced three successive "Queens of the Sound" with names from Massachusetts history—the *Pilgrim* in 1883, the *Puritan* in 1889, and the *Priscilla* in 1893. Each was bigger and better

---

Pouring in the fuel during a race. "Sometimes a loose rivet was driven out with a sudden explosion like that of dynamite. The other wracked boilers would explode in turn, sending the timbers of the hull in a panoply of death."

than its predecessor; the *Pilgrim* was 390 feet, the *Priscilla* 440. Each called for new adjectives to describe its magnificence until, when the *Priscilla* came along, one writer could do no better than dredge up from Shakespeare: *'Tis truly beauty blent.*

The presence of distinguished passengers, right down to the time of its abandonment, was never news on the Fall River Line. Over the years the furrowed, canvas-covered decks and the thickly carpeted corridors were trodden alike by kings and those who had the common touch. People from all over the world traveled on the big white sidewheelers. In addition to Grant, Presidents Arthur, Harrison, Cleveland, and the two Roosevelts made frequent voyages. One commentator

observed, "If you went on a Fall River Liner you hobnobbed with rich and poor alike."

All the Vanderbilts, Astors, Belmonts, and Rockefellers used the palatial steamers—not casually, but month after month, year after year. The list of famous personalities was almost endless; besides Newport's famed "Four Hundred," the Line could count among its clientele prominent Philadelphians like the Lippincotts and Whartons; Chief Justice Charles Evans Hughes; Barclay Parsons, of the Lea and Perrins Sauce Company; General "Blackjack" Pershing; William Burke Miller, Pulitzer prize-winning reporter of the Floyd Collins cave rescue fame; *et al*. Any veteran Fall River Line traveler could add a dozen or two more before you could say *Priscilla*. Perhaps no more aristocratic-democratic institution than the Fall River Line ever was in America.

The final floating palace, the $2 million *Commonwealth*, appeared on the Sound in 1908. Some 456 feet long, she was known as "Charley Mellen's apartment house." Mellen was president of the New Haven Railroad. Perhaps with a subconscious sense that this would be their last opportunity to astound the world, her designers did not limit themselves to one decorative theme. Her various decks and several public rooms represented seven distinct architectural styles—her grand saloon was done in Venetian Gothic, her dining room in Louis XVI, her cafe in 16th-century Italian. Superimposed on the period design was a motif involving grotesquely carved mariners' heads and mermaids snared in fishing lines.

The *Commonwealth*'s main claim to fame was her dining room 50 feet above water, with outer walls almost entirely of glass supporting a ceiling of three great domes. One writer declaimed: "What a brilliant and animated place it was to enjoy caviar, New England clam chowder, or the other delicacies always found on Fall River menus." After partaking of caviar and clam chowder, a combination that marked true New England provincialism, a voyager might pass through "an inviting doorway" to dance in the grill under "an illuminated painting of a Spanish galleon outlined against the setting sun," or stop for a drink in the garden cafe on the main deck, which was "a glimpse of a Parisian sidewalk cafe afloat"; or he might elect to loaf in the "vastness of the grand saloon, done in Gothic style, with its palms, Oriental rugs, deep comfortable chairs, attractive table lamps, and its vaulted ceiling." In connection with all this it should be borne in mind that this was not a crack ocean liner that was being described; it was simply a paddle-wheel steamer that made a nightly trip of about nine hours between New York City and Fall River, Massachusetts.

It is hard to understand why the New Haven Railroad built the *Commonwealth* in 1908, for 19 years earlier it had built something else that ultimately undermined all the Sound steamers. This was a drawbridge across the Thames River at New London, Connecticut, which, in 1889, completed the first through-shore railroad line between New York and Boston. Prior to that time cars were floated across the Thames on barges and the only all-

rail route was a rather roundabout inland course. The Fall River Line's boats were still the elegant and interesting way to travel, despite the need for proceeding on from Fall River by rail. But with fast through-trains running along the coast, the handwriting was on the wall.

The stock market crash and the bankruptcy of the New York, New Haven and Hartford, in 1935, did not improve the prospects for navigation, nor did the rising competition of buses, nor finally the lowered Boston–New York rail fare. In 1931, the sidewheelers of the Bay State Line had stopped running and the New York and Hartford line had died at the age of 107. Now a blight had come to the Providence and New Bedford boats. Yes, and a black plague to the white boats from Fall River.

In 1937 the Union Shipbuilding Company bought the *Plymouth, Providence, Commonwealth,* and *Priscilla* for $88,000—the scrap value of $6 million worth of steamboats. The *Priscilla*'s bow lines were frozen to the dock at Providence and they had to chop them through when a tug appeared in January, 1938, to tow the last of the Sound's palace steamers to the wreckers. It was an ignominious end for the "Opulent Age of Sidewheelers."

The river boats lasted a century, give or take a few years. It was a great century, but it is a past century. The bells, the haunting whistles, the glamour and excitement of the river boats are preserved only in a few yellowed diaries, dusty lithographs, faded memories, and in the incessant waves that gently lap the irregular coastline of Long Island Sound.

My Father Built the
STANLEY STEAMER

This photograph, taken in 1897, shows the Stanley twins in the very first steamer.

Reminiscences of Mrs. Prescott Warren, nee Emily Stanley, daughter of
F. E. Stanley, maker of the famed car bearing his name.

by Arthur F. Joy

It was the era of bicycles," Mrs. Prescott Warren recalls, "and my father, Francis Edgar Stanley (identical twin of the co-manufacturer of the car, Freelan Oscar Stanley) was very athletically inclined. He rode a bicycle beautifully and he wanted my mother to ride with him. But mother was not very agile. She weighed 200 pounds, you see, and did not look with great favor upon cycling. However, she gave in once, and rode until she fell off and got a few bruises and a scare."

This, says Mrs. Warren, was a motivating factor in F. E. Stanley's desire to make a horseless carriage that would enable his wife to ride more safely in the open with him.

"Never mind, my dear," he soothed, "I will build something so that we can ride together, side by side."

In this connection, Mrs. Warren says that he first got the idea from an early car made in Maine in the 1880's, and also from one which appeared at the Brockton Fair, perhaps the Duryea. (Note: In Portland, Me. about this time, Willard I. Twombly invented a motorized bicycle and formed the Lovell Cycle & Ether Motor Co. The generator corresponded to a steam boiler and ether was used to generate the vapor.) He had also been reading about a horseless carriage said to be made in France. He was wondering if he might not be able to make one

23

Prescott Warren, right, and a physician friend, in an early model of the Stanley.

for himself.

"Father began drawing diagrams in his den, lots of them," Mrs. Warren goes on. "This was in 1897, and soon he had actually built a little car, a horseless carriage run by steam, and he took me out to ride in it one day that same year."

That first Stanley steam runabout was equipped with reverse gear, operated by a hand lever, and it was steered by a tiller. F. E. wanted his daughter (Mrs. Warren was also an excellent cyclist) to try it.

"Why should I try it?" she argued.

"Go ahead," he urged. "Drive it! I know you can!"

"Finally I did. I grasped the tiller, put the power on, tried out the foot brake, found it worked, and got underway. It was just like riding a bicycle, only easier. We were on Washington Street here in Newton, Mass., at the time. I drove that car two or three miles. I believe it marks the first time a woman ever drove a steam car. I was thrilled to death!"

At that time, F. O. Stanley, the twin brother, was not too interested in the steam carriage which brother F. E. had made. Besides, the brothers were up to their necks in the photographic dry plate business which they had developed and F. O. was devoting his time mainly to that. He supervised a machine in the factory which coated the film.

F. E., nevertheless, had been bitten by the automobile bug. He couldn't forget it. Unable to deny the urge to create, he began to build another car.

"Finally, even F. O. got interested and put his hands and his mind to it, too, so that by 1898 both were manufacturing automobiles (perhaps half a dozen built that year, with speeds limited to about 35 m.p.h.). Soon after, they were coming out in commercial quantities. I believe," says Mrs. Warren, "that they made two hundred steamers the very next year, 1899. People would stand in line and virtually throw money at my father. But if he felt anything was wrong with a car, he would not accept any cash until the condition was rectified—to his own satisfaction!" The Stanley Steamer was an easy car to run. It had few moving parts and could go like the wind.

George Eastman, the camera and film tycoon from Rochester, N.Y., who later entered into the lives of the Stanley twins in a very intimate way, visited Boston in October, 1899, and while in town called on the twins.

"I was in Boston yesterday," his personal correspondence relates, "and went to see the Stanleys. F. E. Stanley took me for a 10 mile run in 27 minutes. He also took me through the factory and showed me the men turning out the machines. He said they were actually finishing ten a day and certainly everything was going along at a pretty good clip. His vehicle has some notable advantages, one of which in particular is the down-draught which carries the heat away from the back of one's head. I suppose you know all about their machine. They seem to be turning them out rapidly and I believe that the steam machine, at least for a light runabout, is the thing. I tried to get Mr. Stanley to say that he would give me one early but he said they were about three months behind their orders. Have you any pull at the New York end of the concern, which I should judge from Mr. Stanley's remarks is the headquarters?"

Continuing, now with Mrs. Warren's reminiscences.

"At first, we could proceed only about ten miles in the steamers. Then we had to fill up with water. But this was no problem as we would refill from the horse watering troughs along the way. We used to write things on the troughs with chalk: 'I am going to Aunt Clara's,' and things like that."

Both *F. E. Stanley* (*above*) *and his twin, F. O., had beards, dressed alike and had identical handwriting.*

Mrs. Prescott Warren, daughter of F. E. Stanley, believes now that she was the first woman to have driven a steam car.

As time went on, the Stanley twins improved their cars.

"The later ones had condensors so that we could run all day long and the water supply would be used over and over. The burner under the steam boiler was made to burn kerosene and/or gasoline. The last cars father and my uncle made were big, comfortable, and expensive." (Note: a 1917 Stanley touring car, 5-passenger, 20-horsepower, listed for $2,200 f.o.b. Newton, Massachusetts.)

From the Eastman correspondence, the simplicity of the Stanley steamer mechanism is also apparent. In 1901, Mr. Eastman wrote:

Since I have seen a new machine that Stanley is getting out at Newton, I have altogether changed my ideas about steam machines. They appear to have simply eliminated trouble instead of putting on devices to overcome it. I rode in the new Stanley machine and ordered one. He superheats his steam to such an extent that there is little or no vapor. This, of course, is unimportant but he claims the superheating enables him to run twice as far on the same amount of water and to save about one-third of his gasoline. He can carry gasoline for 140 miles of good roads. It is not under pressure except about one pint of it at a time, Cylinder lubrication will lubricate the engine absolutely for exactly 50 miles run. The lubrication of the crosshead has been done away with. No steam air pump is required and the burner is a wonder. In addition to mak-

ing a beautiful flame it cannot be affected by the wind and cannot burn back. If you light the gasoline at the vaporizer it will blow the flame through into the right place, thus lighting itself. The machine is so simple that it almost looks unfinished. I have not yet made any arrangement with Stanley to get a commission but you had better see his machine!

Continuing, again, with Mrs. Warren's reminiscences, she can recall being stopped by a policeman once on Commonwealth Avenue, Boston.

"I was going ten or twelve miles an hour," she says, "and he blew his whistle at me. He ordered me to stop and told me that I was violating the speed limit!"

The Stanley Steamer gained worldwide attention when professional racer Fred Marriott, representing the Stanleys, drove 127.659 miles an hour at Daytona Beach, Florida in January of 1906 to become the first human to travel faster than two miles a minute. Later, he almost lost his life going much faster (some say close to 200 m.p.h.) in a Stanley racing steamer on the same beach.

All of this activity plus a drive by F. O. and his wife up Mt. Washington, the first time this had ever been done, created fantastic interest in the Stanley Steamers (it took them little more than two hours to do it).

Although the favorable publicity resulted in good business for the brothers, nevertheless in 1898 we find them giving in to the clamour of certain persistent financiers who wanted to buy the company. Setting a stiff quarter-million-dollar price for their automobile business, they rather reluctantly sold out to a firm, the Locomobile Corporation, that year.

"So my father, and his twin, my uncle, Freelan O. Stanley," Mrs. Warren continues, "went back to the photographic dry plate business."

So successful were their efforts in this direction that it was not long before George Eastman of the Kodak firm in Rochester began to hear about the competition which the Stanley boys were giving him. He was uneasy over the fact that Stanley photographic plates were outselling at consumer levels his own plates.

Mr. Eastman was concerned enough about this to come here to make a deal. He wanted to buy out the business, but the price seemed high at the time.

From the historical files of the Eastman Kodak Company, there is corroboration of this, as follows:

In 1902, Eastman considered buying the Stanley Photographic Dry Plate business and F. O. Stanley wrote him, "We hope when your experts come here to look over our business you will come with them as we have something new we wish to show you in the way of steam carriages. I had a race yesterday with my old carriage and a 16-horsepower Winton semiracer, and I beat them so badly that I do not believe I shall ever hear from them again. The owner of the carriage claimed he could go 40 miles an hour, but after the race he was perfectly willing to admit that it could go 40 miles, I could go 50 miles an hour."

"Eastman bought one of the new Stanleys and wrote: 'For real dead game sports, the Stanley machine is the only thing. I have just gotten a new one from the Stanleys. If the electric is a 'peach,' the Stanley is a 'peacherina.' "

Stanley dry plates continued to sell at an astonishing rate. George Eastman heard about it and again came to Boston on a personal business trip.

"This time," Mrs. Warren recalls, "he did buy out father and uncle Freelan. But he paid considerably more for the business than he would had he concluded the purchase the year before (sale price rumored to be in vicinity of $800,000.00)."

"After they sold the dry plate business to Eastman," Mrs. Warren resumed, "they went back into the manufacture of steam automobiles. Now, their production ran into the hundreds."

(F. E. himself writes of this: "We sold the dry plate business. My brother and I are now in the automobile business. As to the plant at Newton, the buildings were transformed into an automobile factory. The manufacture of plates contnued at Newton about a year after the sale and then was moved to Rochester. We commenced the automobile business in 1896, nine years before we sold out. We have been in the automobile business ever since.")

Continuing with the story, during this busy period, Freelan Stanley came down with tuberculosis (1903).

"Too sick to drive, he boarded a train for Colorado," Mrs. Warren says. "Once there, he fell in love with Estes Park, not far from Denver. Eventually, he purchased the entire place . . . from an English lord, I believe. It was the right move, for with careful attention to diet, F. O. lived to be 92. At Estes Park, he built a fine hotel. The Stanley Hotel, and there he would stay every summer. Winters he spent at his home in Newton, Mass."

F. O., as a matter of fact, was in Colorado that tragic day in 1918 when his beloved twin brother crashed his Steamer on Newburyport Turnpike in an accident which took his life a few hours thereafter.

"Father was returning from Boothbay Harbor at the time," Mrs. Warren says. "He had planned to go to Vermont where they were setting up a unit car, but something went wrong with his own vehicle and he decided to drive back to Newton and the factory first. He was *not* racing! Two eyewitnesses whom I know were motoring behind him and saw it happen. The road was narrow at that time and while it would permit two cars to pass, there was not room for three abreast. Driving along, father glanced ahead to see these two cars stopped, astride the road in front of him. Apparently the drivers were carrying on a conversation! There was no room for a third car to get through! Father had but one choice, to turn off. However, there was a pile of wood by the roadside at that particular point and this he crashed into when veering away from the parked vehicles. His machine hit the woodpile, veered and plunged down an embankment. I believe that the car may have overturned."

Mr. Stanley was gently picked up and placed in an ambulance, but he died enroute to a hospital in Ipswich.

"We were at Squirrel Island, Maine, at the time and mother was having a dinner party. I was a young woman, then, and was supposed to put some life into the party. Sewell Ford, the writer, was there. So were my two daughters and a few others. I happened to glance out a window and noticed two young men —counsellors at a nearby camp— coming toward the house. They rapped on the door and said that someone in the Stanley family was wanted on the telephone. I remember that Sewell Ford chided me when I rose to take the unexpected call, saying that all I wanted was an excuse to avoid him! I left to get the sad news over the phone. I hated to have to come back and tell mother!"

F. E. was 69 at the time of his fatal accident in the Stanley Steamer. Out in Estes Park, F. O., brokenhearted over the sudden loss of his twin brother, made the long return trip to attend the services.

"Mother lived ten years after that. As for the business, we had to stop making automobiles during the war. But we did sell many steam engines to the government. They shipped the engines overseas where they were used to pump water out of the trenches!"

The Stanley twins had had plans for resumption of business as soon as peace came. But with F. E.'s untimely death, things did not go well. Eventually the business broke up and was taken over by banks.

"For a while after that, my uncle, F. O. Stanley, manufactured violins along with his nephew, Carlton Stanley, in a shop near his home in Newton. This was a resumption of his activities as an excellent wood carver. Both boys were fine whittlers when youngsters. These violins were extremely well made and they sold in fair volume. My mother passed away in 1927. My aunt, Mrs. F. O. Stanley, lived to be 93, and she died in 1940. F. O. himself lived until 1941. He had a beautiful home on Waverly Avenue, Newton. Here, at this resident hotel where I make my own home now, I while away the days in ease and with fondest memories. My sister, Mrs. Edward M. Hallett (Blanche Stanley), lives nearby. Some day, we hope a book, the Stanley family biography, is forthcoming. All the detailed facts are available and I know that it will be a good story, just as the lives of the principals, the Stanley twins, was a good life!"

BIG GENE and the GHOST TRAIN

Engineer Eugene Everett Potter in 1897

NY & NE engine 183

*One half the glories have not been told
Of that wonderful train of white and gold,
Which leaves every day for New York at three,
Over the scenic NY & NE!*

by Francis D. Donovan

There isn't much left of the old New York & New England Railroad today; remnants of its main line exist from Boston through Walpole and Blackstone, Massachusetts, on into Putnam, Pomfret and Willimantic, Connecticut. Beyond, little remains of the trackage between Waterbury and Fishkill via Hawleyville, and the once-busy Air Line route between Willimantic and Middletown dead-ends near Cobalt, and no longer do trains thunder over the great Lyman Viaduct fill near East Hampton.

Be that as it may, the New York & New England, in its day, generated some of the greatest political and financial shenanigans ever known to Wall Street and Beacon Hill; it made and destroyed fortunes and characters but, withal, it produced and utilized some of the finest personnel and locomotives known to railroading through those and succeeding years.

Legend has spun webs of fact and fancy around two of these—the "Ghost Train," and engineer "Gene" Potter. Recollection rests well on the two, and the stories of the White Train flitting through the dusk still enthrall listeners; but the true story of the Ghost Train is only part of a strange and wonderful drama of the time.

Youngsters—and grown-ups, too—who watched in awe as Potter roared past in his engines, recognized a rare combination of courage and daring mixed with, at times, a quiet humor; his associates on the N Y & N E RR regarded him as a competent and dependable engineer, albeit a stubborn man who, disregarding consequence, clung tenaciously to a purpose.

Gene Potter could handle the throttle of a fast passenger train with the same facility he employed in addressing a boy's club, or in reciting the poetry of Ella Wheeler Wilcox,

whose verses filled his scrapbooks. It was a rare and fortuitous turn of circumstance that brought Potter and the Ghost Train together; they were meant for one another, perhaps indicated when Potter said, on first seeing his new Engine 167—"she's a strong, fast engine! By golly, she's just what we need."

Born in 1853, Eugene Everett Potter started firing on the Boston, Hartford & Erie RR in 1872, after serving a machinist's apprenticeship at the Mason Machine & Locomotive Works in Taunton, Massachusetts. The B H & E RR was the financial successor to a series of variously named corporations, stemming from the Norfolk County RR of 1845, running from Dedham to Blackstone. Through construction and merger, the line at the time Potter started firing ran from Boston to Waterbury.

On the road, Potter's ability and interest in his work soon manifested itself, and in 1878 he was set up as engineer of the fast "Washington Express." He thus took his place, at a relatively young age, among engineers noted as "fast runners": Ed Delano of the "Shore Line Express"; Dexter Blanchard of the Boston & Maine's "Montreal Express"; Warren French of the same road's "Portland Flyer"; Charlie Russell's Boston & Albany "Owl Express"; and the Fitchburg's Mitchell Young, running the "Chicago Express" between Boston and North Adams, Massachusetts, on an incredibly fast schedule.

In 1884, the N Y & N E RR, under the brilliant leadership of Charles P. Clark, inaugurated a new fast train called the "New England Limited" operating between Boston and New York over the Air Line

Route between Willimantic and New Haven, and over the New York, New Haven & Hartford RR into New York City. The road and Gene Potter became simultaneously famous from the first day of the Limited's operation—November 10, 1884—and the venture was successful from the very beginning. Trains left New York and Boston at 3 P.M. daily, making the run between the two cities in six hours. The 86 miles between Boston and Willimantic were made non-stop, as the engines took on water "on the fly" from track pans east of Putnam, Connecticut.

The track pans were novel innovations. They were 1500 feet long, 28″ wide, and 7″ deep, and were centered between the rails. When locomotives passed over the track pans, scoops were lowered into them, and at a speed of 40 miles per hour, 2500 gallons of water poured into the tender's tanks in less than 30 seconds.

Operating fast express trains over the old New England road—the later Midland Division of the New Haven RR—was never something that could be described as a relaxing experience. What is left of the line to this day is a snake's trail, hilly and winding, and in view of the route one wonders how trains rolled over it at the speeds the schedules required. Passengers, too, faced hazards, such as on March 10, 1888, when the westbound Limited got stuck in a blinding snowstorm at Hampton Grade, Connecticut, and the 105 passengers spent all night in the coaches because the brakeman who had gone for help had fallen off a bridge and was badly injured.

The railroad profession had its compensations, though, for by 1889, Potter was earning $7.00 per day as engineer, while his fireman, who actually did the hard work, earned only $2.00.

Gene Potter was well known by this time. He possessed a natural flair for showmanship without being a boor. His size and manner contributed to the proper—and required—mien of the "brave engineer," and he hit his stride in earnest when he developed a talent for public speaking and writing. His voice and style of delivery assured him of regular and attentive audiences; always a strong Brotherhood man, he was continually in demand at meetings, marriages, christenings, and funerals, or in doing what he most enjoyed off the road, addressing groups of young people. His talks to youngsters were instructive and inspiring without being sermons. He exemplified the tenets of clean living, personal honor, and religious conviction, and he could express these beliefs in a forceful yet simple manner. There was in him no hypocrisy. Potter loved life, and he had a remarkable ability to communicate his understanding of life to others.

Gene could make newspaper headlines at will. On August 21,

1888, all of the Boston papers noted that Engineer Potter and Fireman Bagley had shaved off their mustaches.

The New England RR knew that it had a valuable property in its Limited and its glamorous engineer, and the road's management did not hesitate to capitalize on both. By choice, President Harrison rode the Limited to New York on August 13, 1890; on that run, Potter was the engineer, Charlie Robinson fired, and Mike Ford was conductor.

Although the new fast train had done much to help the New England road, storm clouds were gathering by 1890. President Clark, who had done his best in building up the N Y & N E line, was called to the presidency of the New York, New Haven & Hartford RR, arch-

---

On March 16, 1891 the "New England Limited" was officially redesignated the "White Train." Engine No. 167 sported 63" drivers, and carried 160-pound steam pressure feeding into 18" x 24" cylinders. She was fast!

rival of the New England. Shortly thereafter, the New Haven denied the New England an entrance into New York City over New Haven rails, and a desperate New England RR employed a cumbersome routing by rail between Boston and Wilson's Point, Connecticut, via Waterbury and Hawleyville, then conveying the trains on car floats across Long Island Sound to Oyster Bay, Long Island, thence via Glen Cove and Mineola into the Flatbush Avenue depot. This route later became known as the Long Island & Eastern States Fast Passenger Express Line; the remarkable difficulties its route engendered soon brought its end, but not before the New England management, in an effort to simulate prosperity, placed dummies at the windows of the coaches.

It was as a result of this sort of frenzied attempt by the New England RR to recapture its passenger business that Potter and the railroad were to achieve their greatest fame, for on Monday, March 16,

1891, the "New England Limited" was officially redesignated the "White Train."

The road overlooked no possibilities in making this change a signal event; the train was made up of seven of the Pullman Palace Car Company's finest rolling stock—parlor car and baggage combine, royal buffet car, smoker, dining car, coaches, and parlor cars. All of the cars were painted white, and were equipped with Baker heaters and Pintsch gas illumination. The parlor cars were fitted out with velvet carpets, silk draperies and white silk curtains; the deep and comfortable chairs were upholstered in old-gold plush. Full-length plate glass mirrors were installed at each end of the cars, causing Potter to remark drily, "there'll be bad luck to spare if we go off the iron and break all these mirrors . . ." He smiled, though, as he regarded himself in the glass; he wore a white duster, white cap, and white gloves. His fireman wore white overalls, and the train crew under conductor Mike Crowley wore white caps trimmed in gold.

General Passenger Agent A. C. Kendall took charge of the parlor and dining cars and handed out ivory and gold menu cards bearing poems:

Spread the glad news wide and fast—
The White Train's come to Town at last!

Such beautiful cars have never been seen
Outshining in splendor the sun's bright sheen.

Without a jar, or roll, or antic,
*   Without a stop to Willimantic,*
The New England's Limited takes its way,
*   At three o'clock each and every day.*

Maids and matrons, daintily dimitied,
*   Ride every day on the New England Limited:*

Rain or snow n'er stops its flight—
*   It makes New York at nine each night.*

Common cars for the hoi-polloi,
*   But for the classical Boston Boy,*
Who will verses of Homer and Virgil sing,

Our new White Train is just the thing!

It was up to Potter and his engine to make the plush and gold and ivory worthwhile, and on that first afternoon, as Gene walked to his locomotive, he believed his engine No. 167 could meet the reduced time schedule—five hours and forty minutes—even with his heavy train. It sported 63″ drivers, and carried 160-pound steam pressure feeding into 18″ x 24″ cylinders. She was brand new, built by Cooke Locomotive Works in 1890.

Potter turned to watch Mike Crowley coming up to the engine. "She's a beauty, Mike," Gene exulted, "a powerful beauty." Crowley looked up at the N Y & N E R R Petee Cross emblem on the side of the tender. "You'll need luck, the both of you," said Crowley quietly, "and I wish you all there is." A few minutes later, Potter, acknowledging Crowley's go-ahead motion, started the train on its way to New York.

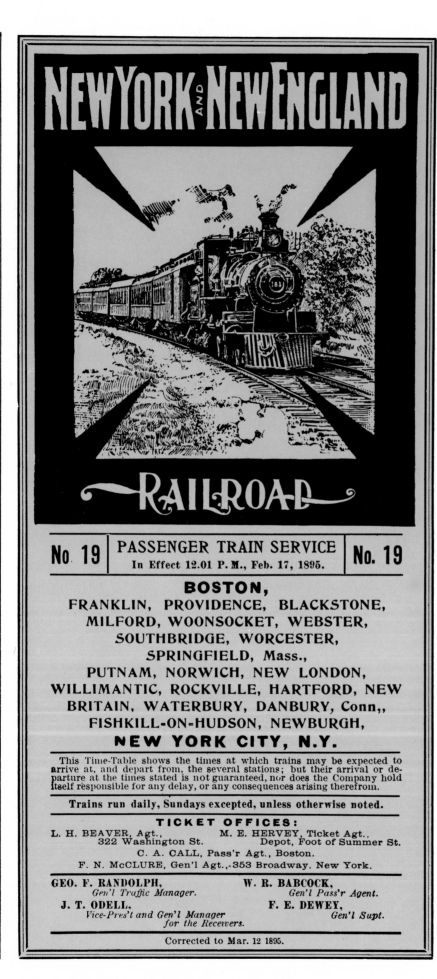

The train soon became known as the "Ghost Train," and even today there is no separating Potter and the Ghost, for as long as it was in existence he was its engineer. More than that, the two were emblematic of the time of which they were a part —an era of vigor and development, a time of heroics strangely mingled with gaudiness and ostentation. It is axiomatic that Potter and the Ghost Train carried one another into fame, but unlike John Luther "Casey" Jones, Potter had no accidents before achieving a permanent niche in history. Those who knew him well said that Potter would have made a capable preacher, lawyer, or businessman, but the destiny that directed him into railroading gave him a life he would not change.

The stories grew about Gene Potter. Railroad men, and after them, townspeople along the line repeated the tales.

One of the best-known yarns concerns the time President Clark boarded the White Train at New Haven and, noting that they were 35 minutes behind schedule, sent instructions up to Potter to make up the lost time. The regular running time between Willimantic and Boston—86 miles—was 135 minutes. On that night, when Potter hooked on, the train was still 25 minutes late, requiring him to make the run in 110 minutes. By the time he had reached North Windham, Potter had convinced all on board that he was doing everything possible to make up time. On through Putnam, Walpole, and Norwood he pounded; sweeping into Boston, he slowed for the curve over the old bridge at

NY & NE Railroad Timetable of February, 1895, featuring Potter and engine #183 on the New England Limited. The original photo for the illustration was taken at Dorchester, Massachusetts.

32

South Boston Cut. He looked at his watch, then shouted across the cab to his fireman, "We mustn't get in *ahead* of time—danged if we didn't gain a few minutes along the way!"

The train sheets for that night showed that Potter ran 62 miles in 54 minutes; the final 51 miles through Franklin to the Summer Street depot were covered in a little less than 47 minutes! On the morning after the scorching run, Superintendent Allen ordered Potter to appear in his office "for the purpose of disciplinary action for excessively fast running." President Clark, hearing of the summons, appeared in Potter's stead, and nothing more was heard of the "disciplinary action."

Meanwhile, the New Haven road was exerting a continually increasing pressure on the New England road—a pressure calculated to reduce traffic and prostrate the New England. To make matters even worse, the New England road, under the control of A. A. McLeod's flimsily financed Philadelphia, Reading & New England RR, was plunged into receivership when the P R & N E went bankrupt in December of 1893. In full awareness of the weak position of the New England RR, the New Haven moved in, and by 1895, the Morgan interests announced they were in control, and Clark became president of both systems.

The situation became even more complicated in that the new "Consolidated" road started running its "Shore Line Express" along the present coastal route to New York at the same time that a new five-hour express was initiated on the New England. The White Train was discontinued on October 19, 1895, and Potter took over the throttle of the "Air Line Limited," the White Train's successor.

Only one stop was made by the new Limited, and thus this train had the distinction of being the only train ever to go through New Haven without stopping. Potter had engine 129 west, Mike Crowley, conductor, and engineer Sam Landon, and conductor Harry Lindsley ran opposite trains. The Boston-end train left the "new and elegant Park Square depot" (near the present site of the Statler-Hilton hotel) and ran via West Roxbury and Dedham, coming onto the main line at Islington Tower in Westwood, Massachusetts, thence on into Middletown, Connecticut. A New Haven engine and crew took over at Middletown, and ran non-stop to New York City.

Potter and Crowley lost nothing in the new arrangement; they ran their schedules like clockwork, and they continued to be written up in the press. The Limited was noted on January 27, 1895, when the city of Putnam, Connecticut, registered an official complaint to the effect that Potter's train was passing the Chickering House block so fast that "it jars the building, shaking paper and magazine stocks from the shelves in Talbot and Chapman's news-room."

But Gene didn't ease up in his fast running; he thrilled to the roar and speed of his express. In 1898, he started running his new "full-blooded" Schenectady locomotive. This engine, the Number 2, replaced his older engine which was scrapped at the Norwood shops. The new No. 2 had 69″-diameter drivers, and weighed about 91 tons. Potter was proud of his engines, and always made sure they were in tip-top condition. His firemen—Pat Barrett, Charlie Robinson, Ed Bagley, and Earl Scott—regarded him as a good engineer to fire for. "Mr. Potter never was a rawhider, but he'd get all the good out of every pound of steam, and always hooked her up real careful so no steam got wasted. He was a fast runner on a fast schedule, and expected full pressure every mile of the way and always got it."

There were occasional accidents, too, and there were some times that Gene wasn't sure he'd ever see his wife or his home again. The few accidents in which his running was involved came about through no fault of his. His most serious wreck occurred shortly before his retirement. On June 20, 1921, he was engineer of Train No. 45 when the coaches went off the rails near East Waterville, Connecticut. Miraculously, none of the derailed coaches tumbled down the high embankment carrying the track.

He kept his record of fast runs intact: "On April 18, 1900—ran 215 miles in 263 minutes. Putnam to Boston 61 miles in 60 minutes. Geo. Brown my conductor."

When Potter retired in 1922, it was with an unblemished record of 50 years' service. He found time to visit with his friends, particularly with Mike Crowley, who by that time was running Trains 119 and 128 between Waterbury and Boston. He continued with his speaking engagements, wrote "pieces" for the Boston papers, and kept up his fraternal society affiliations. Until he died in February of 1928, he acted as consultant to the New Haven RR on fuel usage and route studies.

Gene Potter lived in and was a part of an era that now seems unreal —a bustling time, perhaps best symbolized by the Ghost Train. And if he could be here, one likes to think that Mr. Potter might quote another verse from the old menu cards:

One half the glories have not been told
  Of that wonderful train of white and
    gold,
Which leaves every day for New York
    at three,
  Over the scenic N Y & N E!

ROCKET OF LONG AGO

The "Rocket" weighed 1,600 pounds and was made of canvas and glue, but she carried a "thousand pounds of steam per square inch": enough pressure to break Fred Marriott's own world speed record, as well as his neck, unless he was lucky —————————————————— *by Arthur F. Joy*

He was eighty-three, and he was sitting back in his worn, creaky chair in that office of his and he was talking to me—about the time he broke the world speed record back in 1906.

"I was driving a Stanley steamer," the late Fred Marriott of Watertown, Mass., told me. "It was the 26th of January and we were at Ormond Beach, Florida. When that run of mine was over, I had gone faster than two miles a minute—a speed unheard of up to then."

Fred was right, too. Officially, he had driven the bullet-shaped steam racing car at 127.659 miles per hour, a new time record which stood until Barney Oldfield, a good friend of Fred's, bettered it a few years later in a car made in Germany.

As Fred talked on, I was lost in his world. It had become a dream

world for him—except for old pictures which hung haphazardly on the office walls surrounding him. Everything about that office spelled out the bygone. It was musty, dark, the rolltop desk was out of date, the clock on the wall was an old, hand-wound type. Even Fred Marriott himself talked in a hesitating, old man's tone of voice. Naturally, why wouldn't he? After all, here he was past eighty then, and certainly entitled to the whims and ways of a man that age.

But I wasn't doting on that angle of it. I was with Fred as he was when full of pep, vim and vigor down

Opp. page: Just before the last trial run and subsequent smashup in 1907.

Above: Fred Marriott and "The Rocket" setting the world speed record back in 1906.

there on the sands of that Florida beach so many years ago—a young, alert, vigorous man.

"As embryonic as the automobile business was in those days," Fred murmured, rousing me from my thoughts, "everybody was building one or trying to—and racing with it. The car that seemed to me to be the attention-getter then was the Fiat, from Italy. Then there was the German car, Blitzen-Benz, and those two English cars, Mercedes and Napier."

"How many pounds of steam," I interrupted him, "were you carrying when you made that world's record, Fred?"

"Thousand pounds per square inch," came his drawled reply. "She was called 'The Rocket,' and the top was curved and shaped like a rocket, too. Robinson, the canoe builder,

Right: Fred Marriot at the wheel of his Track Dancing Machine in the Fall of 1907.

Below: Fred's goal was 200 m.p.h., but it was too much for his light machine.

" ... the combination of speed, light weight, and treacherous sand spun me around and shot me eighteen feet in the air."

glued cedar to canvas to make me a durable canopy. I steered by a tiller, not a wheel. She weighed 1600 pounds. Limit was 2204 pounds—to be eligible."

On and on Fred Marriott talked about those hectic, exciting, early automobile days. I was interviewing him for a local paper. The publicity boys down at Daytona Beach wanted him to come there, at their expense, and accept honors for the Golden Anniversary of his feat. It really put Florida on the map, that record run. But I counted him out on getting steamed up over that now. I was telling myself, erroneously as it turned out, that he could no loner generate a spark of interest over present day activities.

"In those days," Fred continued matter-of-factly, "there were hardly any hotels at all down on the beach. And there wasn't a hospital for miles around. I ought to know. When I got hurt—," and then he paused, and an expression of pain, shadowed his pale, haggard face.

But only for a moment.

"I was doing nearly 200 that day," he said, turning to me with a proud glance. "They were calling my machine 'The Flying Teapot' by then. I shouldn't have tried to shatter all records in her like that, though. She wasn't heavy enough."

"What *really* happened, Fred?" I encouraged him, wondering if it was possible for him to catch on fire about anything except this subject —past auto racing.

His eyes glowed.

"I thought I could make her do two hundred. But that confounded combination of speed, light weight and treacherous sand spun me around, shot me eighteen feet in the air. It was the last time I ever raced a car."

I asked him why, hoping he'd come out of the past and inject a bit of the present, or future, into the interview.

His eyes were reincarnating only the moment of that vivid scene again.

"My only thought was to save myself from being decapitated by the force of the fall. In a flash it came to me that I should slide below the height of the boiler, try to save my head. When the machine finally crashed to the beach, the velocity threw me into the surf. That, too, saved my life."

"How do you mean, Fred?"

"Well," he smiled toward me in deep reminiscence, "the water broke the force of my fall. Even so, I blacked out. When I came to, I found doctors bent over me. I was in a room in a hotel. I learned later that when they fished me out of the water, my head was split open, my right eye lay on my cheek, I had several broken ribs, and a fractured collarbone. "That," he finished proudly, "was the 25th of January, 1907."

I shook my head in mock disbelief, but, of course, every word of it was true. Yet there wasn't a trace of the injuries visible to the naked eye.

"You sure pulled through," I told him, getting up to admire the snapshots and old-time pictures on the wall.

But Fred only went on with his reminiscences.

"They were afraid to let me come north. Pneumonia, or something worse," he said. "So I stayed down and recovered in the warm sunshine. Less than a month after the crash, I was umpiring at amateur races down there."

I saw one picture among the old ones on the wall which really had no business being there. It showed Sir Malcolm Campbell in his Bluebird IV at Daytona in 1933. The car was a superb machine—long, sleek, powerful. I remarked on it.

"Campbell . . . Seagrave . . . Cobb. Now, they've got the record up to 396 miles an hour, maybe more. No 'Flying Teapots,' either!" he said.

I had to agree with him there.

"But the fun? How about the pure demon fun of it? Is that still here, today, Fred? Do the modern racers get as big a bang out of sheer speed as you did?"

Fred Marriott shrugged his shoulders again in that I-don't-know-or-care gesture.

"*I* did," he answered. "I know that much. Racing was my meat. I made my mistakes, no doubt about it, but I don't believe I'd ever change anything about those days."

"You still feel that way, really?" I was quite doubtful now that the racing fever remains in a man's blood for good.

He glanced at me, this old man who had startled the world with his speed in his young manhood.

"Certainly I do!"

Then a gleam came into his eyes, lighting up his old face until it was bright and shiny, like a schoolboy's, full of fine spirit and the old fire.

"Ha! But now," pointing with bony finger to the sky over his head, "now, it's jets!"

And in that gleam, and in that bony finger pointed skyward, in those excited words, I had my answer!

ROPER'S
LAST
RIDE

Sylvester H. Roper and his fatal invention.

by Harry I. Miller

Although the steam bicycle invented by New Hampshire's Sylvester Roper cannot be listed among his more useful creations, it did work very well—alas, too well!

In today's frenetic race by Detroit to develop some alternate method of propelling automotive vehicles, and with steam engines and turbines being touted as being suitable power plants, it may come as a surprise to many automotive buffs that the inventor of America's practical steam bicycle was a Yankee from Francestown, New Hampshire.

The son of a farmer, Sylvester H. Roper (later to be identified with inventive greats like Elias Howe, Alvin Clark and Spencer the great gun manufacturer of Hartford) had visited Boston's Charles River bicycle track on June 2, 1896. The 73-year-old inventor had lugged along a bicycle powered by a steam engine, and he besought race officials to let him enter his steed in the races. With some misgivings and protests from the assembled racers, Roper was given the green light. He was pitted against some of the country's outstanding wheelmen, and he spread immediate dismay.

For ahead of him the graying little man pushed a fire-eating, smoke-belching bicycle. Despite catcalls and derisive yells from some of the racers and the laughing officials and spectators, Roper invited the race entrants to follow him around the track. They agreed to humor the old man.

Roper reached into a sack, extracted a handful of coal and tossed it into the tiny furnace of his midget boiler. The other wheelmen started off and Roper trailed slowly behind, as lap after lap went by.

But as steam pressure quickly rose in his compact boiler to 180 pounds—about that used later in the nation's giant locomotives—the little one-cylinder engine perked up and Roper ran three times around the track to his competitor's one.

The racers howled in disgust as they dropped out of the running, but they implored Roper to "let 'er out." Roper did. The amazing steam bike circled the mile track in 2 minutes, one and two-fifth seconds, a phenomenal record.

After clocking off this startling speed, Roper piled on the steam in an attempt to beat his own record.

He did, but the effort killed him.

The huffing, puffing engine was making the bike cut a lively 40 miles-an-hour pace on the back stretch when spectators noticed the front wheel of Roper's steed wobbling uncertainly. Seconds later it veered off the track and onto the sand, overturning and throwing Roper off.

The riders rushed to his rescue. When they lifted the old inventor, only a slight cut above the temple seemed the extent of his injuries. But later medical investigation revealed the New Hampshireman had died of a heart attack while riding, and life was extinct before his wheel hit the dust.

Yet the mechanical genius had had the foresight to prevent injury to other wheelmen and spectators from a bursting boiler, by using his last conscious moment to shut the steam off.

The name of Roper was well known in those early days of steam propulsion, and Roper, a mechanical engineer, had even then been more closely identified with steam engine operation of carriages than any other man in New England.

Back in 1869, Roper had equipped a heavy 2-wheeled velocipede with a steam engine and used it for over a decade. By the time he got around to adapting the idea of steam to a bicycle, bike racing had become a most popular sport and tracks had mushroomed in most major cities.

The farmer's son from Francestown had early shown infinite mechanical aptitude and had learned the machinist's trade in Boston. Elias Howe, of sewing machine fame, and Clark and Spencer, Hartford's great gunmakers, had then begun to startle the world with their mechanical ingenuity. Roper fitted right into such a picture and soon became associated with the manufacture of sewing machines and guns.

Roper, prior to the initial appearance of Howe's sewing machine, is reputed to have built one whose principles appeared later in Howe's machine. He was also inventor of the first practical knitting machine ever used in that part of New England.

The hot-air furnace and ranges were also fruits of Roper's creativity. The steam bike that proved trail's end for the noted inventor now reposes in the Florida museum, Bellm's Cars of Yesterday, Sarasota, and it still runs!

1800 FEET OF BAD LUCK

by Sarah Bridge Graves

Old Orchard's Ocean Steel Pier would be the longest in the world, a man-made peninsula, offering mooring for small boats and a port of call for coastwise steamers. It would have its own restaurant, orchestra, and miniature railroad . . . and be the target for one disaster after another.

The winter of 1898 never went more slowly for any town than it did for Old Orchard, Maine. The town was simply beside itself in anticipation of the beginning of what was to be the largest steel pier in the world. Since 1895 the project had been discussed, argued over and planned, but it was not until 1898 that the contract was drawn up and the construction begun by the Berlin Bridge Construction Company of Connecticut.

The War Department had given its blessing; even an Act of Congress had been necessary before this 1800-foot finger of the United States could be pointed toward Europe. Old Orchard itself turned out *en masse* with the arrival of each new structural member; The Old Orchard Ocean Pier Company was formed and ex-

For a nickel you could ride 1,800 feet out over the ocean in the smallest train in the world. The little locomotive weighed 700 lbs., was capable of hauling twelve cars. It was the high point of the trip for most of the visitors to the Ocean Steel Pier.

clamations of wonder arose from every throat as the structure grew and grew. The first 500 feet of it was "anchored" to a sub-stratum of ledge out into the bay. Beyond that, pilings were longer and increasingly longer. At the far end of the pier, great oak pilings made a fender to be used exclusively as a landing place for yachts, steamers and large sailing vessels. At that point the down-reaching steel pilings extended 50 feet from the promenade deck of the pier to the floor of the ocean where they were bedded securely into the sand.

It was not considered enough just to build a pier. The very fact that it extended a landlubber's strolling habits more than a third of a mile out over the Atlantic ocean brought on other schemes. Fishing boats could dock at small landings alongside the pier. Pleasure crafts could easily do the same. Mooring platforms were fashioned and steel ladders placed at strategic locations. The fishing industry was provided with just about paradise.

Everyone felt like a millionaire . . .

With 17 feet of sea water under them at low tide and twenty-seven at normal high tide, the coastwise steamers readily acknowledged this as a summer port of call. Plying between Boston and Portland they gracefully swung into Saco Bay and added immeasurably to the glamor of the place. Just think of it! You could go to Europe by way of the end of the Old Orchard Ocean Steel Pier!

Of a certainty they would transport you to Boston for the mere matter of purchasing a $1.00 ticket and from Boston surely all the world lay in wait, just like an open book. Boston was the hub of the universe, and any sea captain would tell you about the Boston boat.

On the pier were three pavilions. At the shore entrance they took tickets, arranged for baggage and bicycles. About five hundred feet out and again at the one-thousand foot area from shore, the pier expanded into fifty by sixty-foot platforms where onlookers might enjoy the novel excitement of cages of beautiful birds and cages of monkeys. Their endless antics vastly amused both young and old and provided a never-to-be-forgotten highlight at the beach.

At the outermost end of the pier a great Casino was constructed. It covered an area seventy-five by one hundred and twenty-five feet. Here a splendid restaurant catered to those eager to enjoy the novelty of such appointments, not on a boat and yet certainly out over the ocean swells. An orchestra played each afternoon and evening for dinner and dancing, and life seemed to be joined to fairyland. Everyone felt like a millionaire.

With the coming of night a diamond tiara of electric lights bathed the entire length of the pier in enchantment. Tubs of evergreen trees stood like dark sentinels between benches placed against the protective steel hand rails along the promenade deck. Here patrons of the pier

Stretching out into the ocean for more than a third of a mile, steel pilings became longer and longer. At the far end of the pier, pilings extended 50 feet from the promenade deck to the floor of the ocean.

Below: Old Orchard as it looked before the great pier was constructed. Old Orchard Beach, Me.

sat to enjoy the stars and to watch the reflected glory of the great structure swimming on the night tide below.

Over this new and attractive avenue of approach thousands of summer visitors did indeed come to visit Old Orchard. Here was the superlative pleasure of seeing and being seen on the longest ocean steel pier in the world. This was the height of fashion.

All of this had come to pass in an incredibly short span of time. It seemed only the day before yesterday that something was planned and now Old Orchard had new claims to glory. For the time being, anyway, these augmented and almost outshone its wonderful hard-packed sandy beaches, already world renowned as the finest sort of place for a span of horses to draw carriages at low tide. The very placement of supporting piers on the mainland had been designed to allow free wheeling and turning for the handsome equippages. In all of New England there

Below: The Old Orchard Steel Pier, as it looked before 1898 when it was almost completely destroyed by the same storm that sank the Portland.

was not an equal to this seven miles of gently sloping, tow-free, warm, expanse of ocean and shore.

All went so well bigger plans were made for the coming season. Each person told another how much business had been realized by the exciting new pier at Old Orchard. It was truly a drawing card of the first magnitude. But so was a storm that brewed in the sea on Thanksgiving night 1898. At the height of the gale a raging ocean swept away the brand new Casino 1800 feet from shore.

Next morning the beach was littered with window frames, splintered chairs and tables, oddments from the gift shops and all manner of lumber in every state of destruction. Trains waited at the railroad station to give passengers a chance to view the debris from the storm. However it was only superficial damage and could be repaired. The structural steel of the pier was undamaged. Such was not the fate of the steamer *Portland* (See Yankee, November, 1956), abroad in the same cruel storm. It sank with a total loss of life. Old Orchard felt it had been spared the brunt of the storm that terrible night.

Old Orchard began to consider itself the playground of two nations . . .

As spring came along in 1899, a new Casino was built and completely fitted out ready for another wonderful summer season. Now the great pier had a past! It had withstood the perilous encounter of the sea. People wanted to stand at its outermost end and ponder upon waves that had swept away a building the size of the Casino.

In the early summer of '99 everyone succumbed to the charm of a darling little live-steam locomotive. This innovation pulled a miniature train right down the middle of the promenade deck on the Old Orchard Ocean Steel Pier. For the sum of five cents, anyone could ride from the main entrance of the pier straight out over the brawling Atlantic ocean.

This little train went hissing and puffing along, bedanging its brass bell in the best tradition of railroading. It was capable of hauling twelve cars besides the tender. The steel locomotive weighing 700 pounds was about six feet long. The top of the smokestack reached halfway to a man's waist. The gauge was slightly more than 12 inches. The tracks were of steel. The tender carried twenty pounds of coal and three gallons of water.

The eager little train was temporarily fitted out with wooden rails because a shipment of special steel rails was delayed in arriving. Meanwhile the train chuffed back and forth and delighted both passengers and onlookers on the sea-going pier.

In July of 1899 this particular little train held the enviable distinction of being the smallest train in the world. Souvenir china was made in Germany and the image of the little locomotive was hand painted on countless pieces of Dresden. Each passenger felt very sure that their nickel's worth of railroading was a devilishly exciting maneuver.

Summer followed summer in a bright succession of prosperity and Old Orchard expanded by day and night. More and bigger hotels came into being. Cottages sprang up. Tourists continued to stay for the entire season and lasting friendships sprang up between them and the townspeople. Each welcomed and respected the other. Bilingual shopkeepers numbered many Canadians among their clientele. Canadian money was passed as freely as coins of the United States. Old Orchard began to really consider itself the playground

of two nations who lived and thought much alike and were friendly as could be.

Then came August 15, 1907. Summer was such a pleasant time, and August the elegant month of the year. People were dressing for dinner and a round of evening festivities when about seven o'clock fire broke out in one of the wooden hotels near the pier. In a matter of minutes the town was ablaze. Over five thousand guests, summer visitors, tourists, townspeople, store owners, shop keepers, cafe and restaurant personnel and hotel staffs were driven into the streets and held at bay by one of the costliest fires ever to occur in the state of Maine.

Where moments before all had seemed luxury, prosperity and a wonderful summer season not yet drawing to its close, now a raging holocaust consumed hotel after hotel. Businesses went up in flames in the wind-fed fire. The magnificent Hotel Velvet, show place of the town, burned flat in thirty minutes, its entire contents a charred loss. This was the sumptuous place that molasses candy kisses had made possible. It had been the scene of some of the gayest times in a town full of summer gaiety.

Flames from this hotel licked onto the shore end of the steel pier. The superstructure was burned. The booths extending out on the pier for nearly a hundred feet shared the same fate. Only by ripping up the flooring of the pier beyond that area was it possible to confine the fire and prevent it from flowing out the entire length of the pier and taking the Casino at the end.

The season ended as a saddened, blackened ghost of itself. But the debris was carted off and plans were formulated to make out of this chaos a bigger and better and more beautiful and fireproof town to take the place of the burned area in Old Orchard. What could be repaired was made good as new. The rest of it was new. The pier was given a new superstructure and some new promenade decking and a cluster of new booths at the shore end. Business got under way the next summer. Trains ran, people came, salt water taffy was in

OLD ORCHARD BEACH, ME.

every mouth. A staunch admiration and respect for Old Orchard was felt by all who saw what had been accomplished. A miracle had come about. A miracle through hard work.

On March 25, 1909, the Weather Bureau in Boston posted "Northeast storm warnings at 10 A.M. Block Island to Eastport, strong to high northeast winds probably tonight." For fourteen hours, rain, accompanied by a terrific gale gave the New England coast and the Old Orchard area the worst storm since 1898. Many of the seashore residents insisted this was the hardest blow they had ever known. The Saco river rose 30 inches in 24 hours.

When morning came a great many people went down to see how the pier had come through the storm. They discovered to their fascinated horror that the first pavilion, about a thousand feet off shore known as "White City," still full of its amusement penny arcade picture machines, and 300 feet of the pier structure had been torn away by the powerful seas.

Bad luck still continued.

On the 30th of April six carpenters were rowed out by boat to the outer portion of the pier to check over the Casino and make any needed repairs. The small boat originally engaged to transport the workmen to and from the pier capsized on its return journey inshore. The boatman almost lost his life. A storm brewed all day and by night the men could not be removed from the pier. There was no possibility of a small boat surviving the raging water which continued for 3 or 4 days.

When the deep turbulence finally subsided a boat from the Fletcher's Neck Coast Guard Station at Biddeford Pool was able to come alongside the once proud pier and rescue the men. After this, plans went forward and later the whole Casino was dismantled and brought in shore piece by piece and rebuilt at about the 800 foot area. The remaining 1,000 feet of the supporting trestlework and piling was removed inland to prevent its becoming a hazard to navigation in Saco Bay.

Today, Old Orchard is still old Orchard, sea and shore and holds faith with that part of what was once the longest and proudest ocean steel pier in the world . . . the marvel of the Gay Nineties.

During the summer, thousands of health and pleasure seekers came to Old Orchard but June 26th was traditionally the most popular bathing day. It was believed that on this day the water was endowed with special healing properties.

Some adaptations and institutions in Section II proved impractical. Their stories are one . . .

. . part of THE FORGOTTEN WORLD OF STEAM today.

THE NANTUCKET CAMEL

During the early 1800's, the tonnage of whaleships and barques greatly increased. Because of this, it became difficult for these vessels to cross the so-called bar at the entrance of Nantucket (Mass.) Harbor—unless the cargo was partly unloaded outside. In fact, the inner harbor, itself, was only about seven and a half feet deep at low tide.

In order to overcome this problem, a Nantucket man designed what might be called a floating drydock; it was called a "camel" because this double barge held so much water. The so-called "camels" were the extraordinary invention of Peter F. Ewer and were financed by fifty Nantucket people. The plans and construction were carried out by J. G. Thurber at Nantucket and in a short time these floating barges, steam propelled with a rudder and water gates, were ready for service.

After a whaler had signaled its arrival outside of the harbor, the "camels" maneuvered along the main channel under their own power to meet the inwardbound ship. They made a speed of about two knots. As they approached the vessel, the "camels" separated, lengthened their connecting chains until these very heavy chains hung in a loop deeper than the keel of the whaleship. They then passed along underneath it, one on either side until the whaler was well within. At this point the water gates were opened so that the "camels" could be filled with their long drink of salt water. This was the camel-drinking episode. When the barges were full they would sink below the surface of the water. The chains were then tightened by means of thirty windlasses, steam pumps pumped the water out of the barges at a rate of thirty barrels per minute and, as the lightened barges or "camels" rose, the ship became steady and secure between them supported by the fifteen heavy chains. After the operation was completed, the whaler, "camels" and all, could easily pass over the bar into the harbor, propelled by the engines of the "camel" and helped by the flat-bottomed towing steamboat. This floating drydock enabled large vessels to go right to the wharf for unloading most of their cargo. The invention was considered most remarkable at the time as whaler, "camels," and all, did not draw more than five feet of water.

Unfortunately, the "camels" proved to be most unprofitable for lack of patronage and eventually all of them simply went to rest alongside a dock as the whaling business made a rapid decline.

by Vincent Short

COMPLETE ON THIS SPREAD

How can we describe the "Camel"? To begin, she was steam propelled and functioned rather like a floating wet drydock . . .

The *Massachusetts* tows the *Nantucket Camel* into Nantucket Harbor. The "camels" were 135 ft. long, 19 ft. wide and 29 ft. deep. Whaler, "camel" and all, did not draw more than five feet of water.

LOMBARD'S IRON MONSTER

by Walter M. MacDougall

A steam log hauler would have to lay its own wide rails. It was something that Lombard had watched when a boy that gave the answer—a horse-driven treadmill . . .

The sun sets on a cloudless horizon, red but without warmth. The road, stretching like a ribbon of ice between the silent spruce and fir, is in blue shadow as if the marrow-reaching cold had a color. Then the silence is broken. The pounding of rapid exhaust blasting up into the pale sky, the clank of moving metal, and the complaints of heavily loaded sled runners grows and fills the evening. Over a knoll comes a monster —the most dramatic creation of iron that ever invaded the woods. With a surge of flying sparks flung against the first stars of night and with the powerful thudding of lags, Lom-

bard's steam log hauler passes and disappears followed by its long train of sleds.

Although Lombard's iron horse had a brief history and passed leaving few cherished memories, it does hold an important place in the annals of advance. Lombard's great contribution was not the engine but the means of locomotion, the lag tractor tread—a mechanism which was to end the deadlock in the miserable trenches of France and was to bring into existence the bulldozer and that host of lag-driven machines which grind and move to the bidding of man.

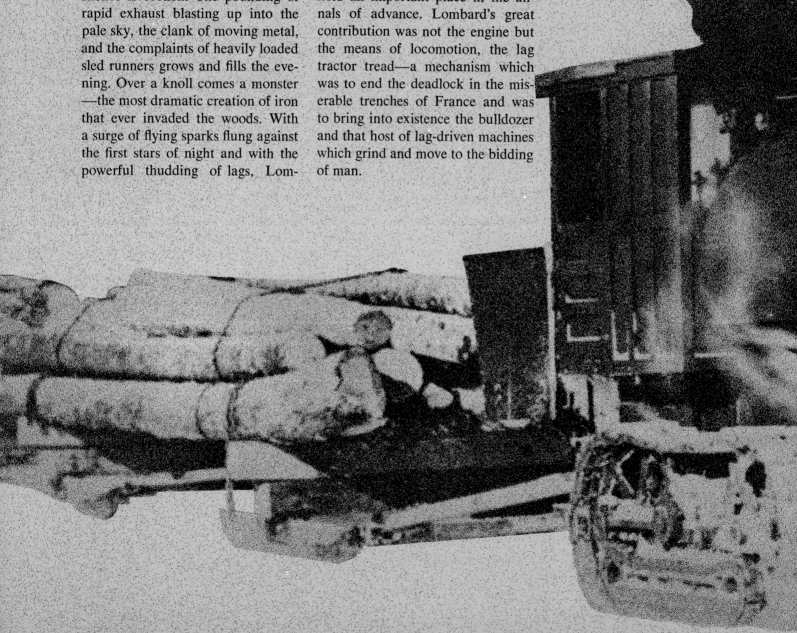

There was nothing particularly unique about the engine, but its means of locomotion, the lag tractor tread, was the forerunner of the bulldozer and the many other lag-driven machines we still use today . . .

Coal was the usual fuel for many haulers because it was easier to maintain pressure, but in timber, burning wood made a log hauler truly independent.

The story begins on a small farm in Springfield, Maine, with the birth of Alvin Orlando Lombard. The date was February 21, 1856. There was nothing prophetic in that birth unless it was the name chosen for the boy—that does have a ring. Alvin's father was a blacksmith and the operator of a small sawmill. It was in a world of turning wheels and sparking iron that the boy grew up and began to tinker and invent. On a small hillside brook running across his father's farm, Alvin built his first mill. It featured a steel brace from a hoop skirt and sawed cucumbers into straight cucumber boards and timbers. At his father's mill he rigged a power churn, liberating both himself and his brother Levi from a chore. By the time he was old enough to vote, Alvin Orlando Lombard had joined the ranks of Yankee inventors. Perhaps the die had been cast in that small brook on his father's farm. At any rate, Lombard was destined to make a great contribution.

In 1899, Lombard was living in Waterville, Maine. His inventions had run to paper machinery. His patents were taking on the form of iron in the foundry of the old Waterville

Iron Works. There were machines to strip bark from pulp and to sort out waste from the chipped wood destined for the sulfide digesters. Perhaps most successful was an automatic control for waterwheels and turbines—a mechanism which is still in use at hydroelectric plants across the nation. Success, a rare commodity among inventors, had come to Alvin Orlando.

It was a chance conversation that made Lombard determined to build a log hauler and emancipate the horse from the killing hauls over tote roads. Some reports claim that Alvin Orlando went home from that conversation and began work without eating his supper; but, regardless, within two days he had his plans drawn and a wooden model sitting on a desk at the Waterville Iron Works.

Steam was the logical choice of power, but the big problem lay in weight and traction. Alvin had already experimented with steam power. Before the Stanley Brothers, Lombard had built a steam car.

Building a log hauler, however, was another story. In some way the weight of a boiler and fire box had

If one had three log haulers on a job, he might hope to keep two in operation

Capable of hauling 300 tons of wood at a speed of 4–5 m.p.h., Lombard's iron horse required a crew of four to keep it working: an engineer, a fireman, conductor, and steerer.

to be spread out over a large area and a tractive mechanism devised which would not only grip but also adjust itself to any irregularities beneath. A steam log hauler would have to lay its own wide rails. It was something that Lombard had watched when a boy that gave the answer—a horse driven treadmill.

The "Mary Ann," the first Lombard hauler, had been built in time for the winter season of 1900–1901. There followed a period of trial and error, that old stand-by for inventors who lacked technical training. At first the horse was not entirely eliminated. Lombard's first plans called for a team of horses hitched in front

of the engine to do the steering. For the horses it must have seemed as though they had gotten out of the pan only to land in the fire. Now there was a pushing, steam-breathing devil tied to their tails. This steering experiment failed and the horses were replaced by a man who bent over a wheel and wrestled to keep the steering sled's runners in the proper ruts while sparks from the smoke stack landed on his Mackinaw

—the only bringer of warmth to his bitterly cold job.

During the next few years, Lombard set up his own works on the sight of the present Keyes Fibre Plant between Fairfield and Waterville. The company was a family concern and never what one would consider a big operation. After building an engine, Lombard waited for a buyer and counted his cash to see if there was enough to build another hauler. Experimentation went on.

There were no set specifications on iron in those days and parts were often faulty. In the cold of winter cast iron parts would break. As one old-timer put it, "Those sprockets would snap like a 'T.D.' pipe stem on a frosty morning." If one had three log haulers on an operation, he might hope to keep two in operation. But despite all this, the Lombard was a worthy machine. On the iced tote roads of New England, Canada, and as far west as Wisconsin the log haulers began to haul their trains of sleds.

As long as a log hauler ran, she could do the work of scores of horses.

Of all the problems which Lombard encountered with his log hauler, the most serious was that of his patent right; it was wide open to infringement. Alvin's patent had been taken out on May 21, 1901. By the time that Lombard's Traction and Engine Company was getting into high gear, lag tractors were appearing in California.

Meanwhile, back in the woods, the Lombard haulers were moving a pile of stuff. All across Maine during those first two decades of the twentieth century, the whistles and exhausts of those engines were echoing off the snow-blanketed mountains. In the deep wilderness of the Allagash, log haulers pulled two standard-gauge locomotives from the Canadian border to Churchil Depot for Lacroix's logging railroad.

At each location the story was much the same. A log hauler crew consisted of an engineer, fireman, conductor, and the steerer. Close to the rear, the conductor rode the sleds communicating with the cab by a bell rope which ran along the sled stakes. Should one of the wooded reaches break on a curve, the unleashed sleds would head for the undergrowth and the conductor was left to jump. From the cab the engineer worked the throttle, watched the lags turning below him, and swore at the fireman when the occa-

sion arose. Up front in the dubious place of honor huddled the steerer. There were no brakes on a log hauler or on its train of sleds, and nearly every road had its downgrade that made steerers pray that should they live through this once more then they would find some other way to make a living. Down grades were sprayed with hay to help hold back the sleds, engineers could put their haulers into the "britchen"—an art of reversing the engine and gingerly cracking on enough steam to "pillow" the pistons —and the fireman in a real extremity might shovel out coal to help trig the following sled runners if he had not already jumped, but run-a-ways usually went hell-bent-for-election.

At night when the cold made the hard woods crack, the roads were watered. Icers, long tanks mounted on sled runners, were hauled over the road spraying water, which froze and glinted in the moonlight. When the sun rose, the Lombards were back doubling up the grades and sluicing down the mountain sides.

Anyone who went out to repair a stranded log hauler could appreciate Dante's lowest level of hell. Crews were often forced to build bonfires along both sides of the engine to thaw out parts and keep themselves from freezing. After crawling around with jacks and blocks, handling ponderous, ice-cold hunks of iron, one

yearned for the warm, living smell of horses.

On larger operations coal was the usual fuel, but many haulers on the smaller jobs burned wood. It was easier to maintain steam pressure with coal, and there was no danger of ramming out a boiler plug while stuffing the fire box, but in the tall timber burning wood made a log hauler truly independent.

Nineteen twenty-eight saw the last big operation for Lombard log haulers at a place called Cooper Brook in Maine. The Northern Paper Company hauled nine hundred tons of coal into the woods for their twenty-ton Lombards, built a wooden trestle 1250 feet long and removed 42,000 cubic yards of dirt and rock to ease the grades on that haul to Upper Jo Mary Lake. On such a large operation as this, the trains were run by dispatchers who sat at a desk fronted by a map of the road and flanked by up-right phones from which they issued orders. "Gobacks," or turn-out roads, were used to route the returning empties so as to give the loaded sleds a clear run. Once a train was started, it was better not to stop. The runners of loaded sleds had a way of freezing in.

By 1930 the story of steam log haulers was over. Gas engines were the coming thing. Lombard, himself, held races to prove that the new engines were better, and sometimes he won. The importance of Lombard's tractor tread grew and kept growing while the inventor was all but forgotten. At Vassalboro, Maine one can still visit the dam and experimental station where Alvin Orlando did his testing and inventing. But it is doubtful that many stop to look or, if they do, they would know that here worked the Yankee genius who first gave the lag tractor tread to the world.

BOYNTON'S DREAM ENGINE

by John H. Ackerman

COMPLETE ON THIS SPREAD

This is Locomotive No. 1 of the Boynton Bicycle Railway Company — a monumental piece of Yankee ingenuity that never made the grade.

As sightseeing attractions in Portland, Maine went, the rather gritty surroundings and yards of the Portland Company, builder of steam locomotives and other machinery, was not highly rated. But on this one particular day in 1889, almost everybody in Portland seemed to be down by the factory yards, looking in wonder on a machine the likes of which had never been seen on land or sea —the Boynton bicycle monorail locomotive.

What they saw was the brainchild of a persevering, earnest, and rather humorless man named E. Moody Boynton. In the 1880s, he began to stir public interest with his outspoken comments about the railroads of America—they needed fast, lightweight trains. Such trains, he stoutly maintained, would cost less to build and operate, and would encourage the railroads to expand and improve their service. Viewed from the vantage point of today when federally encouraged lightweight flyers are testing 150-mile-an-hour runs between New York, Washington, and Boston, Boynton's opinions bear a haunting resemblance to the current emanations of sundry public relations departments with an interest in the new speedsters.

Boynton's dream engine was built for him at the Portland Company's works after a Newburyport, Massachusetts shop threw up its hands and quit. A staid, old-line locomotive and machinery builder with an excellent reputation, the Portland Company tackled Boynton's engine gingerly in what must have represented the triumph of Yankee curiosity over Yankee skepticism.

The engine scored an immediate success in one respect; it drew crowds to the factory to see it run on a short stretch of specially built track. What the crowds saw was a locomotive with a single 8-foot driving wheel slung between two parallel boilers just ahead of a two-story cab. Cylinders and main rods mounted beneath the smokebox and boiler drove the single driver along a single running rail, while a guiding rail overhead, supported by arches, steadied the engine. Boynton rode in the second story of the cab, wearing a fur hat, yelling at small boys to stay off the track, and looking, so one onlooker said, more like a minister than an inventor.

Later that day, Boynton gave an optimistic interview to the press. He expected, he said, that his bicycle engine would pull four cars carrying 88 passengers each at 100 miles an hour. To reach this speed, unheard of in 1889, Boynton relied on his engine's single driver: it would cut friction so much that the engine's power would be utilized solely for pulling. Its light weight would greatly reduce building and operating costs, he enthused, while con-

struction of a right-of-way for his four-foot-wide, 14-foot-high cars would involve no expensive grading. He dreamed of his skinny cars and their skinnier track threading their way through once inaccessible gorges and over tall mountains with never a tunnel needed.

Boynton's bicycle railroad, he added, would operate with unusual efficiency thanks to a telephone system he would also devise. Using it, engineers could call a station or another train while running at 100 miles an hour. (This became reality decades later.)

Despite his optimism and his correct enough analysis of the virtues of lightweight trains, Boynton and his bicycle railroad dropped into obscurity after the brief triumph in the Portland Company's yard. The reasons for the curtain's sudden fall are not hard to discern. In his haste to eliminate friction, Boynton forgot that some friction is necessary if an engine is to pull a train. His one-wheeled locomotive, like a one-legged horse, was woefully lacking in adhesion and pulling power. Even as Boynton experimented, the practical locomotive most closely resembling his design was losing the battle of tractive effort in England. There, engines with a single pair of seven- or eight-foot driving wheels had long pulled crack expresses. But the coming of longer, heavier trains saw the once fleet singles spin and stall or require double-heading.

Boynton passed over lightly another major objection to his system —the fact his engines and cars were not interchangeable with conventional railroad rolling stock. (This same criticism continues to stall development of monorail systems today.) Costly and time-consuming transfers of passengers and freight —a major factor in the demise of the narrow-gauge railroads of Maine and the West—would have been required. With millions invested in conventional equipment and roadbed, the railroads were hardly prepared to junk their rolling stock.

Boynton's claim that his right-of-way would cost less to build than a conventional right-of-way must be viewed with skepticism. The erection of miles of arches to carry the overhead guide rail and the grading needed for the single running rail could easily have cost more than a conventional roadbed.

For years, Boynton sought legislative permission to build his bicycle railroad. He never received it. And he died, a disappointed man who never lived to see lightweight trains embodying his beliefs go into service. Now, time has proved his fundamental thesis correct. As lightweight silver cars flash by at two miles a minute, there's likely a smiling ghost in the offing—E. Moody Boynton, vindicated after all these years.

HOTTER THAN HELL

The Plunger *was a complete system of problems but its major flaw was the time needed to extinguish the fires and vent the steam. And if you waited until the firebox cooled, this made the diving period longer than most wars.*

by Robert A. Granato

It was a stormy birth, at the turn of the century, for the United States Submarine Fleet, the first in the world, when John P. Holland, after years of frustration, finally convinced the Navy and Congress to add the submarine to the nation's naval arsenal.

On April 11, 1900, after a quarter of a century of designing, constructing, testing, and political battling, the peppery Irish inventor presented the Navy with its first submarine, the *USS Holland*. Appropriation hearings in Congress were concluded in June and final contracts were awarded.

Pop-art posters across the nation's college campuses today picture a comical-looking, Charlie Chaplin-type man, with his head peering out of a hatch on the submarine. Few know who he is or what his contributions were to revolutionizing modern, naval warfare. While many of his scientific contemporaries gained recognition, the man who fathered the forerunners of our present nuclear submarine fleet remains in obscurity.

Born in County Clare, Ireland, on February 29, 1840, he grew up in the turmoil of that country's struggle with England. Strongly anti-

John P. Holand, father of the American Submarine Service.

British, as a young man he saw the significance of the *Monitor-Merrimac* clash of ironclads during our Civil War. He began to apply the principles of the ironclads to the development of a submersible.

His strong anti-British feelings led him to fear the growing might of the British fleet. Holland, from his experiences in Ireland, saw the British as the threat to world peace.

Immigrating to the states in 1872, he approached naval officials with his designs and received his first setback when they were rejected. Utilizing private capital, Holland built "Boat #1," in 1878, and tested the craft by sitting on the bottom of the Passaic River in New Jersey for 24 hours. The fiery Irishman countered the rejection by stating, "The Navy doesn't like submarines because there is no deck to strut on."

Most naval officers opposed the submarine with the opinion they were "death traps when they were not toys." Strategically, the surface Navy was viewed as a defensive force with its primary mission to defend the nation's coastline and important harbors. Few thought the submarine practical for harbor and coastal work in shallow waters.

By the late 1880s, influential naval officers began to think of the submarine as a possible auxiliary craft to the fleet. Even with this slight

change in thought, naval officers never looked upon the submarine as an offensive weapon prior to World War I.

As late as the opening stages of World War II, differences of opinion as to the submarine's offensive capacity still existed. The battleship, with its protective screen of smaller craft, was thought to be the nucleus of naval seapower afloat. The disaster at Pearl Harbor and the ensuing record of the submarine fleet action as the only remaining offensive potential in the early stages of the Pacific conflict was to rewrite naval warfare tactics.

Holland's disappointment at the Navy's rejection of his submarine design did not hinder his efforts. Still concerned over British seapower, he turned to the Fenian Society, an Irish revolutionary group, which financed the world's first practical submarine.

Constructed and tested by May, 1881, the 31-foot *Fenian Ram,* was stolen by a competitive group of Irishmen from Connecticut. It later was abandoned in New Haven and is now on display as a memorial in Westside Park in Paterson, New Jersey.

As naval authorities began to see a practical use for the submarine, a competitive contest for the design of a boat was held in 1888. Holland's design won and he formed the J. P. Holland Torpedo Boat Company. He won a second competition in the early 1890s, and was awarded a contract in 1895.

The contract was awarded with the stipulation that Holland construct the boat along lines of the Navy's specifications. Holland, however, doubted its performance and while he embarked on the $150,000 Navy contract for the *Plunger,* he started construction on his own design with his own resources.

The *Plunger* was to be propelled on the surface by a steam engine and switched to electric motors powered by batteries while submerged. The first trials proved it was impracticable, as the time needed to extinguish fires and vent the steam made the diving period too long. Once submerged, the heat remained in the firebox, making the submarine unbearable.

Upon completing his own design, he said, "I do not think I can improve on the arrangement or general features of this design . . . it represents a powerful and effective boat." He offered the design to the Navy, but was again rejected. Using his own financial resources, estimated at $1 million, he went ahead with the construction of his own submarine in Elizabethport, New Jersey.

Holland's boat was the first to be propelled on the surface by an internal combustion engine, which set an important precedent for the future development of submarines. The gasoline engine could be shut down instantly for submergence and transferred to electric drive with batteries as the power source.

The 53-foot boat had a diameter of 10 feet and displaced nearly seventy-five tons. Lack of a periscope hindered maneuverability while submerged and the craft had to be in an awash condition for the captain to look out the portholes in the conning tower.

Holland had offered his design to Assistant Secretary of the Navy Theodore Roosevelt. While Roosevelt praised the concept of a submersible, the Navy withheld a decision.

Holland, a mechanical genius, was unable to cope with the political scene in Washington and win favorable publicity to gain the support of Congress. In the late 1890s, he merged with the Electric Launch Company to form the Electric Boat Company, the forerunner of the present Electric Boat Company, a division of General Dynamics in Groton, Connecticut.

The merger brought Isaac Rice, a financial expert who knew the political trails around Washington and had a flair for publicity, into action. He immediately sent the *Holland* to Washington for exercises on and under the Potomac River in full view of newspapermen, Congressmen and the military.

Congress was impressed with a series of trials and a number of key naval officials added their "brass" to the weight of the decision. Appearing before an appropriations hearing of the House Committee on Naval Affairs in June, 1900, Admiral George Dewey, the Spanish-American War hero of Manila Bay, gave his endorsement to Holland's submarine. He said, ". . . if they had had two of those things in Manila, I never could have held it with the squadron I had."

The appropriation was passed and five submarines, ordered. The Silent Service was born.

Lt. Harry H. Caldwell, an observer aboard the *Holland* during its trials and a key witness at the hearings, assumed command. In fleet maneuvers with the Atlantic Squadron off Newport, Rhode Island in September, he came alongside the "hostile" battleship *USS Kearsage* while submerged.

Surfacing, he shouted his message to the flagship's bridge, which electrified the American press: "Hello *Kearsage.* You are blown to atoms. This is the *Holland.*" Editorial writers across the nation attacked the expenditures for "floating fortresses" sinkable by an insignificant 53-foot submarine.

John P. Holland was not to witness the submarine in battle. He died on August 14, 1914, at the age of 74. A month later, German U-boats sank three British cruisers with a loss of 1370 lives. The age of submarine warfare was upon us.

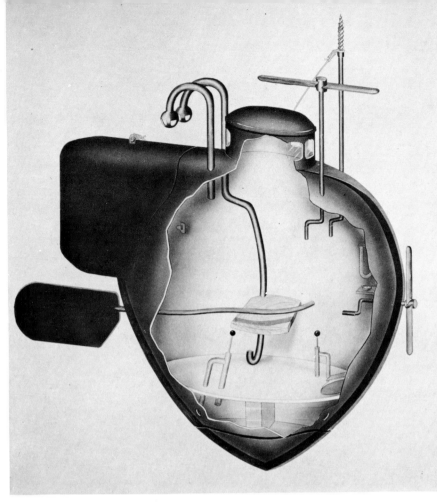

Left: The first American submersible, the Turtle *was built by David Bushnell in Saybrook, Conn., during the Revolution. She made one unsuccessful attack against a British frigate in an attempt to break the blockade of New York Harbor.*

Below: The cumbersome 85-foot Plunger *was the first submarine ordered by the U.S. Navy. Delivered in 1903, it never got beyond dock trials. Elaborate plans called for three screws. Two were driven by two steam engines each, a third by two electric motors for submerged running. Before the* Plunger *submerged, an electric motor drew smokestack and air tube into its superstructure and slid the cover over the hatch.*

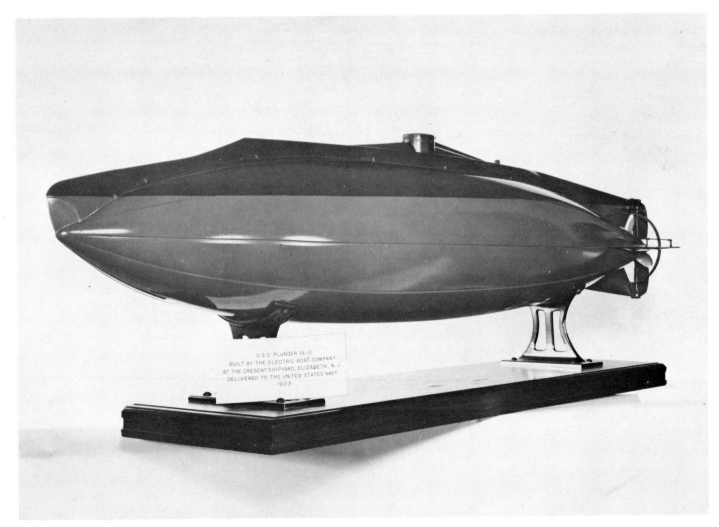

U.S.S. PLUNGER (A-I)
BUILT BY THE ELECTRIC BOAT COMPANY
AT THE CRESENT SHIPYARD, ELIZABETH, N.J.
DELIVERED TO THE UNITED STATES NAVY
1903

LUXURY ON RAILS

*What could be more luxurious than chartering
a private railroad car and attaching it to one train
after another in order to see the country?*

by Willard Allphin

The excursion car 'City of Worcester' will start on its trip to the West today, going as far as Bismarck, Dakota [Territory] for an absence of about ten weeks. The car will go to its destination over the Boston and Albany, New York Central, Chicago and Northwestern, St. Paul and Pacific, and Northern Pacific Railroads. The party will consist of Mr. and Mrs. Jerome Marble, Miss Nella Marble, Miss Marble, Mrs. C. C. Houghton and daughter of this city, Mr. and Mrs. John Babcock of Boston, Mrs. H. H. Bigelow, Miss Addie Bigelow and Master Irving Bigelow. Mr. C. C. Houghton will join the party some weeks later."

This item from the Worcester (Mass.) *Daily Spy* for September 2, 1878 marks a little-known chapter of American railroading. From 1876 to 1894, if cost was no object, you could hire a private railroad car

and take your family and friends anywhere the tracks went. Not only that, you could live in an atmosphere of plush and tassels.

Your travels were likely to be reported, as in the continued story of the above trip. For example, the *Spy* of September 11 said, "The excursion car 'City of Worcester,' when it arrived at Minneapolis last Friday with Mr. Jerome Marble's party on board, was taken to the fair grounds, where President Hayes and party were being received. The car was opened for the inspection of visitors, and attracted a great deal of attention."

It was the idea of the private car which was new. According to Charles F. Carter in, "When Railroads Were New," Josiah Perham, a Maine woolen manufacturer, was the first to organize cheap excursions, just before 1850. At first the

railroad officials were astonished at the way Perham's plan caught the popular fancy, but they were soon doing everything they could to help it along. His first excursions were to Boston, but before long they were extended to all of New England, and to New York, Niagara Falls and Quebec. In twelve years he is said to have made a fortune.

At least one excursion by sea was operated on a more exclusive basis, and was reported in a book, "The River and the Sound, an Account of a Steamboat Excursion by a Party of Ladies and Gentlemen from Worcester, Mass., in the Summer of 1869." The book opens with this statement: "The party was mainly made up of some of the best citizens of Worcester County; not people of wealth and social position merely, but those whose hearts are in the right place, and who never for a

The Worcester Excursion Car Company's annual hunting trip to the Dakotas.

moment forget the amenities of life."

Excursions by land offered attractions of a different but no less interesting sort; and what could be more luxurious than chartering a private railroad car and attaching it to one train after another in order to see the country? The Worcester Excursion Car Company rented cars by the day, week or month, depending upon the whims and purses of those who chartered them.

The company was formed by Jerome Marble and Charles B. Pratt in 1878. Marble had a conventional career, clerking in his father's store in Charlton, Massachusetts, and in a Boston paint store. In 1853 he moved to Worcester and became a partner in and later the owner of a paint, oils and chemical business.

Pratt's career was anything but conventional. He was a diver for many years and owned a salvage company which repeatedly and unsuccessfully attempted to raise the *Hussar,* a British pay ship which sank at Pot Rock in the East River near New York in 1780 with 980,000 pounds aboard. As he grew older he became more settled in his ways and his business in Worcester prospered. He was City Marshall and later Mayor for three terms. He was president of the street car company and treasurer of the Worcester Excursion Car Company.

The excursion company's first car was the private car of Jerome Marble, who had prospered in his enterprises and had admired the private car of a railroad president. Marble had one built in Wilmington, Delaware in 1876 and called it the "City of Worcester." He thoroughly enjoyed taking a party of friends and cruising over the rail lines or heading for Dakota Territory to hunt buffalo and antelope. However, being a good New England businessman, he no doubt thought that it was too bad not to turn an honest dollar on the idea, so he tried renting the car to others.

The idea caught on, and in 1878 the Worcester Excursion Car Company was organized. Within two years the company was operating eight cars. According to accounts of that day, this was enough to attract the opposition of the Pullman Company, which prevailed upon some of the railroads to stop hauling the cars. This reduced business to the point that the company was dissolved in 1894.

Perhaps it is better that it died abruptly rather than staying alive to sicken gradually with the decline of the American railroad as a passenger carrier.

Steam was dangerous. In Section III boilers blow, bridges collapse, and boiling seas . . .

. . . run high. DISASTER AND TRAGEDY strike New England.

STRANGE
VOICE
TO
STARBOARD

by Malcolm MacDuffie

*There are lines of ships we never knew, ships that lived for
many lovers and died as all ships die, some in
the full pride of power. To what ghostly limbo do old
paddlers go, and do they ever return? For those of you
who do not believe in ghosts, we dedicate this story.*

We old-timers remember them still, the side-wheel steamboats that once served the coast of Maine. There was something stately, purposeful, energetic about them that none of the later screw steamers could equal. Maybe it was because we were very young and sailing from schoolroom discipline to vacation freedom, and the tall ship waiting at the Boston wharf was an argosy of adventure, her heartbeat responding to our own excitement. Maybe it was because so much of her vitality was exposed, the great paddlewheels visibly thrashing the water into a long, double track of creamy suds, her "walking beam" atop the hurricane deck meanwhile rocking vigorously like a young farmer striding across his ploughed fields in the joy of the morning.

It is so that we remember the flyers: *Ranson B. Fuller, City of Rockland* and *City of Bangor*. And so we remember their smaller sister, *J. T. Morse,* the fabulous sidewheeler that connected with the "big boats" at Rockland and paddled swiftly eastward through the island thoroughfares with their way landings to Bar Harbor. But there is a long line of their forebears we never

knew, ships that had their own personalities, carried on their own arduous duties, lived for many lovers, and died as all ships die, either by mischance in the full pride of their power, or at the hands of the cruel ship-breaker. *Chancellor Livingston, Harvest Moon, City of Richmond, Penobscot,* to what ghostly limbo do the old paddlers go, and do they ever return to the waters where bell buoys watch for them and the sweet call of their whistles brought welcome to so many wharves and villages?

With one such ship and with such a return I believe I had an experience once. The old side-wheeler *Mount Desert* left the Down East coast when I was only one year old. She went to New York to try her hand at the excursion business. But there are those who say she died soon after of a broken heart, homesick for the pink granite ledges, the high-perched lighthouses, and the air like old wine from the slopes of the tall island for which she was named.

But this yarn begins in the middle 1930s when I was the happy owner of the stout little yawl *May Mischief.* My boys were small in those days, and their mother stayed ashore with them at the Southwest

Harbor cottage. I went singlehandedly much of the time, beating to the westward as long as time would allow, anchoring of nights in delightful small ports and squaring away at last for the "down-hill slant" home.

One early October day I was returning from the last cruise of the season to the westward. Time was running out with the unpleasant necessity of getting back to work and, as often happens, the weather was not cooperating. I had laid two days, fogbound, in Tenants Harbor with the wind southeast, a welcome excuse to take comfort and go clamming. Now, the fog scaled up a little and a light air came in from the south'ard; I got under way across Penobscot Bay for the thoroughfares. All that day I fanned along with the booms broad off or checked in a little as the wind hesitated about going back into the wet quadrant.

I had hoped to get into Southwest Harbor by night, but late afternoon found me crossing Jericho Bay in a heading and dying air with the fog creeping down over Swans Island like a dirty mop. The best I could do was to work into York Narrows where the tide carried me in behind Orono Island, a deep-water passage

The sound was unmistakable, the pounding tread of a sidewheel steamer not far away and nearing.

much used by yachts in summer. Perforce, I anchored in a flat calm on the east end of the shoal between Orono and Round Islands, quite out of the channel. It was seven o'clock and a "dungeon" of fog as I lighted the Shipmate to heat a belated can of corned beef hash. I ate my pilot bread deliberately, with strong coffee, while the fog dew dripped off the boom on the cabin overhead.

About nine o'clock I checked the riding light, which was visible from the companionway only as a dim halo of light, and prepared to turn in. I remember standing with my hand cupped around the chimney of the cabin lamp, fairly puckered to blow it out, when I heard that faint, persistent sound I never expected to hear again—the tread of the wheels of a sidewheel steamer not far away and nearing. Of course, it was impossible. The dear old *Morse* had paddled westward for the last time years before. Yet I had heard that rapid plowter too often to be mistaken. There is a queer, characteristic check in it at regular intervals, caused by the pause as the big beam-engine crank passes its "dead centers" in each revolution. It could best be described as the sound of a man running through crusty snow— six thumping steps and then a pause to balance, then six more. Only the thing is quicker than any man can step, for these thumps are the buckets hitting the water with all the spring and thrust of steam behind them.

"Well," thinks I, "what do you know about that? They must have put the old *Morse* back on a freight run." But there was something wrong with this explanation. The rapidly strengthening sounds of paddles were coming down the inside channel close to the yawl's berth. And the

Morse never came this way; she always used York Narrows over to the northward. She made no calls at the old Swans Island landing of Atlantic, to which this back passage gave access. Thinking thus, a draft of air came from the southeast, *May Mischief* swung a little at her anchor, and I got the unmistakable acrid whiff of soft coal smoke coming down-wind. Now the fire in my little stove was out—I checked it. Moreover, I had burned hardwood that night.

About then I heard the voices, though I can't be sure of the precise order of events. A woman's cry came out of the murk to starboard, young, nervous, pleading, "Fred, oh *Fred,* I don't like this a bit." Then, after a pause and in a higher key, "Fred, she's bearing down on us!"

Right then, not a hundred yards abreast of us it seemed, the whistle sounded, a frightened, gulping, sibilant whoop in the thick dark. Almost immediately there was a thin, woody shock, a thin, pitiful scream, and a strong, man's hail, "There, damn ye, ye've done it now!" The beat of paddles altered a little, as if the man running over snow stumbled the least bit before recovering his stride. Then near and clear came a hurried clang of engine bells from that unseen ship. But I might have been aboard her, so familiar and so vivid is the scene of emergency; seen the skipper leaning out of the middle wheelhouse window, the lookout peering over the bows, the mate and a couple of hands craning overside and aft at the freight deck gangway, the engineer at his lever anxiously watching his "rods" as he caught the great piston into reverse. Certainly I could hear the smother of water behind suddenly checked paddles and the

firmer beat as they took hold to back the ship's way.

Then—silence. It might have been a dream. It must have been a dream, my body so paralyzed between incredulity and helplessness and the suddenness of it all that I could not come to decision. I waited, transfixed, half in and half out of the cabin. The night wind blew cold about my shoulders. A halyard slapped gently at the mast. A spatter of drops fell all at once on the deck from the fog-drenched rigging. The night was empty once more. I might have been the last man alive, and floating on the last ship to drift off into space on a dissolving ocean.

If it was indeed the awakening from a dream, there was one more curious incident that cries aloud for explanation. Before I could pull myself together and come to grips with the world of reality, there came the chuckling of an urgent wash against the yawl's broadside. She lurched suddenly, as from an eddy from another direction, and I could feel her swing to her anchor. There came a faint hissing from overside. I looked, and even in the dark I could see the water creamy with suds, boiling as surely as it ever boiled under churning iron paddles of the ships of long ago. And while I wondered, the deck under my feet stirred. The yawl's bows rose smoothly, and she curtseyed profoundly, three distinct times, to the following wake of a ship that was not there, to a ship that must already be four hundred miles away, rotting at some deserted wharf, or lying stripped on some dismal mudbank, lax timbers spreading under her sodden weight.

I should not dare to tell this story for fear of being thought a queer one, given to nightmares or an overworked imagination. But there are some interesting developments that encourage me to go on. The first came in connection with some collecting of steamboat history that I indulge in from time to time. An old timetable of the Boston and Bangor Steamboat Company came into my possession. Among its tattered folds, along with stateroom plans of the big "outside" paddlers, there was a map showing connecting lines from Rockland. And here was a broken line clearly printed in red showing the course of the steamer *Mount Desert*. At the turn of the century the old *Mounty did* call at Mackerel Cove, Swans Island. And she *did* use the deep passage behind Orono and Round Islands, passing within a hundred yards of where I lay in *May Mischief* that night.

But did the *Mounty* ever pass that way in early evening, at such a time as I had heard the sounds and felt the surge? Ordinarily, the steamers left Bar Harbor about 2 P.M., and would be passing this point a couple of hours later. But there were often irregularities. Delays in the arrival of the morning boat from Boston, extra-heavy freight to handle; such circumstances could, and sometimes did, mean very late westbound passages. It was not beyond the bounds of any possibility.

I began to haunt Swans Island in later summers. I found the rubble of an old, stone-crib wharf, and learned that once steamboats had landed here. I asked questions of oldsters, not daring greatly, but hoping I would hear some tale that bore on my strange experience. At last, this fact fitted into place like the last crooked piece of a puzzle: back in the '90s of the last century there was a fish weir on Pond Island, across York Narrows from Swans Island. It was owned by a Bangor dealer who sent down a young man to camp on the island and tend the weir. He was no stranger there, having sailed on

The Mounty *walking the waters in 1891. Old timers will recognize the Bar Harbor background.*

one of the company's mackerel schooners and harbored often at the Old Harbor. Indeed, he was already mighty sweet on an island girl, and at last there came an early October day when the two were married in the Methodist church on the hill. The circumstance was remembered because of its tragic aftermath. After the customary jollities, Fred Cozzens was rowing his bride home to the camp on Pond Island when their peapod was run down and trampled under by the *Mount Desert*. The ship had paused only briefly as the officers had been quite uncertain that it was a boat that they had struck. The broken bodies of the couple had been recovered by a lobsterman not long after—the first that the island people knew of the accident.

One more word and I am done. A number of years ago I met an old sailorman, Dennis Hogan, who was a patient in the Ellsworth hospital. In beguiling his last hours with stories of the days he loved to remember, I started to tell him this yarn. I had got to the point where I told how I anchored behind Orono as night fell, when he broke in, "I know what you are going to tell me; you heard the voices!" I asked him how on earth he knew, and he went on like this:

"When I was cook in the old

coaster *Satellite,* we ran out of the channel one night when we missed stays, beating through. Before we knew it there was no room to try again and we had to fall off and let her go between Orono and the big island where we anchored at the tail of the nine-foot bank. Tide was ebb, so we lay there that night. Along about nine o'clock and all turned in, along comes the Old Man a-running and a-banging on the house door, hollering that the steamer had run down a boatload of people. We turned out and got the boat over as soon as ever we could, and a couple of us rowed around for an hour and didn't find nothing. The captain said the steamer had gone off. I thought he was mistook, but he claimed he had heard the poor souls screeching as plain as could be. The next morning a lobsterman towed us out of there with his power boat. We asked him about the drowning, but he said we were crazy. The steamboats never went through there no more."

Be all that as it may, there are winter nights when I awake in my safe bed with a seaman's instinct of disaster. It may be the wind has come to the eastward, bringing fog, and the curtains stir a little at the window. But I seem to hear the tread of paddles once more, and smell the tang of soft coal smoke, and hear that thin cry, "Fred, Fred, I don't like this one bit." And a soft blow, and a man's strong hail, "Damn ye; now ye've done it!"

INVITATION TO DISASTER

by Winston Pote

"Old Peppersass" could climb Mount Washington at only 2 miles an hour, but it could come down a lot faster ... particularly when the teeth broke on the gear wheels ...

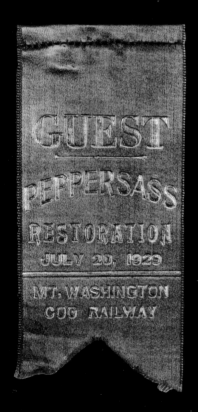

In July of 1969, the famous Mount Washington Cog Railway would have completed 100 years of carrying passengers safely. But on September 18th of 1967, this record ended with the tragic accident which involved about 70 passengers. On July 20th of 1929—Old Peppersass, the first locomotive to climb a mountain—ran away down the steepest grade—and the writer was a survivor of this spectacular accident. The ancient wood-burning engine was not a passenger carrier, so had nothing to do with any safety record. But this is a story of frightful speed down the steep mountain side—of a wild ride on this strange engine—and a flying jump over jagged rocks!

It all started back in 1852, when Sylvester Marsh climbed Mt. Washington on foot and found the view magnificent, but the climb far too strenuous. He thought it was entirely practical to build a railroad up the mountain. It so happened that Mr. Marsh was a successful inventor and a wealthy business man. He was a native of Campton, N.H. and a self-made man, who had walked to Boston to get work, and went to Chicago when it was a small town. His inventions, one of which was in the meat packing business, made it possible to retire when he was relatively young. So he built a model and with enthusiasm developed the rack rail and cog wheel engine, and used his own capital to the extent of $139,000. He overcame

Jacob's Ladder *is a trestle of varying heights above the ground, reaching a maximum of twenty feet and pitched on a grade of nearly thirty-seven per cent . . . an altogether poor place for a locomotive without brakes.*

and 500 official guests

ridicule and despite the Civil War, completed this unique railway in 1869.

The first locomotive was built in Boston and shipped to Littleton, N.H. and then hauled 25 miles to Mt. Washington piecemeal, by ox teams. When assembled, it was soon nicknamed "Peppersass" for its resemblance to an old fashioned peppersauce bottle. The "bottle" or boiler, was mounted on trunnions to keep it vertical, regardless of grade. It was a wood burner and was used to push the building material up the completed portion of track on a flat car. It had no tender at the time, so wood for fuel was picked up along the way. It had a cog wheel in front and pulled itself up the track.

The first passenger trip to the summit was on July 4, 1869. During

Above: In charge of her last trip up the mountain was engineer "Jack" E. C. Frost and fireman William I. Newsham, both of Concord, N.H. Mr. Laurence Richardson, Chief Mechanical Officer of the Boston and Maine Railroad, sits on the woodpile.

Left: Six trains wait at the Base Station to carry guests to the summit. The flat car in the rear of the last train was arranged for photographers and newsreel cameramen.

its early years in passenger service, Peppersass was accompanied by three other vertical boiler locomotives of an improved type, with enclosed cab and a much larger cog wheel in the rear, which gave more speed. Peppersass would travel only 2 miles an hour. In 1878 a fleet of much improved horizontal boiler engines were adopted, and the original engine was retired. There are many safety devices, such as steam compression braking, and the engine pushes the car and thus is always in the downhill track position.

After the death of Sylvester Marsh, the Boston & Maine Railroad bought the Mount Washington Cog Railway and continued operating it until 1930. It was then sold to Colonel Henry Teague, who tried to make it pay during the depression era. One improvement was the turn-outs to allow trains to pass, thereby permitting more trains to operate. Before this, they all went up together and returned in the same procession. The cars are braked independently, and not coupled to the engine. The switches to operate regular rails and the central cog rail are complicated, and require nine separate operations, with seven planks and two levers to move. According to passengers and pictures it was this cog rail switch that caused the September 1967 accident. The locomotive was derailed just below the switch and overturned beside the track, allowing the car to roll free. Part of the switch or the cog rail section was not in place. Seemingly the hand brake was not used quickly enough and did not stop the car.

It was late in the day and the car was crowded, with some standing in the aisle as the train began its descent. Gathering dusk may have contributed, but all witnesses and passengers able to describe the accident, seem to make it clear that human error existed and that nothing had broken. The car rolled down the mountain some 500 feet with its screaming load of 70 or more passengers. Some tried to kick out windows. "The car shifted"—it was said, which would indicate that many people moved to one side. This may have saved many lives, as the car flipped over and landed on its side, on a shallow curve. Otherwise it could have gone down a steeper grade. Everything was chaos with people piled together in a wrecked car. Those who could, started passing people out the windows. Many were cut and some seriously injured. Others were able to get around or not hurt at all. Eight persons were killed, including three children. It was about two hours before a train came up the mountain with first aid equipment.

Now, may I take you back almost forty years, to the first locomotive again,—and the historic events at the beginning. For a number of years, Old Peppersass was "lost." After being exhibited in 1893 at the Columbian Exposition in Chicago, it remained in that city for eleven more years. In 1904 it was displayed in St. Louis and then went to the Baltimore & Ohio Railroad, where it was forgotten.

It was the late Rev. Guy Roberts of Whitefield, N.H.—who in 1916 had come to the rescue of the crumbling Old Man of the Mountains at Franconia Notch—who took the initiative in the twenties, in finding Old Peppersass and returning it to New Hampshire. The locomotive was shipped to Concord, N.H. repair shops of the Boston & Maine Railroad, and thoroughly overhauled and redecorated in gay colors. This was done under the eye of E. C. "Jack" Frost, who was to be the engineer on the memorable trip up Mt. Washington.

According to Frost, some trouble was experienced in getting up steam, during tests. The water foamed! They bored a hole in the wrought iron boiler, to find the cause of this. They discovered the boiler was half filled with nuts and cherry stones stored there by squirrels, some fifty years before when the engine had been on display at Bretton Woods. The repair crew also had to weld part of the frame which held the forward wheels and drive shaft —worthy of note in view of what happened later.

Elaborate plans were made for the return of Old Peppersass and the Base Station was decorated with flags and bunting. The gala day was Saturday, July 20th 1929. Governors from six states were invited and 500 official guests. The day was clear and without wind—perfect. Six trains were decorated and waiting to carry guests to the summit. There were many news photographers and correspondents. Four newsreel cameramen were on hand and even sound equipment, as this was in the early days of sound movies. Arrangements were made to have photographers shoot pictures from a flat car in the rear of the last train. The Base Station never had such a gathering— thousands of spectators and distinguished guests.

Old Peppersass came chugging up the track, blowing her whistle in answer to the cheering crowd. Engineer Jack Frost and fireman William Newsham were dressed in bright red shirts and tall beaver hats. The exercises were at two o'clock, and Colonel William Barron of the Crawford House presided. He had obtained a bottle of water from the Lake of the Clouds, to christen the engine. Governor Charles W. Tobey officially received the locomotive for the state of New Hampshire, and it was christened by President George Hannauer of the B. & M. Soon after, the six trains were loaded to capacity with guests, and what a scramble for space on the small trailer car. Photographer E. D. Putnam, of Antrim, N.H. had found a place and asked if I was going. I managed to squeeze in behind the newsreel cameras and a lot of folding camp chairs. I carried a Graflex camera, a doctor's leather bag full of extra lenses and film, and a Filmo movie camera. In my haste to get pictures of the ceremonies I had not taken time to eat and now I realized that my lunch was in the car. There would be no food for several hours, and the hunger that followed played a fateful part in decisions that afternoon.

The original intent was to run Peppersass a short distance, but all these photographers would never be satisfied, and engineer Frost had wanted to make one last trip to the summit, which could be seen clearly

Patrick Camden, former roadmaster of the Cog Railroad, is seated on a "slideboard" or "Devil's Shingle." The slideboard was a sled of wood and metal designed to fit onto the rails and used by railway employees for sliding down the mountain. Its speed was controlled by lifting up on the friction brake handles on either side. The record slide from the Summit to the Ammonoosuc River, a distance of three miles, was two minutes and 45 seconds. Use of these slideboards was finally forbidden, after the accidental death of an employee.

Sylvester Marsh, successful inventor and wealthy businessman, sponsored his own idea: Peppersass, *the original cog railroad engine and "The Mount Washington Cog Railway."*

above us. So we started on the bumpy ride, with frequent stops to allow Peppersass to catch up, which gave us a chance for pictures. All trying to shoot at once, some hopping off and even hitching rides on the old engine. At the Waumbek water tank, an official appeared to signal for Peppersass to go back. This last train was far behind the others and would be due on the summit. But Frost continued on upward to the Halfway House, a small building near the track. A stop was made for more wood, and I suspect that Frost had arranged for this. Starting again, and climbing a short distance, we all heard a loud bang, as though something had broken. "That doesn't sound so hot!" exclaimed a newsreel camera man. But the old engine was

coming along alright. I was to hear a very similar sound to end normal descent, late that afternoon.

So on we went, another quarter mile and then across Jacob's Ladder and what a view from this flat car! Peppersass followed slowly in the distance. Engineer and fireman were busy waving those tall hats and blowing the whistle which made little white puffs in the almost calm air. Here was the place for pictures and we stopped above the trestle. Rev. Guy Roberts climbed off and so did photographer Putnam. I had one leg over the rail to follow, but my Graflex had slid under those camp chairs and all the feet, and I couldn't get it because of the angle of ascent. I almost left the camera, but the thought of trying to find it later, and

perhaps walking down on an empty stomach caused me to stay aboard. That decision cost me what could have been the most dramatic movie sequence of my career, for later on Peppersass flew by this spot completely out of control. It also almost cost me my life! Ironically—the only thing that went to the bitter end on the old engine, was my camera.

We continued up the steep "Long Trestle" to the Gulf Tank, where Peppersass stopped to take on water. I got movies of this and they filled it so full that it ran over and poured down the sides of the tender. My train moved off toward the summit, leaving me with no definite plan. Oh—for a sandwich! By now it was five o'clock. Frost had evidently received orders to go down, but he looked longingly toward the summit. Should I try to ride down on this old engine? At least there was that lunch down below. As I watched, Peppersass took on two passengers —the engineer's son Caleb, a boy of sixteen, and Daniel P. Rossiter, who was official photographer for the railroad.

My decision to ride down was delayed by circumstances. I finished up a movie film in showing it starting away from the water tank, and so was not ready. Finally I grabbed two cameras and the large bag and tried to run after Peppersass. A very strange chase over the rocks! Moving only 2 miles an hour, it should be easy, but I stopped twice, as though to give up. There seemed to be some restraining force, holding me. Must be an empty stomach, so I ran on. Finally I caught up and Frost stopped and then reached down with a helping hand. My gear was landed on the pile of wood and there was ample room. With a clank, some grinding, and a roar of steam, we started off down the mountain.

Watching Peppersass from the flat car, I hadn't realized that a ride could be so rough and so noisy. Conversation was limited to shouting.

Frost had a huge oil can and tried to use it. Newsham, the fireman, tossed a chunk of wood into the flaming firebox. Sparks flew. What close-up shots!

We passed two climbers, who waved. Soon we reached the top of Long Trestle, where a 36% grade started, and that was quite a view! I stood close to the engineer and so could just barely hear his words as he yelled to Newsham: "How do you like the looks of that!" I was not alone in feeling apprehensive about this ride. Down we dropped—a different kind of jolt now. Rossiter sat near the doorway, holding his camera. I don't recall seeing him move from there, but within three minutes he was killed, thrown from the side of the tender, where he tried to hang on and drop.

There was a loud crack, like a sledge hammer blow! We seemed to bounce a bit and lurch to

Mount Washington, the "Crown of New England," rises 6,293 feet above sea level. Hundreds of peaks and pinnacles can be viewed from the summit. The oldest Cog Railroad in the world is seen in this view, winding its way to the Tip Top House.

Above: For many, the climb up Mount Washington would be far too strenuous, particularly in a dress of fashion around 1890. (Notice the horizontal boiler engines in the background.)

Left: The second type of cog-road engine used in 1873 offered refinements on Old Peppersass. The upright boiler was retained but the smokestack has been changed, an enclosed cab added, and an improved type of tender adopted.

77

Right: As a result of a derailment on September 18, 1967, eight passengers were killed and a number were seriously injured. Had it not been for this tragic accident, the Mount Washington Cog Railway would have completed 100 years of carrying passengers safely.

Below: A Cog Railroad train prepares to leave the Base Station for the Summit in the summer of 1930.

one side. As we picked up speed, there was an ominous grinding sound. Frost grabbed the old hand brake wheel, which spun loosely and had little or no effect. I could see his mouth opening, shouting "JUMP, JUMP!" I'm sure I didn't hear the words, so terrifying was the clatter! Struggling to the woodpile, I grabbed the bag of film, carefully threw it out the doorway and watched it roll over on a grassy place. I should have gone with it. Caleb was impressed by this and was the first to jump, and so escaped with only a torn shirt, as he landed in bushes. The brake must have been holding partially, or something dragging; we were not going more than fifteen miles an hour —but it was awfully unpleasant!

The engine rocked violently, and pieces of flaming firewood and masses of embers flew from the firebox. Afterward I was to find burnt holes in my clothing. Rossiter still sat there with his camera. I jumped back onto the woodpile and reached for the Graflex. As I tried to grab it I was high enough for a terrifying sight! There was Jacob's Ladder— and that was no place to jump! I forgot the Graflex, fastened the wrist strap on the movie camera, and scrambled around. The pieces of wood were tumbling. But we were going too fast now! Then something else happened—we started to roll freely, a sudden drop, like an old elevator. (I believe an axle had broken and the ends of it had dragged on the ties, which were splintered for a long distance. Later I saw a trainman with one wheel and part of the axle, wrapped in a newspaper, and it showed an old progressive break.) Surely the engine would tip over! And the sensation was hopeless—as trees and rocks whizzed by. Engineer and firemen clung to the doorways, looking!

Down we rushed—first a deep hole in the mountain, then blurred rocks nearby! I jumped from the woodpile, but caught one foot on the Peppersass sign. So—it was a dive—head first—but with no sensation of falling, as we were already falling! There was a mixture of sky and rocks—then a huge rock coming fast, as I tried to throw my head back. I seemed to land mostly on the left jaw, so had turned around with head toward the track. Lots of stars, but remember seeing the engine, like a rocket with a long trail of steam! Should have been knocked out, but a witness said I got up and pulled a handkerchief from my pocket. Soon knew the jaw was broken, because I could hear the bones rattle. Tried to find the camera, but something was wrong with one knee.

I was very close to Jacob's Ladder, and some time later recall seeing the engine's smokestack under it. It was here, at the first curve, that Rossiter was thrown off, after hanging on the side of the tender. He was killed instantly! Both engineer and fireman jumped just before this and suffered broken bones, but recovered. Frost had made a miraculous 30-foot jump on the north side. Old Peppersass shot off the track on the reverse curve, just below Jacob's Ladder, the boiler bouncing into the scrub trees, where it was hidden for a time. Photographer Putnam was near this spot, and it must have been a terrifying thing to see. He said: "She rocked wildly, and the air was filled with embers and wood, and in falling, it passed within twenty feet of me!" All that remained on the track was the ash pan, which slid 900 feet, or nearly to the Halfway House.

What followed was extreme excitement and confusion. I remember a hiker hurrying down with my black bag. He told me to sit down and he would find the camera, but dashed off in the wrong direction. Getting around was painful and the next day I learned that a knee cap was fractured. The jaw fracture was a compound one and I walked around holding it together with one hand because it felt heavy! (Have never had normal feeling in lip or chin since.) Somehow I climbed up the mountain far enough to endure a long ride back on the first excursion train. I was on this train before passengers knew what had happened, and when it stopped to pick up the engineer and fireman, who had been sitting near the track, I heard Frost warn them not to go down there. But they thought he was in no condition to know, so they went! It had seemed to me that we must go up to the summit and down the road. Eventually, that is what happened.

On the summit we found a little frost on the board walk. The hotel was packed with guests—most of them staring at me. I was told later, that my head was swollen up like a balloon. Couldn't swallow milk— and so it was for several days. If I had only eaten that lunch! It was a rough ride down the road for me, and we reached the hospital in Berlin, at one o'clock in the morning.

I heard about it all later, and the mountainside swarmed with souvenir hunters, who carried away anything that was light. Fortunately, most of the engine parts were heavy. The steam gauge went across the Presidential Range, while the whistle found its way into Pinkham Notch. I often wondered where my Graflex camera landed, but pieces of it eventually turned up at the University of New Hampshire. I never found the lens, but Putnam said it was alright.

Before the summer was over, parts of Old Peppersass were assembled in the Concord repair shop, and finally it was placed on display at the Base Station, where it may be seen today. It should never have made that last climb up the mountain. The slowest locomotive ever built, but it surely finished in a blaze of speed! We all missed the big picture that day. But I was fortunate indeed to live and be able to tell about it.

NIGHTMARE AT DEVIL'S BRIDGE

It was a bright, moonlit night. The Captain knew every rock and ledge through Vineyard Sound. The five-mile-wide channel was plainly marked with buoys and lights. Then why, on that tragic night, did the big steamship run aground?

by John Mason

The Steamship City of Columbus *of the Boston and Savannah line.*

In the year 1884, there was a man named Bunker living up in New Market, New Hampshire. He worked in the machine shop over in Newfields and was never late or absent —until Friday, January 18, of that year. That day he didn't show up for work. The boss sent two of the men around to his house to find out if he was sick.

They found Mr. Bunker in bed, shaking and sobbing on account of three dreams he'd had which were all mixed into one frightful nightmare. He motioned the men to sit down by his bed and in a choking voice said:

"I guess you fellers know that my daughter got married a few days ago to Lou Chase. Well, yesterday they started on their honeymoon. They went down to Boston to sail to Savannah on the *City of Columbus*." He paused, wiped his eyes, and went on:

"Last night I dreamed I was standing on a high, wind-swept cliff looking down on the ocean and some jagged rocks. All of a sudden I saw a big black steamboat all lighted up coming towards me. She was headed straight for the ledge and was *inside* the buoy. I yelled, and I guess that woke me up. Well, I got to sleep after a while and this time I dreamed the steamer struck the ledge and began to sink. I could see men, women, and children, all struggling in the water, and the wreckage everywhere. I woke up in a sweat.

"After a long time I drifted off again and dreamed I was on the wreck, and there was Lou Chase, trying to help my daughter into a lifeboat but a big wave came along and swept everything away. I'll never see them again. They're both dead. I know they be."

The men tried to tell Mr. Bunker that he'd had a nightmare; that the *City of Columbus* was a fine, big, seaworthy ship; that no storm had been reported along the coast; that it was, in fact, a bright moonlight night. But he would have none of it. His dear ones were gone and that was all there was to it. So they left him sobbing and went back to the shop to report to the boss.

The next morning when the Boston papers came in, there were the big, black headlines:

CITY OF COLUMBUS WRECKED
OFF GAY HEAD. 102 DEAD!

I heard about this strange dream several years ago and ever since then I've tried to find out *why* such a first-class steamship should run aground on the Devil's Bridge off Gay Head, when at that point Vineyard Sound is almost five miles wide and plainly marked with buoys and lights.

Even if it hadn't been a bright, moonlight night, the Captain knew every rock and ledge because he'd sailed through the Sound hundreds of times. Okay then, what did happen on that tragic day 85 years ago this month?

I'm afraid that question will never be answered. Some who could have talked died in the wintry seas; the few who did survive gave such conflicting testimony that it was impossible to fix the blame. I've spent a lot of time looking up the records on this wreck only to find that one story contradicts the next. Some of the men I've talked to say the officers had been drinking; others claim that Captain Wright was a teetotaler and above reproach in any way.

There was a long and rigid investigation, of course, and the officials did decide that Captain Wright was "derelict in his duties," so he was deprived of his Master's license and ended his days working as a stevedore on the wharves at Savannah, Georgia.

Naturally, some facts about this tragedy are available, and here they are:

The *City of Columbus* was a 2,000-ton steamer, 270 feet long with a 30-foot beam. She had accommodations for 75 first-class cabin passengers, and room for 50 more in the steerage. All her equipment, such as pumps, boats, life rafts, rockets, etc., was strictly up-to-date and for 10 years government inspectors had given the *Columbus* an A-No.-1 rating.

When she sailed from Nickerson's Wharf in South Boston on her regular run from Boston to Savannah, Georgia, at quarter past three on Thursday afternoon, January 18, 1884, there were 135 souls on board, including 87 passengers and a crew of 48. There were several children but nobody knew the exact number.

A strong nor'west wind was blowing when the *Columbus* passed Boston light, then Harding's Ledge, and Minot's. She headed across the Bay for Race Point at the end of Cape Cod and, about midnight, passed Cross Rip Lightship. Shortly after that, the beacons on East and West Chop came into view and, of course, they could easily see the powerful light on Gay Head. The *City of Columbus* was now half way through the Sound.

Shortly before noon, the U.S. Revenue Cutter Dexter *arrive*

...nder forced draft and lowered her boats for rescue

Jutting out from Gay Head there's a ragged reef of rocks called Devil's Bridge. At low tide the rocks are visible, but during a storm they are covered with flying spray from the surf that continually breaks over them. Black Nun Buoy is on the outermost point of this sunken ledge.

About quarter of two that morning Captain Wright, who claimed at the inquest that he had been on the bridge for ten hours, went into the pilot house and, just as they came abreast of Nobska Light, he said to First Mate Edward Fuller, "When Tarpaulin Cove bears north, change the course to west sou'west."

But the Captain didn't wait, as he was supposed to do, for that order to be acknowledged. Instead, he stepped down into his cabin under the pilot house and promptly fell asleep, sitting on the floor with his head up against a steampipe. For two whole hours he was unaware that the course had not been changed. Asleep on the floor of his cabin was hardly the place for the captain of a coastwise steamship like the *City of Columbus* to be!

According to the official testimony of Ned Leary, the lookout, it was quarter to four in the morning when he sighted the buoy on the outside ledge, off the starboard bow. He yelled, but the wind was blowing too hard for him to be heard, so he ran to the pilot house and pounded on the window.

Gus Harding, the Second Mate, jumped up and, seeing the buoy on the wrong side, yelled: "Hard a-port!" All this shouting woke up Captain Wright. He poked his head into the pilot house, repeated the order, and then gave the signal to stop the engines.

By now, the Devil's Bridge was dead ahead and, although the quartermaster put the wheel over as fast as he could, they struck the sunken ledge at a 15-knot clip with a terrific crash, tearing a great hole in the side and bottom.

Then Captain Wright made his final, fatal mistake. He ordered the engines reversed! The fast-filling *City of Columbus* backed twice her length into deep water and settled rapidly. (She finally came to rest with just her bow section and two masts above the angry water.) Had he remained on the ledge instead of backing off, it is almost certain many could have been saved. At the inquest, Captain Wright testified that he carried a full equipment of flares and signal rockets, but couldn't get at them because of the rising water.

Divers at work

When asked if he sounded a "distress" signal on the steamer's whistle, he replied, "No, I didn't pull the whistle cord because I didn't think it would do any good." Then he added, "I have yet to learn what the 'distress' signal is on a steamboat whistle."

Purser William C. Spaulding testified that he occupied a cabin on the hurricane deck and left it when the ship struck. With Edward Fuller, the First Mate, he tried to arouse the sleeping passengers. "But," said Mr. Spaulding, "she listed so quickly the whole port side was under water and all the people in those staterooms must have drowned immediately."

Spaulding said when he rushed on deck that he saw at least 60 men, women, and children, all thinly clad, slipping and sliding over the icy deck, moaning pitifully, and praying for help.

"Then," he said, "I saw a big wave coming—its foamy crest sparkling in the moonlight. I swung myself into the shrouds and climbed up as fast as I could. The wave struck us broadside and, when I looked down again, not a soul was to be seen."

Lifeboat No. 5 was manned and got away without capsizing, but all other boats were smashed, and six men on the life raft were washed overboard.

A group of 20 terrified passengers sought shelter on top of the upper cabins, but they were washed overboard in a tangle of ropes and wreckage. Out of 135 passengers and crew, only 28 had the strength to pull themselves into the shrouds and out of danger. Captain Wright was with this group. As soon as they leaned against the rigging, their wet clothes froze solid and held them there. All through the long dark night these frightened, freezing survivors watched the brilliant beacon on Gay Head less than half a mile away—and prayed their hearts out that someone would see them.

One steamer came within hailing distance, but she failed to notice the masts of the *Columbus* rising from the sea. And no one heard the faint, pitiful cries of "Help" that came from the crosstrees.

As the night wore on, several of the men weakened, lost their grip, and fell into the sea. Others died, and hung head downward, their frozen garments holding them fast to the rigging.

When daylight broke over the desolate scene, the keeper of Gay Head Light, Horatio N. Pease, discovered the wreck and sent his men out to rouse the villagers. A boat was

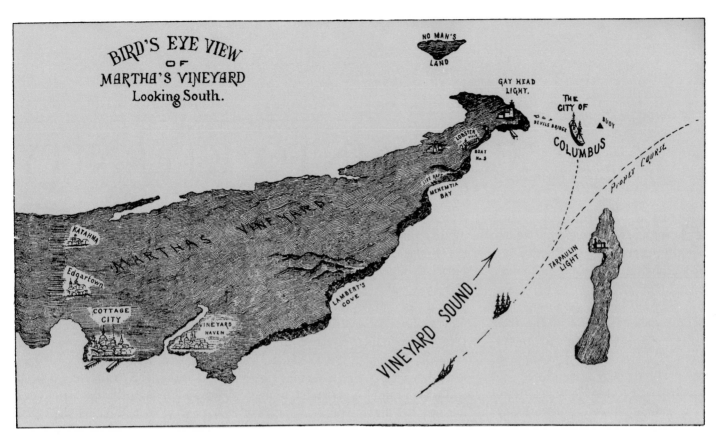

BIRD'S EYE VIEW OF MARTHA'S VINEYARD Looking South.

Jutting out from Gay Head there's a ragged reef of rocks

launched into the raging surf and after a terrific two-hour battle with the elements, seven of the men in the rigging were rescued. They jumped, if you please, onto the crest of an on-rushing wave and were washed within reach of the surfboat.

The empty life raft came ashore at Menemsha Bight; and under the cliffs on Martha's Vineyard, Lifeboat No. 5 struck some rocks, overturned, and spilled its all-but-dead occupants into the surf. A party of brave Gay Head Indians waded waist deep into that icy water and pulled them out onto solid ground. One was beyond all help, and only two of the others were able to walk. The Indians carried them up the cliff and took care of them for three days in their homes until help arrived from the mainland.

Other Gay Head Indians yoked up a pair of oxen and plodded 12 miles through the deep snowdrifts to fetch the lifeboat from Edgartown.

Shortly before noon, the U.S. Revenue Cutter *Dexter* arrived under forced draft and lowered her boats to take the remaining men from the rigging.

Lt. John Rhodes, a Connecticut boy, bent a line around his waist, dived overboard, and swam to the wreck twice to make heroic rescues. Later he was honored by his home town of New Haven and given the Massachusetts Humane Society's Gold Medal for bravery.

Captain Wright was the last man to leave the wreck. He was taken out of the rigging at half past three in the afternoon, having been aloft more than 12 hours.

All of the old newspaper clippings say: "Not a single woman was saved from the *City of Columbus*"

—but that's not so. Fred Cowden of New Bedford wrote to me that Mrs. Eugene Williams of Tatnuck was saved with her husband. This has been verified by her daughter, Mrs. Frank Smith of Worcester, who adds: "Mr. and Mrs. Williams were one of several honeymoon couples on their way to the sunny South."

* * * * *

A few days after the *City of Columbus* was wrecked, with a loss of 102, old Mr. Bunker up in New Market, New Hampshire, scanned the newspapers for news of his loved ones. It didn't take him long to read the names of those SAVED, for there were just 33. Turning to the list of those LOST, he found what he knew he would find:

"J. Lewis Chase and wife, New Market, N.H."

18 *HURLED* INTO ETERNITY

A fearful accident by which eighteen men were hurled into eternity" proclaimed the *Daily Times* of Burlington, Vermont, on December 12, 1867.

It was, indeed, a strange and fearful event and one of the most bizarre that ever transpired in Vermont. Even today no one seems to know exactly why it happened, but it is believed to have been the result of appalling human frailty. It was the sort of monstrous disaster which sometimes occurs when imperfect human beings have control over powerful machines.

Nineteen years before this event, two railroads had engaged in fierce competition, each trying to be the first to reach Lake Champlain and thus open up trade to the Middle West. One railroad, the Rutland and Burlington, laid its tracks through Vermont via Bellows Falls and Rutland. The other, the Vermont Central Railroad, constructed its line from Windsor via White River Junction, and Northfield to Burlington. So fierce was the competition between these railroads that tracks were laid and bridges built as fast as crews of men could construct them.

Harlow Bridge, about a mile and a half south of Northfield, on the Vermont Central line, was erected at that time. Of wooden structure, the bridge stood on piled granite block abutments 60 feet high on each end and a 75-foot-high granite pier in the middle, the bridge spanning a chasm some 300 feet in width through which the Dog River ran.

On December 8, 1867, as a wood-burning engine coughing fire and smoke rumbled across the bridge during the night, sparks from its smokestack set fire to the bridge and burned it completely. The iron rails fell into the chasm, some of them twisted from heat, others stuck in the frozen ground with jagged ends upright.

This was no time to lose business to its deadly rival, the Rutland Road, so the Vermont Central at once poured about 100 mechanics and laborers into the rebuilding of the bridge.

Train travel was very heavy in those days, but passenger service continued in spite of the lack of a bridge. Traveling to Boston or New York from the north, one would ride as far as a landing near the gap, alight from the train, then walk across a flimsy footbridge high above the river to a landing on the other side. There one boarded a train which had been run up from nearby Roxbury to take passengers south. Workmen carried baggage, the United States mail, and express the long way around. Steps were cut in frozen ground, stakes driven in the sides and ropes attached for those too timid to cross the shaky, wind-

Right: Harlow Bridge, circa 1890. Opposite page: On December 8, 1867, the Harlow Bridge was destroyed by fire, but the tragic accident occurred three days later, on the 11th. This photo was taken the next morning.

Here is a story by JULIA W. McINTIRE *of one of Vermont's most bizarre and monstrous disasters—the kind which sometimes occurs when imperfect human beings have control over powerful machines.*

tossed temporary bridge. Railroad officials supervising the work were Maj. Harvey Tenney of St. Albans, Vermont, master bridge builder, and Horace H. Locklin, Assistant Superintendent of the Road.

The fateful engineer was Francis B. Abbott of Northfield, 40 years old, at one time selected to run the "General Sheridan," a crack engine on the Central. His usual job was to run a 6:30 A.M. train from Northfield to St. Albans, return that afternoon to Roxbury, there to Northfield where he could spend the night with his family. His special duty on this occasion was to run a small construction train, consisting of engine, tender, and passenger car, carrying workmen and materials back and forth from the bridge to Northfield.

On Monday and Tuesday after the fire, Abbott ran the train about eight times each day. When carrying heavy timber, he backed the train to the abutment and there tipped the materials over the edge, thus saving carrying materials past the engine. Since there was a rising grade of 50 feet to the mile leading to the abutment, it was not considered necessary to put up "bunters" (now called bumper blocks), heavy posts fastened on a rail even with the drawbar of a car, to prevent a train going any farther.

On Wednesday, the 11th of December, Engineer Abbott ran his train three times in the morning. At noon he took the workmen for their dinner at the Northfield House, a pleasing colonial hotel built by former Gov. Charles Paine on the village common across from the depot. The men arrived just before 12:30. The hotel dining room could not accommodate them all at once, so about 90 men went in for the first sitting. Abbott ate his dinner on the engine. Major Tenney, who boarded at the William Smiths' near Harlow Bridge, had come to town that day only to be shaved. Anxious to get the men back to work, he told Abbott about one o'clock to ring the bell to summon them, because, as Abbott said later, "he wanted me to carry that lot up and come back and get some more that had not et their dinner as quick as I could."

When the men, lingering over their dinner, heard the bell, they straggled out of the hotel to board the train. William Taft, a bridge carpenter, saw that the passenger car was crowded, so he got onto the engine. Major Tenney also got aboard the engine, sat in the fireman's seat, and said to Abbott, "Blow the whistle and wake them up!" According to Taft, "the whistle was blowed and the bell rung." James Farwell, a fireman, got on next, followed by Sidney Bliss, normally a fireman but on this trip just a passenger on his way home, accompanied by Daniel Lyman—five men in all, plus the engineers, even though rules posted on the cab allowed only the engineer and fireman.

The train proceeded north across the village common. When Tenney asked Abbott why he went north, the latter replied that he had

to go up another track west of the depot as a rail was broken. Here he slackened speed. More men boarded the passenger car and Tenney ordered, "Keep going and ring the bell." So with a screeching and a clanging, the train left the village.

Assistant Superintendent Locklin sat on the forward part of the crowded passenger car with the brakeman, Samuel Fox, and other workmen—between 80 and 90 men aboard in all. The car, heated by a wood-burning stove, was warm and cozy, the men relaxed after their good dinner, enjoying a respite before returning to work in the numbing December cold.

Engineer Abbott, having worked up a good head of steam, started towards Harlow Bridge, backing the train at a brisk pace. It was just a short run, usually at a speed of 12 m.p.h., certainly not over 18 m.p.h. Even express trains on long runs did not go over 27 m.p.h. in those days of Lilliputian, primitive "hay-burners."

As the train rounded the first curve towards Elbow Bridge (about three-quarters of a mile from the depot), named because of the elbow curve of the Dog River near the bridge, it had increased its speed to 20 m.p.h. Bliss asked Abbott how he enjoyed his work and the two carried on a slight conversation until Bliss, worried, noticed the excessive vibration of the boiler in its frame, or cradle, as more steam was generated to increase the train's speed. He told Abbott it looked to him "as though she was coming out of her frame," but he was assured the boiler was all right. By the time the train approached the second curve, everyone knew it was going too fast; that is, all except the oblivious Abbott. He, of course, could not see where he was going unless he looked out the window. The chasm was in plain view to the others as the train sped towards its fate.

Locklin, now standing on the passenger car platform, waved his arm frantically, signaling the engineer to stop, but was unheeded. Taft jumped for the brake on the tender, shouting to Farwell, "We shall run off!" and to Abbott, "Shut off!" By now the train was only 60 rods from the chasm. Fox, in the passenger car, electrified by the danger, jammed on the brake. Still Abbott pushed his speed to 25 m.p.h., unheeding the shouts and warnings from the terrified men. In desperation, one of the firemen threw a stick of wood at him. Abbott, finally realizing the terrible danger everyone was in, turned around, opened the furnace door and reversed the engine.

Past the point where the train usually stopped, Tenney jumped from the engine, followed by Lyman, Bliss, and Farwell. In the passenger car, now but a few feet from the yawning abyss, Locklin and the others on the platform leapt for their lives.

Only a few men now had time to smash windows and jump, one or two just as the passenger car hurtled to the gap, turned sidewise and plunged over. As the center of the car struck the bank of the precipice, it broke into three pieces, the roof sliding ahead. The forward half of the car fell onto a shelving rock, spilling out men, seats, and the hot stove into a pile. The rear half of the car fell on top of that and then bounced a few feet beyond, where it lay on the river bank.

The sudden reversal of the engine had snapped the cast iron coupling between the car and the tender with a shuddering crack. The tender hung for a moment over the edge of the chasm, then plunged to the ledge on top of the men who had been spilled from the car, killing many of them instantly.

The big driving wheels of the engine, sliding ahead because of the frosty rails, went to within four feet of the chasm. Here Abbott jumped. The engine stopped at the very brink and then slowly, very slowly, started downgrade.

Charles P. Smith, who lived nearby, had seen the train coming at express speed toward the gap. He heard no whistle sounded, no bell rung, and he knew the train was doomed. He ran to help and heard the dreadful groaning of the men beneath the tender.

Marshall Hopkins, farmer, standing between his house and his barn near the bridge saw the train racing along the tracks. He said later that, although he had seen a thousand trains pass over there, he "seldom see one smarter." As the car and tender crashed into the chasm he ran to the schoolhouse beyond the bridge to help.

George H. Slack was a little boy sitting at his desk near the window in the little schoolhouse and heard the crash when the passenger car went over. He saw the tender hang for a few seconds and then fall, bottom up, on top of the hapless men lying in a pile. He could see the wheels of the engine spinning furiously to keep the car from going over the edge of the embankment.

Abbott had jumped back into his engine and quickly ran it to Northfield for help. Another car and engine from the roundhouse, ropes, equipment, and doctors were hurried back to the disaster. As many injured as could be rescued were carried into the small schoolhouse and the nearby homes on Stony Brook.

Some of the men were still pinned beneath the tender. Ropes were put around it and the engine strained to raise it. Up came the tender, slowly and painfully, then the rope broke and the tender fell again upon the men. After many tries it was pulled back onto the track. The dead and wounded were brought to Northfield by sleighs and passenger cars and the village was turned into a veritable hospital. Every room "with a fire" or some sort of heat at the Northfield House was used for the injured. Seven of the severest cases were placed in the hotel's barber shop and five in the reading room. Engine House #1 was used as a "dead house" under Dr. George Nichol's care.

The horrified trustees of the Vermont Central sent all possible help to Northfield. A special train carrying the company doctor and needed medical and hospital supplies was dispatched from St. Albans immediately.

Eighteen men were killed in the catastrophe and nearly 40 wounded. By this accident, reported the *Daily Times,* the Vermont Railroad lost or killed or wounded every foreman and master workman on the bridge except Major Tenney, Master-in-Chief. Assistant Superintendent H. H. Locklin, also had jumped to safety.

A Court of Inquiry was set up at once in Northfield by the railroad officials in an attempt to determine how this accident could have happened and why.

Engineer Abbott, called first, testified that he never left his engine that noon, that he had not had anything intoxicating to drink for six months, that perhaps he had hurried the train a little faster than he in-

tended to; that he had previously run an engine he was not used to when the lever flew back and his engine hit another tender and shoved an engine through the backside of the end of the engine house. This was at Northfield. He protested vehemently in his own defense that if the railroad had put up the "bunters" at the north side of the chasm, as he thought they should, the accident would never have happened.

Assistant Superintendent Locklin testified that it was Abbott's business, not his, to look out for the train and that Abbott went much too fast —nearly twice as fast as he should have—that when he jumped he did not think the engine had even been reversed.

Major Tenney said he had nothing to do with putting up bunters, that Locklin was in charge. He had told Abbott to hurry up the men but did not mean for him to run excessively. He thought Abbott just forgot the bridge was gone. He had had a presentiment that something dreadful was going to happen that day and had said so to one of the Northfield doctors. He said, "I knew the fate of the train when I looked out and saw Hopkins' house."

Other railroad men testifying were pretty much in agreement that Abbott's excessive speed was due to his nervousness at having Major Tenney aboard. The public had other theories—that Abbott was exhausted from his duties, that he had had an hallucination, that he could not stop because of a defect in the engine which ran out of control, and that he was insane. None of these theories seems to fit. The only clue, and a very slight one at that, comes from Major Tenney's testimony at the Court of Inquiry when he stated, "He

[Abbott] ran out north to get on to this track and I asked him why he went that way. I did not discover as Abbott was cross and I was not." It is possible that there had been previous trouble between the two men resulting in a clash of personalities and that Abbott, angry and upset, forgot what he was doing.

Abbott was immediately discharged by the railroad. He sold his property in Northfield and moved to a small farm in Roxbury. For a time he was said to have been "half crazed" by the terrible result of his lack of vigilance which shocked the entire country and left a gloom over sorrow-stricken Northfield.

Hundreds of the curious rushed to the scene of the disaster and "like wolves," said George Slack, soon stripped the passenger car, lying on the riverbank, of most of its wood for souvenirs.

Harlow Bridge was finally rebuilt with a central pier of piled granite blocks supporting a heavy bridge with wooden siding beneath the tracks. In 1899 this bridge was replaced by an iron one. In 1930 the bridge was again rebuilt, this time supported by two concrete piers.

As the tiny "hay-burners" went out of fashion, they were replaced by heavy locomotives, many of them named for prominent Vermonters. For many years powerful engines carried long passenger and freight trains as they thundered across the high bridge above the Dog River.

Today the passenger trains are gone in Vermont but long freight trains still travel swiftly and safely over the chasm, looking down upon the little schoolhouse nearby.

Never again was there such a railroad disaster in Northfield as that of Harlow Bridge in 1867.

*"For God's sake, Staples, port the wheel!"
Anson screamed. Then beams cracked,
timbers splintered and the sea began
pouring into the galley. Here are the
terrifying details of the last twelve
minutes of the notorious* Larchmont.

ONLY 19 LIVED

On August 10, 1959, died the last survivor of one of the nation's worst sea disasters. He was eighty-year-old Captain James E. Staples of North Brooksville, Maine, a veteran of forty-five years on the water.

Fifty-two years before, on the clear, starlit night of February 11, 1907, Staples was quartermaster of the steamship *Larchmont* as it proceeded down the Rhode Island coast with an estimated 300 passengers and crew, bound for New York.

At approximately 10:45 the coal schooner *Harry P. Knowlton* loomed out of the darkness and crashed into the port side of the steamer forward of the paddlebox. The *Larchmont* went under in just twelve minutes.

Only nineteen lived through that fateful night. The exact number that perished was never accurately determined. The passenger list sank with the ship.

In effect, this is James E. Staples' story.

Early in February, 1907, a low-pressure front formed over the Great Lakes. On the 11th it moved into New England bringing below-freezing temperatures. In Providence snow began to fall at 6 P.M., quickly reached blizzard proportions, then ceased abruptly. On the *Larchmont*, tied up at her South Water Street dock, small drifts collected around the pilot house.

Staples, standing the gangway watch, shuddered involuntarily as he looked at the gray sky. "We're in for a rough one tonight," he murmured to himself. Scores of ticket holders elbowed their way past him, eager to get aboard where it was warm.

In the interior of the *Larchmont* porters scurried here and there trying to keep track of the passengers' luggage and answer innumerable questions. "Is there a bar on board?" one drummer asked. There was, and business would be brisk. There's nothing like a sea voyage to raise a thirst, said another.

Many of the overnight trippers were Italian laborers on their way to Gotham to find work. Others, full of wine and cheap whisky, had to be assisted on board. The Joy Line was

by Norris Randolph

Here in the main saloon, ruptured boiler pipes released deadly steam and trapped many of the passengers before they could escape.

interested in making money. The carriage trade could look elsewhere.

At 7 P.M. the gangway was taken in. The steamer, backing slightly to clear, swung out into the Providence River. She was already a half hour late; the snowstorm had delayed freight loading operations.

The wind out of the northwest rose perceptibly as the *Larchmont* rounded treacherous Point Judith and nosed her way into Block Island Sound.

Lunging and rolling, she bucked into the teeth of a violent, fifty-mile gale which whipped the angry sea into a boiling tumult. Salt spray from towering waves lashed out savagely, coating everything on deck with a fine layer of ice.

High above the masts the stars seemed to glitter like sapphires in the winter night. The *Larchmont*, making maximum speed, with all her lights showing, was now running on time.

To the superstitious, a study of the *Larchmont*'s past performance would have proved a singular fact: the ship was a Jonah.

She was built in Bath in 1885 as the *Cumberland* for the International Steamship Company's Boston–St. John route. A sidewheel, three decked, two-masted steamboat, she registered at 1,605 gross tons and was 252 feet long. Her hull was of white oak. The vertical beam engine capable of 1,000 horsepower allowed a top speed of twelve knots.

For seventeen years she plied from Boston to Nova Scotia without mishap—until a foggy morning in July, 1902. Pulling away from Bos-

Capt. Frank T. Haley of the Knowlton *was used to near-collisions on the Sound. His orders to Johnson were to "keep her on course."*

ton's Commercial Wharf, the *Cumberland* was struck without warning by the United Fruit Company steamer *Admiral Farragut*. She reversed course and limped back to port, the forward compartment filling rapidly.

The next day, on being towed across Boston Harbor for repairs, the after bulkhead gave way and she went under.

The *Cumberland* was overhauled in New York, but the owners had second thoughts about returning her to service. When word got around that the Joy Steamship Company was in the market for a steamer on the Providence-New York route, the *Cumberland* switched hands.

She was re-christened the *Larchmont* and on September 4, 1902—five days after her maiden voyage as a Joy liner, a pile of mattresses caught fire in the men's cabin

. . . and the two vessels were steering a collision course

causing minor damage.

On January 24, 1904, she ran aground in Narragansett Bay near Bristol, R.I. Two weeks later, five miles from Bristol, the *Larchmont* ran aground again.

October 11, she collided with the lumber schooner *D. J. Melanson* off Stratford, Connecticut. The pilot was George W. McVay.

John A. Hart, 25, a Providence engineer, was asleep in stateroom "12" when he was murdered and robbed on February 19, 1905. The crime was never solved.

Fire broke out again January 11, 1906, caused by a defective electrical connection. It was soon brought under control.

Now only the final act of the *Larchmont* drama remained to be played.

"What damnable weather, eh, John?" said Staples as he gripped the wheel against the force of the storm. "What? Oh, yeah, Jim, it sure

is," replied pilot John Anson, thinking of his fiancee back in Providence. This time next month they would be married.

In the saloon deck below, Millard Franklin, seventeen, of North Attleboro, Massachusetts, billed as the "Young Houdini" and en route to an engagement in Trenton, New Jersey, was mystifying the incredulous with his feats of legerdemain.

From one corner came the sound of tambourines and accordions. A dozen Salvation Army lassies were practicing songs they would sing tomorrow at the Army's Scandinavian Congress in New York. One of those who lingered and listened was Captain George W. McVay, an intelligent, imposing figure

---

The ill-fated Larchmont *was called a "floating death trap," due to her lack of such safety devices as wireless equipment then coming into use on most steamships.*

whose rise up the chain of command in the Joy Line had been meteoric. Fellow captains of the Sound regarded him with awe as a "boy wonder."

In another corner sat Jacob and Sadie Michaelson, holding hands and talking in whispers. In twelve days they would be man and wife.

The dining room was closing for the night. It was 10 P.M. Freight handlers, their back-breaking labor over hours ago, had gone to the fo'c'stle. They had to be up early. The *Larchmont* was due to dock at pier 28 in the East River at 7 A.M.

Most of the fifty-man crew were either asleep or beginning to yawn as the *Larchmont,* valued at $125,000 and carrying a $45,000 cargo, steamed majestically into the night.

Allowed by law to carry 593 persons, she was far from crowded. There was nothing to fear. Didn't the *Larchmont* come equipped with eight lifeboats, four life rafts and four cork rings, as well as 635 life preservers?

Finishing his rounds, Capt. McVay returned to the wheelhouse. He stopped briefly to comment to Staples on the foul weather—it was then 3 degrees below zero—and went to his cabin.

McVay had taken off his coat and vest when he heard the *Larchmont*'s whistle sound. Four blasts—the danger signal . . .

The *Harry P. Knowlton*, built for the South-American trade, was a three-masted coal schooner, 317 tons and 128 feet long, or half the length of the *Larchmont*. Owned by George B. Dunn, of Houlton, Maine, she hailed from Eastport.

On February 7, bound for Everett, Massachusetts, she had taken on 453 tons of bituminous coal (a lighter load than usual) and sailed up to City Island, New York from South Amboy, New Jersey. Ice, however, prevented her from entering Long Island Sound.

The *Knowlton* managed to get free by 10 A.M. on the 11th. Crowding on all available canvas, the coaster began to beat her way up the Sound at a 10-knot clip to make up for lost time.

The seven-man crew was commanded by Capt. Frank T. Haley, at sixty a dour, hardened skipper who could count a forty-five-year career in the coasting trade.

At the wheel stood Carl V. Johnson, thirty-seven. Unfamiliar with the waters of Block Island Sound, he had all he could do to keep her on course due to the gale winds.

At 10:35 P.M., mate Frank Govant, of Bangor, was standing watch. Idly, he noticed the green starboard light of an oncoming ship. She was about a mile off.

Believing the officer in charge had missed seeing their starboard signal, Govant called out to the lookout and asked if it was working.

Govant's question seemed odd to Haley and he came rushing on deck. The port light of the *Larchmont* was visible less than 400 yards away. The two vessels were steering a collision course.

Haley was used to near collisions on the Sound. One more wouldn't make much difference. "Keep her on course," he ordered Johnson.

"Aye, sir," Johnson replied. Then he heard the high screech of the *Larchmont*'s whistle and his knuckles grew white as he clenched the wheel.

Pilot Anson released the whistle cord. "For God's sake, Staples, port the wheel, port the wheel!" he screamed. Staples shoved her over as far as she would go, hung on, and prayed.

Anson's order was a frightful mistake. It drove the *Larchmont* to starboard—directly into the path of the onrushing *Knowlton*.

McVay reached the wheelhouse, but there was nothing he could do. It was too late. "My God, John," he said, "what have you done?"

His words were drowned out in the deafening crash. Beams cracked. Timbers splintered. The schooner's bowsprit ripped into the *Larchmont*'s hull about twenty-five feet forward of the paddlebow tearing a jagged gash above and below the waterline. The sea immediately began pouring into the galley.

The main steam pipe, the major source of power, was ruptured. The paddlewheels continued to turn, slowed, then stopped; the engine was dead. Lights all over the ship flickered and went out. Huge clouds of scalding vapor spread slowly up from the engine room.

McVay grabbed the speaking tube and demanded the chief engineer's report. There was no answer. He ordered Staples and second pilot James S. Wyman to investi-

gate. The steam prevented them from getting further than the saloon deck.

Caspel Hest, first assistant engineer, of Albany, New York, gave a damage estimate and advised McVay to "beach her on the mainland, she's sinking fast." With the power out and the current against them, the plan was hopeless.

The *Knowlton* had swung away to starboard; the *Larchmont*'s momentum had carried her forward of the schooner's stern. The *Knowlton*'s crew saw the steamer enveloped in a white, heavy mist and apparently undamaged. They shouted to be taken off their disabled ship.

Neither vessel sent up distress signals which could easily have been seen by surfmen at the Lifesaving Service's Quonochontaug station, three miles to the east. Nor was the *Larchmont* provided with wireless just coming into use on steamships.

On the doomed steamer, mounting confusion gave way to panic as passengers streamed on deck frantically seeking an avenue of escape. Those who had not been suffocated in the cabins or lounges fought their way topside.

Harris Feldman and his wife, Bertha, of New York, were awakened in their stateroom by the crash. Both got dressed and ran out into the main saloon.

"I pulled myself together," he was to tell a Providence Journal reporter, "and decided that only those who kept cool heads would have much chance of getting out . . . alive."

They and thirty-three others clung to the after housing of the hurricane deck as it broke away. The *Larchmont* started to go under.

Capt. McVay and six crewmen, including Staples and Young, swung No. 1 lifeboat from its davits and tried to pull around the bow to leeward and pick up those struggling in the water, but the wind was too strong.

The Harry P. Knowlton *beached on the Weekapaug, Rhode Island, coast shortly after the disaster. She'd been built for the South American trade but on her last voyage she was bound for Everett, Massachusetts, with a cargo of coal.*

As the lifeboat was carried away by the current, McVay turned his back as the *Larchmont* disappeared bow first beneath the frigid waters of Block Island Sound. The climax had come. It had taken the *Larchmont* twelve minutes to die!

The *Knowlton,* her hull having shipped three feet of water, headed for the Rhode Island coast. A mile off Quonochontaug, the crew took to the dory.

At 1:30 A.M. Haley spotted a lantern glow. A surfman was making his western patrol. Bordering on collapse, they made it ashore and reported to the officer in charge.

It was just a bump, nothing serious, Haley said. The steamer had stayed on course. She wasn't in trouble.

On Block Island Sound the *Larchmont*'s lifeboats drifted toward the island. The stars looked down on a scene of utter desolation. The living and the dead alike resembled human sculptures carved from ice.

To the east, faint rays of the rising sun outlined two men as they tottered along the beach. It was McVay and Staples. Then, for the first time since the *Larchmont* had plunged to the bottom seven hours before, the full scope of the tragedy unfolded.

The grim story of the disaster broke in the afternoon editions. For the next six weeks the press had a field day. Editorial writers from Chicago to Kansas City assailed the country's steamboat lines as unsafe, their ships "floating death traps." The word "cowardice" was frequently flung at the *Larchmont*'s crew.

It was rumored that McVay had made a hasty exodus from the pilot house. Reports had it that his boat was one of the first over the side.

Lawsuits were leveled at everyone in sight. The Joy Line brought action against the *Knowlton*'s owner for $125,000 charging improper navigation and negligence. The survivors sued the Joy Line for $100,-000. In most cases, the plaintiffs were happy to collect enough to cover lawyers' fees.

The Board of Steamboat Inspectors started an immediate inquiry at New London. On April 22, after hundreds of pages of testimony, the federal agency handed down its verdict.

The hapless pilot, John Anson, was alone to blame. Anson made a good scapegoat. Being dead, he wasn't available to testify.

Today the *Larchmont* lies in 114 feet of water. Only her rusting boilers mark her grave. When the sea is calm, commercial fishing boats hover over the spot. Below, schools of cod and flounder keep company with the dead, the known and the nameless.

THE WRECK OF THE ROYAL TAR

by John Mason

COURTESY OF THE BLACKINGTON COLLECTION

Some seamen still believe that birds, snakes, and brass bands are unlucky for a vessel, and to take them aboard on a Friday is tantamount to collective suicide.

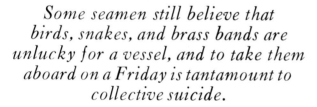

Many years ago, Mr. Roy Coombs of Vinalhaven, Maine saw some queer-looking rocks lying on the beach. He picked them up. They were "white stones," four or five inches long, and quite smooth. As he had never seen anything like them before, he put a couple in a candy box and mailed them to Harvard University to see if the professors knew what they were.

He nearly fell off the porch when they came back from Cambridge. The accompanying letter said: "The specimens you sent us are teeth from a hippopotamus."

Mr. Coombs was well aware that hundreds of years ago camels roamed around New England, but a "hippo" on Vinalhaven—well, that was something to talk about.

He took the biggest tooth and carved it into a handle for his favorite knife. When he proudly showed it to an old-timer down on the wharf, the old duffer said, "Pshaw, that's nothin', I know where there's part of an elephant's leg, and a lot of bones that come ashore from the wreck of the *Royal Tar*. She was the circus boat what burned up right off Widder's Island in October of 1836. That's where them teeth come from."

And the old fellow was right. The *Royal Tar* did burn with a circus on board, and the elephant's carcass came ashore later at Brimstone Island. Two of the bones of his front legs were saved by the Islanders. (One was owned by the late Alton H. Blackington.)

96

The side-wheel steamer, the Royal Tar, *burning in 1836.*

The *Royal Tar* was built in St. John, New Brunswick in 1836 at a cost of $50,000. She was one of several sidewheel steamers then running between St. John and Portland, Maine. She was 146 feet long on the keel, 160 feet over-all, had a 24-foot beam, and was listed as 400 tons burden.

Above deck, at the stern, was a canvas-covered pavilion (or tent with a wooden frame), then a big open space amidship. Up near the bow were two tall funny-looking smokestacks with a mast between them. She carried one square sail on that mast and a couple of jibs running to the bowsprit. (The sails were used when the engines failed to make headway against the tide.)

The skipper of the *Royal Tar* was Capt. Thomas Reed, as fine a man as you'd want to sail with. It was criminal the way folks talked about him after the fire. All sorts of lies were told about him, but when the survivors presented him with a purse of $750 in gold for his bravery and he was made Harbormaster at St. John, the rumors died down and Captain Reed lived to a ripe old age —loved and respected by everyone.

While many of the old-fashioned superstitions of the sea have long since been chucked overboard, some sailors and skippers still believe that birds, snakes and brass bands are unlucky on a vessel—and to take them aboard on a Friday is nothing but an invitation to disaster.

Captain Reed didn't believe in such foolishness, and on Friday, Oc-

" . . . *man the buckets, men, and get a chain on that elephant.*"

tober 21, 1836, he sailed the *Tar* out of St. John with the biggest and strangest cargo that ever buckled the gangplank of his little sidewheeler.

The whole town turned out that bright October day to watch the brass band of "Dexter's Locomotive Museum" go aboard, followed by "Burgess' World Famed Circus" and "Menagerie of Wild Animals, Birds and Reptiles."

There were red and yellow wagons, and golden cages containing cobras and pythons, two big lions, a spotted leopard, a Bengal tiger, and many smaller animals.

Next came a pair of proud pelicans, a lot of chattering monkeys, six beautiful Arabian horses, two awkward, lumbering camels, and "Mogul," the elephant!

As if this were not enough to tax the capacity of the little *Tar,* there was a very large passenger list and a crew of 21.

All told, there were at least 100 men, women, and children—besides the animals—all jammed into the *Royal Tar* as she headed for Penobscot Bay and Portland that Friday afternoon. Many passengers, moving from New Brunswick to Portland for the winter, did their cooking in the crowded steerage quarters.

As the elephant was too big to go below, he was chained out on deck. The other animals, and the birds and snakes, were stored between decks.

After things got settled down, the brass band came out on deck and gave a concert. As the heavily laden steamer sailed slowly down the coast, the music was wafted toward shore where the natives gathered excitedly on the wharves to wave and wish them "Godspeed."

On Sunday, the blue October sky became flecked with mackerel clouds and a raw wind whipped up the sea. The tigers and lions stirred restlessly, and the womenfolk got seasick, what with the rough water and the combined smells of wild animals, and of cabbage being cooked. Who wouldn't?

Captain Reed, kind man that he was, put into Eastport and stayed there until Tuesday, giving the passengers opportunity to go ashore and the animals a chance to exercise.

Tuesday afternoon they sailed again, heading south for Penobscot Bay through choppy seas and a spanking off-shore breeze that soon developed into a first-class gale.

In order to get into the lee of the islands, Captain Reed steered the *Royal Tar* toward Fox Island Thoroughfare and was just abreast of Channel Rock when the assistant engineer burst into the pilot house, white and shaking.

What's the matter, Marshall? Seasick?"

"No, Captain, it's worse than that. We've got to anchor and fill the boilers."

Captain Reed said, "Well, we'll ease along till eight bells when we'll be close to Vinalhaven, and then we can water up."

"No! We can't wait that long. We've got to anchor *now!* The boilers are red hot, sir, red hot and smoking!"

Captain Reed looked hard and long at the engineer, finding it hard to believe that the boilers were in such condition. As he turned the *Tar* toward Isle au Haut, he said sharply, "Go back to the engine room, Marshall, and tend to your duties." A few minutes later he gave the order to drop anchor.

After all these years, it's nigh on to impossible to get all the details of what had happened. Most folks agree (from stories told by the survivors) that the night before the chief engineer had been up all night fixing a leak in the boiler. When he turned in, he left his assistant, Mr. Marshall, in charge. This careless officer failed to notice the water was running low and when the alarming condition was brought to his attention he muttered resentfully: "Oh, don't worry about that. We've got water enough."

But they didn't have! And every minute that went by, the water in the glass dropped lower and lower. Why that man didn't report this state of affairs—for which he was responsible—will never be known.

The anchor had barely gone overboard when the dread cry of "Fire" was heard below decks and a puff of creamy brown smoke mushroomed from the companionway, followed by a tongue of flame which licked along the main deck.

When Captain Reed came out of the pilot house and looked down through the iron grating, he saw rolling flames and heard the screams of the passengers and the terrified cries of the wild animals, trapped between the decks.

Choking from the thick smoke, he made his way aft and ordered the frenzied crew to lower the lifeboats, recalling then, to his horror, that three of the boats had been left behind in St. John to make room for the circus wagons and cages.

"Throw the wagons over. They'll float—and those poles and ropes. Man the buckets, men, and get a chain on that elephant. Hoist the distress flag. Get that longboat overboard."

Through the stifling smoke he saw one of the boats some distance away from the ship. The assistant engineer had taken it and, with several men, was rowing desperately toward Isle au Haut.

Captain Reed took charge of the longboat and picked up those who had jumped overboard at the first flash of fire! He then returned to the ship. Had there been anyone to man the pumping engine or direct the wildly rushing people, many could have been saved. But with the thick smoke swirling around them—and flames pouring from the portholes—and the elephant trumpeting and pulling at his chains and the air filled with cinders and shrieks—it's no wonder that strong men jumped overboard and women tossed their children into the wind-whipped ocean.

When the wind suddenly changed, Captain Reed strode to the stern, cut the cable, and yelled to the quartermaster to hoist the sail. But before he got it up, a hot-air explosion ripped off a forward hatch and the sail went up in flames.

By now the whole mid-section of the *Royal Tar* was burning furiously and, instead of "steaming" to the shore, as Captain Reed had planned, when he slipped the anchor, the *Royal Tar* was now drifting toward the open sea—a hopeless, helpless, burning wreck.

On board, except for the crackle of flames and an occasional cry from the elephant, silence had settled over the circus ship.

Below decks, all of the poor dumb beasts had perished in their twisted cages; above them, separated by the furious fire amidship, a dozen or so passengers huddled at the bow and stern. Cut off from each other by the flames that worked closer and closer, they made ready to drop over the side into the cold waters of Penobscot Bay. Those who jumped first were so numbed by the cold that they sank immediately. A few who waited (and kept their heads) were eventually saved.

One foolish man rolled 500 silver dollars in his stocking and tied it around his waist. Then he lashed his leather trunk to a plank and, with it, dove over the side. The trunk floated—but he went to the bottom like a silver-plated rock.

A young girl with two small children pushed them over the stern. The youngsters managed to cling to a bale of hay and were picked up by Captain Reed in the longboat, but the girl drowned.

H. H. Fuller, manager of the menagerie, stayed on the quarterdeck till his clothes caught fire, then lowered himself over the side with a piece of rope, making one end fast to the tiller chain—and there he hung. Fearing he might weaken and lose his hold, he passed the rope around his waist and over his neck. This nearly cost him his life because other passengers were also hanging onto ropes which burned through, plunging them into the sea. Three of them grabbed the rope Fuller had wound round his neck and nearly choked him.

As there were still women and children on the smoking deck, Captain Reed had his men make a raft from floating timbers and wreckage. When they finally got it alongside the circus ship, they saw "Mogul," the old elephant, silhouetted against the flames with his two front feet firmly planted on the rail.

He must have thought the raft was for him—for just as it grazed the side of the *Royal Tar*, the elephant gave one mighty roar and plunged headlong onto the raft, smashing it to kindling and crushing two of the crew. After swimming around for an hour or so, "Mogul" struck out for land. A week later he washed ashore at Brimstone Island.

Many of the victims were hauled from the water by the crew of the United States Revenue Cutter *Veto*, which sailed through showers of red-hot embers in spite of the fact that she carried a deckload of gunpowder.

The *Royal Tar* blazed far into the night as she drifted by Saddle Back Light, and then she went down. Years ago, I learned that Capt. John G. Snow of Rockland believed he had located part of her hull, off Widow's Island, and I'm wondering if that is the same wreckage that I saw on Widow's several years before that. Come spring, I hope I can go out there again and take a look.

THE DISASTER THAT LAUNCHED A CAREER

Unlike news stories, an action lithograph was hung on the wall and often remained there for years or until a building was razed. Here's how it all began ...

by Robert C. Baur

Remembered as one of the world's great marine disasters, the burning of the steamship *Lexington,* on January 13, 1840, is lesser known for launching the career of Nathaniel Currier, who, later, teamed with James Merritt Ives and hung Currier and Ives prints in American parlors from Maine to California.

Three days after the side-wheeler burned and sank in Long Island Sound, a broadside bearing Currier's Spruce Street address appeared in New York City. Commissioned by *The New York Sun,* the broadside, entitled "The Extra Sun," featured a lithograph of the blazing ship and five columns of copy describing the catastrophe that stunned the nation. So vividly had artist W. K. Hewitt portrayed the *Lexington*'s eleventh hour, one could almost hear the crackling flames and the despairing shrieks of the doomed passengers. A drawing of Long Island Sound helped readers pinpoint the disaster area.

Anxious relatives scanned the casualty list—but only four survived the *Lexington*'s last voyage. Although Currier listed 87 passengers and a crew of 40, the death toll is believed to be about 140.

Heading this grim roster was Dr. Charles Follen, the theologian, and the wife and children of Russel Jarvis, editor of *The Evening Tattler.* Equally shocking were the untimely demise of comedian Henry J. Finn and of Charles Eberle, the actor. Adolphus Harnden, President of Harnden's Express, perished with a fortune in currency he was delivering to the Merchant's Bank of Boston.

Also aboard were a number of sea captains returning from overseas duty, as well as a funeral party escorting the body of the deceased to Providence for burial. For a time it was feared that Henry Wadsworth Longfellow, an enthusiastic steamship traveler, had booked passage aboard the *Lexington.*

Readers wept over frozen child victims in scorched night clothing so vividly described in flowery Victorian prose. Unbelievably harrowing were the experiences which the living had so miraculously survived.

With frozen hands and feet, Stephen Manchester, the *Lexington*'s pilot, was found floating on a cotton bale the next morning, by the sloop *Merchant.* Manchester said that he had remained at the wheel until burned out. Anticipating his superior's command, he had headed for the Long Island shore before Captain Child gave the order. Then, with the help of the baggagemaster and Adolphus Harnden, he made a futile attempt to lower the lifeboats.

Before abandoning ship he saw passengers throwing water on the flames with a broken specie box. (Possibly the express company cash box which Harnden was hoping to save, suggesting that the money strewn upon the deck sank with the ship. This evidence continues to intrigue treasure buffs, for $18,000 in coins has never been retrieved.)

The *Merchant* also rescued Charles Smith, fireman, and Capt. Chester Hilliard, a passenger.

David Crowley, the Second Mate, washed ashore at Riverhead, Long Island, 50 hours and 50 miles after leaving the blazing vessel. All four survivors harmoniously agreed that the *Lexington*'s skipper, Capt. George Child, died courageously at the wheel.

The *Lexington* was last sighted about 3 A.M. in the vicinity of Old Field Point, Long Island. It is believed her charred hulk is resting today four miles north of Old Field Light.

Soon after the disaster, the steamship *Statesman* returned to New York with five bodies and considerable luggage. The search party reported that passenger luggage was being looted on the beaches. Dr. Follen's trunk had been found in the woods, emptied of all but the pastor's papers.

Public indignation boiled further after Currier reported that Capt. William Terrill, of the sloop *Improvement,* was nearby but failed to aid the stricken *Lexington.* His reason, according to Currier, was that he would have lost his tide into port, "and accordingly he pursued his inhuman course, leaving upwards of one hundred persons to die the worst of deaths. The circumstances of this unparalleled cruelty will hereafter be more clearly exposed, and I trust he will receive his merited deserts. This conduct of Captain Terrill has elicited a universal burst of indignation against him in this city; and for his safety's sake we advise him not to venture too much in public here."

Hawked by vendors, "The Extra Sun," sold out as soon as it appeared on the streets. Currier and his staff worked around the clock to meet

by W.K Hewitt
N. Currier Lith & Pub. 2 Spruce St. N.Y

Awful Conflagration of the Steam Boat **LEXINGTON** *In Long Island Sound on Monday
Eve.g. Jan.y 13th 1840. by which melancholy occurrence; over* 100 **PERSONS PERISHED.**

Commissioned by The New York Sun, *this broadside by Nathaniel Currier was illustrated by W. K. Hewitt and enjoys the distinction of being the first illustrated "extra" in the history of news reporting. The* Lexington *prints were selling 11 months after the fire.*

the demand. Recalling those hectic days, Mr. Currier later told how he helped tie bundles for distribution. Nor was the market confined to New York, for Boston, Philadelphia, and other cities proved equally receptive.

When the initial demand had slackened, a second printing was made. Omitting the title of "The Extra Sun," it featured the testimony of Chester Hilliard, the only passenger to live through the ordeal of fire, water, and subzero cold.

Hilliard, a rugged 25-year-old sea captain, wasn't overly concerned when the fire alarm sounded about 7 P.M. (minor fires from tilting oil lamps were common shipboard occurrences.) However, hurrying to the promenade deck as the shouting and confusion increased, Hilliard found a bucket brigade futilely watering an inferno flaming from the cotton cargo. Pushing through the hysterical throng to the pilot house, he found Captain Child trying to beach the ship entrusted to his care. Then, before the ship could be turned, the tiller rope gave way. The captain's command to shut down the engines went unheeded because the intense heat had already driven the firemen from the engine room.

Although the *Lexington*'s three lifeboats might have carried everyone to safety, Hilliard observed that the passengers were stupidly determined to destroy themselves. The two smaller boats swamped from overcrowding, and the larger boat, capable of seating 40, was smashed in the revolving sidewheel.

Hurling cotton bales overboard, Hilliard urged everyone to save himself. He thought he abandoned ship about eight o'clock, lowering himself with the aid of a fellow passenger, on a bale tied to the rail.

Having been attracted to Mrs. Jarvis in the dining room, Hilliard recognized her clinging to a cotton bale, an infant in her arm. She implored him to bring her the other child, whose lifeless body floated nearby. When his companion died, Hilliard floated alone through the ice until rescued the following forenoon. None the worse for his experience, he returned to New York the next day.

Hilliard cited the captain and crew of the rescue ship *Merchant* (which suffered the misfortune of breaking from the icebound Southport, Connecticut, harbor, only to run aground. She was floated free too late to save the lives of more than three).

Other Connecticut shore residents saw the fire too; but, like the keeper of Norwalk's Sheffield Island Light, they were unable to help because their boats were frozen to the moorings. (Death, it seemed, had underwritten the *Lexington*'s rendezvous with destiny, determining grimly that the carnage be near complete.)

Monday, January 13, may have been the unlucky finale for the *Lexington* and all who boarded her. But for Nathaniel Currier it was the be-

ginning. The *Lexington* disaster not only earned Currier a national byline, but the distinction of producing the first illustrated "extra" in the history of news reporting.

The popularity of Currier's broadside continued throughout the eight-day investigation called by the New York City coroner to determine the cause of the tragedy. Likely, irate Bostonians carried the lithograph to historic Faneuil Hall, where they protested the practice of carrying inflammable cargo on passenger ships.

We know that the picture was still selling 11 months after the fire, from a bill submitted to Currier for coloring 125 *Lexington* prints.

Success of the *Lexington* street sales sent peddlers daily to Number 2 Spruce Street to stock their pushcarts. Special news prints were tacked to the side of the cart, with other selections being based upon prevailing cultural tastes in the individual salesman's territory. Deposits paid on each print were refunded for unsold pictures.

When James Merritt Ives joined the firm in 1857, the partners didn't know their business alliance would be incorporated into Webster's Dictionary. Currier and Ives were far too busy recording the many facets of contemporary 19th Century life. Specializing in new pictures patterned after Currier's *Lexington* bonanza, they rushed artists to sketch fire scenes and other spectacular events. These drawings were expertly engraved on stone by name lithograph-

ato Webster's Dictionary.

Commodore Cornelius Vanderbilt, the nineteenth century shipping tycoon and former owner of the Lexington, *had raced the trim craft on Long Island Sound.*

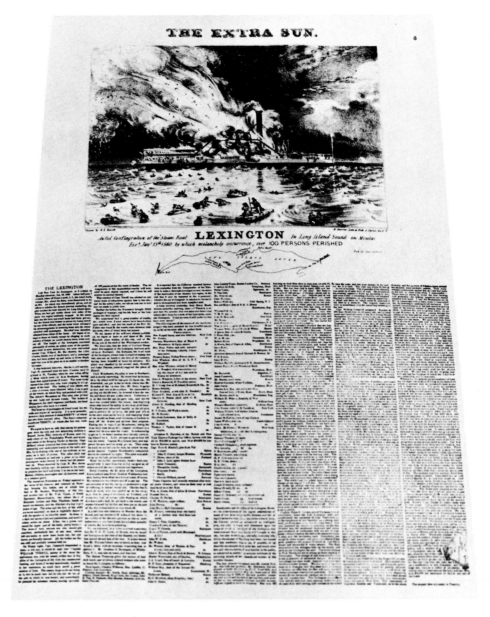

ers like Napoleon Sarony, who had executed the *Lexington* print.

Illustrating subject matter similar to that appearing in the Sunday supplements, these news prints were noted for their longevity. Unlike news stories, which are discarded after being read, an action lithograph would remain wedded to the walls of the livery stable or corner saloon, often until the building was razed.

As a listening post, the lithograph shop drew the ear of Phineas Taylor Barnum, Horace Greeley, and other distinguished contemporaries. Soon Currier and Ives were dispensing prints in many American cities in sales set-ups similar to the

Lexington pushcart system. Eventually a London office was opened for overseas distribution.

When the business was finally liquidated by heirs in 1907, the vast accumulation of lithographic stones was sold by the pound. Fast photographic news service had surpassed Currier and Ives, as a source of information, but their efforts were not forgotten.

The lusty adolescent nation Currier and Ives had so meticulously recorded on stone emerged from the Treaty of Versailles, in 1918, as the dominant power. Aroused to a newborn national pride, the Americana craze was on, and Currier and Ives

were included in its very beginnings for they *were* America. How the partners would have smiled to see collectors searching dusty barns and attic rafters for their handiwork. More astounding would be the prices paid for prints not old enough to be antiques.

One hundred and twenty-six years have erased all but a few copies of Currier's famous *Lexington* print. Many more may have survived —but like Mr. Harnden's treasure, you will have to hunt for them.

THE DAY THE WEATHER

The late E. B. RIDEOUT, the author of this article, was the last
of those who knew the REAL reason why Capt. Blanchard
decided to put to sea in the face of ominous weather reports.

November 26, 1898

Almost 60 years ago, I first heard the facts that led to the sinking of the Steamer *Portland*. The *Portland* had left her berth at Boston, Massachusetts and steamed down the harbor in the early darkness of Saturday, November 26, 1898. Portland, Maine was her destination—but she never arrived there, for, as she turned her course northeastward toward Maine, she plowed into the teeth of one of New England's heaviest November snowstorms of record. Never before, nor since, was there so much snowfall in the Boston area in one single November storm, with such terrific 60- to 80-mile winds as there were in that memorable storm—since known as the "Portland Storm." Of the 200 passengers and crew aboard, not a single soul survived. In that same storm, about 140 other craft were either blown ashore or sunk off the New England coast.

For a great many years after, three questions were topics of endless discussions: (1) Why did Captain Blanchard sail in view of the ominous weather reports, or not turn back when he first ran into the fury of the storm, or why didn't he turn in toward Gloucester? (2) Just where did the steamer go down? (3) Could she have collided with another ship?

I base my story on the remarks made at different times by three Weather Bureau men, all of whom claimed to have heard the statement of Capt. Hollis Blanchard a short time before his last sailing.

Captain Blanchard had the reputation of being a man of reliance, with experience on sidewheelers. Before the turn of the century, there were few propellers. Side wheels were the means of propulsion for ships in those days, except on river boats where the paddle wheels extended the full width of the broad stern of a boat. These steamships had big paddle wheels enclosed in fancy ornamented paddle boxes on each side of the ship, and were not seaworthy in rough weather. Captain Blanchard knew this. Realizing his responsibility, he would not willfully attempt to match the unseaworthiness of his ship against the elements. That is why he became a staunch friend of those at the U.S. Weather Bureau in Boston and abided by their advice before sailing.

About 1908 I became acquainted with three Weather Bureau men who knew Captain Blanchard, when I was less than 20 years old. My greatest interest then was the weather, and already I had become a weather crank. Therefore, I located the Weather Bureau in Boston and introduced myself as such to the first man I met. He gave his name as Mr. Crosby, and he was then the oldest employee in the Boston office.

We had a very nice chat, and quite naturally our conversation drifted to the *Portland* tragedy, which had occurred but 10 years before. Mr. Crosby was the first to tell me why Captain Blanchard had sailed, and he made my visit so pleasant that it wasn't long before I became a daily caller during my lunch hour. Then I met Mr. John W. Smith, who had been the official-in-charge at the Boston office for about 30 years of his more than 40 years with the service. He told me the same story about Captain Blanchard that Mr. Crosby had told me. And later the same story came from Mr. Mark T. Nesmith as it was told to him by the Captain. I will now state the facts as they were so frequently repeated to me by those who had talked with Captain Blanchard within a few hours of his last sailing.

BUREAU WAS RIGHT

Left: The crew of the Portland.

Below: Launching of the steamer Portland, *1889. Nine years later she went down in one of New England's worst blizzards.*

He must act quickly by first calling for help, but where would it come from?

Many readers already know that the *Portland* ran her maiden trip in 1889. She was considered a very fine ship of her kind, with all the latest furnishings, including electric lighting. Captain Blanchard appreciated the gracefulness and fanciful beauty of his ship, but, more seriously, felt his responsibility to his passengers and freight. It was several years before the disaster that the Captain began making calls to the Boston Weather Bureau. He became very friendly with the entire force, and John Smith would explain the morning weather map as it was made from the latest reports. The Captain became familiar with the map and through Mr. Smith's instructions was able to draw his own conclusions as to whether it would become rough and the winds unfavorable for sailing. He learned much from the daily morning scratch map as to the direction of the wind and what its strength would be for his evening's trip to Portland. If the wind, according to the barometric pressure lines and gradient, would be too strong from abeam, then he would not risk it because he knew that there was danger of getting into the trough of a sea, which was always a very weak point in the navigation of a side-wheeler. From his familiarity with the daily weather map and the advice from the Weather Bureau, plus his knowledge of the *Portland*'s weaknesses, Captain Blanchard was a cautious man.

However, there came a day when Captain Blanchard was called "on the carpet" and was told that he was really being too cautious in view of the fact that the alternate and competitive route would be by rail. He would henceforth sail on *their* orders. He felt that sooner or later these orders could well be against his better judgment. He told his friends and advisors at the Boston Weather Bureau about this meeting, and this is how the Weather Bureau men got the facts from the mouth of Captain Blanchard—and how I in turn was told the facts. The Captain continued his daily trips to the Weather Bureau every day before sailing.

On this Saturday after Thanksgiving, there were a great many passengers in Boston anxious to get back home to Maine before Sunday. The morning of that terrible night dawned with sunshine, except for some very thin cirrus clouds that caused a faint ring around the sun. It was a quiet morning with little wind. At the Weather Bureau, the Captain recalled a slight disturbance in the eastern Great Lakes region the previous morning; but it had moved east-southeastward with a very rapidly increasing secondary development by Saturday morning.

"It looks bad," Mr. Smith said when he finished drawing his map. Captain Blanchard was solemn, but he told them he was following orders. He went out the door, saying he hoped it would go off the coast and that he would get his passengers home. Warnings had already been ordered at Washington for a Northeaster along the New England coast. That morning special observations were ordered. Before noon, additional warnings for the increasing severity of the storm were telegraphed from Washington. Immediately Mr. Crosby called Captain Blanchard by phone at the wharf. When he received the information from Mr. Crosby, he thanked him and said, "I am going." Obviously he had been ordered to set sail.

Other than a slowly disappearing sun behind steadily thickening cloudiness, the day remained quiet. Evening settled in. The *Portland* left the wharf at seven o'clock. A very light, gentle snow began which blurred her rows of deck lights from those remaining at the wharf. Soon she disappeared from view as the snow began to thicken. Barely within an hour after the handful of onlookers had seen the *Portland* disappear in the falling snow in the inner harbor, the ever-thickening snow began swirling with an increasing wind. The storm continued to increase as thick snow and a lashing gale suddenly swooped down along the entire Massachusetts Bay and coastal areas. Soon it reached hurricane proportions.

Very few knew that there was a steamship with nearly 200 lives aboard just off the coast in that death-dealing storm, for there was no wireless or radio in those days. However, in the late evening, Mr. William J. Hackett, living in Gloucester at the time (and who became my father-in-law 10 years later), was one of several in Gloucester who heard repeated blasts of a steamship whistle. Many times, after I was married to Laura, he told me

The Portland *was considered an elegant ship with all the latest appointments and furnishings, including electric lights.*

that he recognized the whistle as that of the Steamer *Portland,* as she used to salute Thatcher's Island twin lights on clear nights on her way to Portland. The night of the storm, he knew that her whistling repeatedly meant she was in distress. It finally became fainter—and then died away. No sound but the roar of the storm shrieking outside was heard thereafter.

The constant whistle blasts of the only steamer out that night indicated that Captain Blanchard was calling for help. In those moments he must have reached a point of desperation. What was in his mind? He must act quickly by first calling for help, but where would it come from in an increasing hurricane wind? Further progress into such a blast would exert great pressure on his paddlewheel shafts, which would render his ship wholly at the mercy of the storm if they should break. Therefore, he had to abandon hope of getting his passengers home for Sunday. He must have known it would be disastrous to turn his ship toward rockbound Gloucester and get into the trough with the wind hitting his ship broadside. The only thing that remained, which involved an equally great risk, was to turn around and head for the end of Cape

Wreckage from the Portland *found on the shore of Cape Cod, near Orleans, a few weeks after the disaster.*

Cod, with the wind astern as much as he could keep her that way, thereby taking off much of the strain on her engines and paddle shafts. Then, if he had to, wouldn't it be better to beach her since her chances of rescue would be better?

Was that his final thought in those whistle-blasting moments of desperation off Gloucester?

The second and third questions mentioned before were answered some years ago when divers discovered the hull of the *Portland* with a hole in her side. A sworn statement by the diver is that she lies 4½ miles from Pilgrim Monument and 4½ miles out to sea from Highland Light and that she collided with a granite ship seen just before during a lull in the storm by a man at Highland Light.

The fact of finding the *Portland* beneath the sea off Truro makes it seem likely that Captain Blanchard did head for Cape Cod. The terrifying idea of turning his ship around and then across the gale-driven, snow-blinding blackness of Massachusetts Bay surely very grimly confronted Captain Blanchard. The absolute fact that this ship lies so near Provincetown proved he had to cross Massachusetts Bay. None can realize what a night of horror it must have been aboard. But how did she make it? How much of the way was she aided by the terrifying gale from

astern? Did her engines fail her at any time? How much coal was still available in her bunkers to keep steam up? One thing is certain: Captain Blanchard was tortured by these stark realisms during every moment of guiding his ship to what evidence practically proved to be his hoped-for destination.

But piecing together the evidence of what Captain Blanchard did and what he may have intended to do is indeed difficult. However, to me one thing is certain; and that is his courage and attempt to get his ship so near to a beach was a miracle. I feel he might have been successful in beaching her and rescuing those aboard for, like other sidewheelers, she was a wide-bottom ship with paddlewheels on both sides and probably would not have listed much once she was driven well onto a beach.

However, a little more than 24 hours after she left India Wharf in Boston against—as we now know—the better judgment of Captain Blanchard, a great misfortune overtook her in that blinding storm and blackness. She was struck by another ship which tore a big hole in her side and landed her beneath the waters off Cape Cod, where she still lies after nearly 75 years.

The whole era was "strategic." In Section IV machinery plays the principal part during the great . . .

moments WHEN STEAM CHANGED HISTORY dynamically.

Mr. Lincoln's Flagship:

the "RIVER QUEEN"

Some of the most dramatic moments in Abraham Lincoln's life took place aboard the little steamer which years later endeared herself to New Englanders as the boat to Nantucket and the Vineyard . . . .   *by Edouard A. Stackpole*

Despite the spate of books about Abraham Lincoln and the Civil War there are only fragmentary accounts of one important period— the time he spent afloat aboard the steamer *River Queen*. True, this was only a brief interlude, and yet it contained some of the most dramatic moments in a life which was in itself a compelling drama. It took place during the closing scenes of the Civil War; a few days in which Mr. Lincoln escaped the crowded events of the land to enjoy the comparative serenity of the water.

·It was the second of February, 1865, that he first went aboard the *River Queen*. The trim sidewheel steamer, now to become his "flagship," was a new vessel, having been built at Keyport, New Jersey, in 1864; soon after to be chartered by the Federal Government for use as a regular dispatch boat between Washington and General Grant's headquarters at City Point on the James River. But it was Lincoln's part in her history, rather than Grant's, which became the more important. It was a time when, more than ever, his mind was anticipating the great problems of post-war years. He realized that the war's end involved more than the laying down of arms and that both the North and the South would be inevitably concerned with grave decisions. Whether to bring about a negotiated peace with the Confederate States (all too apparently the great hope of the South) or to force the issue through sheer press of arms was the great question facing him. At Richmond, Jefferson Davis, realizing that time was running out

for the South, finally assented to Lincoln's tacit agreement to an informal discussion on terms of peace. But Davis was soon to learn it was not between "two countries," as he would have it, but for the benefit of "one common country," as Lincoln insisted.

Davis appointed three peace commissioners: Alexander H. Stephens, Vice-President of the Confederacy; R. M. T. Hunter, President *pro tem* of the Confederate Senate (and a former U.S. Senator); and John A. Campbell, Assistant Secretary of War (and former Associate Justice of the U.S.). Their letter of appointment as Commissioners included the phrase: "In compliance with the letter of Mr. Lincoln you are hereby requested to proceed to Washington City for conference with him upon the subject to which it relates." But Davis could not re-

sist using again the phrase ". . . of securing peace to the two countries."

Upon formal application by the Commissioners to enter the Union lines, Lincoln sent to General Grant one of his trusted aides, Major Thomas T. Eckert, with the stipulation that they be admitted only if they agreed in writing that they were to confer for the purpose as specified in his original proposal.

The three then applied to General Grant for admission, referring to Lincoln's note, and Grant admitted them. Accordingly, Lincoln sent Secretary of State Seward to Fortress Monroe aboard the *River Queen,* with instructions to greet the Commissioners but to make them realize any conference on a basis of peace must be on his original terms—not as an armistice; that the war was to "cease on the part of the government

. . . With characteristic simplicity, Lincoln replied that the only way (to end the war) was for those who had resisted the United States of America's constituted laws and who continued to resist, to stop resisting.

Federal troops attack an enemy train.

112

whenever it shall have ceased on the part of those who began it." Further, Lincoln cautioned Seward not to "assume to definitely consummate anything." At the same time he reiterated to Grant that military action was to continue and to agree to no armistice.

While, on the evening of February 1, 1865, Secretary Seward and Eckert conferred with the three Commissioners before Fortress Monroe, Lincoln, in Washington, was engaged in an interview with Gen. James W. Singleton, of Illinois, a "notorious Copperhead," according to one newspaper, and a man dedicated to a negotiated peace, as stated by another. Singleton had been to Richmond to confer with Jefferson Davis and reported to Lincoln the Confederate President's willingness to a negotiated peace—which would ultimately include "reunion" and the

"abolition of slavery," two of Lincoln's minimum requirements—provided that the slave owners were compensated and the Southern States be allowed to retain their rights to determine all questions of local or domestic government, slavery included.

Lincoln had apparently decided to leave such negotiations up to Seward and the three Confederate Commissioners when, on the following morning (February 2), he received three telegrams—one from Seward at Fortress Monroe, stating the "Richmond party not here;" the second was from Eckert, stating he

At the second famous conference aboard the River Queen, Sherman, Grant, Lincoln, and Admiral Porter met in one of the Civil War's most fateful conferences. The painting, by George P. A. Healy, hangs in the White House.

was detaining the Commissioners at City Point. Upset by this apparent diplomatic stalemate, Lincoln was about to recall both Seward and Eckert when the third telegram arrived. It was from General Grant, and he urged the President to come to Fortress Monroe and confer with the Confederate Commissioners personally, as he was "convinced, upon conversation with Stephens and Hunter, that their intentions are . . . sincere to restore peace and union." This telegram determined Lincoln, who trusted Grant's judgment in matters other than only military, and he immediately wired Grant and Seward that he would come to Fortress Monroe to meet the "Richmond gentlemen."

On the morning of February 2, Lincoln took a train for Annapolis, Maryland, and upon arrival there boarded the steamer *Thomas Coll-*

yer. As the vessel made her way down the Chesapeake, the President withdrew to a stateroom. He realized that his forthcoming conference had a great bearing on the military as well as the diplomatic situation. Certain powerful figures in the North were anxious for peace, notable spokesmen for this group being the newspaper editors Horace Greeley and James Gordon Bennett. On the other hand, the radicals in Congress, such as Thaddeus Stevens, would criticize the effort as dangerously conciliatory. But Lincoln, with his yearning for the war's end, was thinking of a basis for peace which would be predicated on his two fundamental requisites—reunion and complete abolition of slavery.

Early that evening the steamer arrived off Fortress Monroe and Lincoln went immediately aboard the *River Queen* for a conference with Secretary Seward. After dinner aboard, the two men were closeted until late at night. From Seward's report it was evident that the Confederate Commissioners were not all in accord as to the Southern stand on the subject of peace. Stephens, the titular head of the group, was willing to concede to a peace which would guarantee state rights and constitutional liberties. There was evidence that he shared Jefferson Davis' belief that Lincoln was behind an idea proposed by Francis Blair, a self-appointed Northern emissary, who had gone on a recent peace mission to Richmond. It was Blair who had suggested a truce, during which the Confederate armies with Northern aid would enter Mexico and drive the French out—with the annexation of Mexico to the United States, under a protectorate, as a result. Such action, Blair believed, would be a justification under the Monroe Doctrine and would in itself constitute a

means of bringing the Great War between North and South to a conclusion without loss of prestige to either side.

It was in an atmosphere of such fantasy on the part of the Confederate Commissioners that, on the evening of February 3, 1865, the now famous Peace Conference took place in the saloon of the *River Queen*. No written record, unofficial or otherwise, of this historic event was made at that time. The only report of what transpired was that given in retrospect by the Confederate Vice-President, and summary reports made afterward in Washington by both Seward and Lincoln, and in a letter to Charles Francis Adams by Seward at a later date. There was a strained sense of courtesy throughout the whole transactions at the outset, some old recollections were mentioned, and then the group got down to the subject at hand.

Stephens asked the main question—the way of "putting an end to the present trouble"—and Lincoln, with characteristic simplicity, replied that the only way was for those who had resisted the United States of America's constituted laws, and who continued to resist, to stop resisting. The Mexican situation was brought up, but Lincoln quickly dispelled the illusion that he was behind Blair's proposal. Restoration of the Union was the only basis for any settlement of the War by cessation of arms. Seward quoted the President's own words, contained in his last message to Congress—". . . the war will cease on the part of the Government whenever it shall have ceased on the part of those who began it."

Clinging to last straws the Commissioners brought up the matter of slavery—would the Emancipation Proclamation apply to slaves freed

during the War or would it continue to be in effect after the war? Seward wryly announced that Congress had passed a proposal, only a few days before, which paved the way for a Constitutional Amendment abolishing slavery. According to Stephens, Lincoln hinted that a return of the Southern States to the Union might enable them to legally postpone such an amendment. What about property rights? Both Seward and Lincoln were reported as confident the confiscated properties would be returned to their owners by Congress and the courts.

At 5:00 o'clock on the evening of February 3, the *River Queen* left Hampton Roads for Washington, bearing Lincoln and Seward. All through the night the trim white steamer made her way up Chesapeake Bay while the gaunt President slept and Seward lay in restless semi-slumber. It was 7:30 in the morning when they arrived at Annapolis and the two boarded a train for Washington.

And so the Peace Conference ended almost as it began, with no agreement. But it did reveal that Lincoln's basic premises were more clear-cut and vital. If it had any lesson for the Southern States it was in their realization that the Mexican intervention was a fantasy, the dream of independence was unreal, and that their hope of "peace with honor" was doomed. It had a dual effect in the North. The "Peace Democrats" were forced to realize the South would accept no terms aside from recognition and separation; the Radicals, although they disapproved of the President's action in attending the Peace Conference, now admitted that he would not compromise his original principles.

But there can be no question that the conference in the little steamer's saloon on that February night made a lasting impression on Lincoln. In his shrewd analysis of the Southern Commissioners' attitude he saw the glimmer of a "just and lasting peace." The fact that, on the day following his return to Washington, he presented to the Cabinet in an evening meeting his ideas on compensation to the Southern States, in the event of the abolition of slavery, shows that he saw a place for a lever in negotiating that peace. What he wanted with all his heart, as well as his brain, was to end the War by having the South lay down her arms and recognize the authority of the Union, and this was the quickest way to restore them as sovereign members of the United States.

Lincoln's proposal was that Congress, in joint session, empower him to pay the southern slave-holding states $400 million in government bonds, half that amount if they ceased their resistance before April 1, 1865, and the remaining half after they ratified the Thirteenth Amendment; that all political offenders be pardoned; and that all property, except slaves liable to confiscation, be released—and other liberal terms. The President's proposed terms were unanimously opposed by the Cabinet. In accepting their decision, Lincoln probably merely laid aside the plan for a more propitious moment.

But, on March 4, a month later, when he delivered his inaugural address, the thoughts of that Peace Conference were still in his mind, as the immortal words of that remarkable document revealed.

The Great War was coming to its climax. Every day the military ascendancy of the North was more marked. Sherman's success in the South and Grant's relentless pressure

on Richmond foretold the final phase. Lincoln was anxious for the end to come as quickly as possible—to terminate the tragedy.

Once again, the little *River Queen* played her part. Upon invitation by General Grant to visit his headquarters, Lincoln telegraphed a quick acceptance and went aboard the steamer (at the foot of Sixth Street in Washington) shortly after noon on March 23. He was accompanied by Mrs. Lincoln and Tad. Filled with the anticipation of being able to observe the men at the front, Lincoln's eagerness was checked by a sudden attack of biliousness, thought to be caused by the drinking water. Upon arrival at Fortress Monroe, the next morning at 9:00 o'clock a fresh supply of water was put aboard the *River Queen*, supervised by William H. Crook, the President's bodyguard. The steamer then proceeded up the James River to City Point, Grant's headquarters several miles below Richmond.

Lincoln was still not feeling well; but on the next morning (March 25) he arose early to walk the top deck and look out over the peaceful river. The early spring had already touched the banks on either hand. As the songs of birds came across the quiet waters, the cares of Washington behind him and the torment of war, just ahead, seemed remote. The haggard President, worn by his spiritual as well as physical problems, sat quietly at the breakfast table, eating little. Later that morning, Rear Admiral Porter came aboard to greet him and accompany him ashore, where a group of officers had assembled to walk with the President to General Grant's headquarters.

A special train then took the party to General Meade's headquarters, and along the way were ob-

served the fresh evidences of recent fighting. At the track's end, President Lincoln mounted a horse and rode over to a portion of the battlefield where the dead were buried. When the train returned to City Point some of the cars carried wounded men and prisoners. Weary, worn by what he had seen, Lincoln declined Grant's invitation to supper and went aboard the *River Queen*. After sending a telegram to Secretary Stanton in Washington, he retired to his cabin.

For years after, the stateroom which Lincoln occupied was noted as such by the steamer's owners, but it was never restricted as to use. The satin draperies which hung about the mahogany bedstead in which he slept, the walnut wash stand, the gilt-edged moulding, even the heavy framed mirror, always remained in place. Today, the only relic preserved is the mirror, a proud possession of the Old Dartmouth Historical Society in New Bedford, Massachusetts.

It was two days later (March 27) that Gen. William T. Sherman arrived from Goldsboro, North Carolina, for a conference with Grant, having come by sea aboard the captured steamer *Russia*.

On that next day occurred the second famous conference aboard the *River Queen*—then moored each night at anchor in the river, for security reasons. Grant and Sherman, accompanied by Porter, boarded a small tug and were taken out to the steamer. In the after stateroom they met with Lincoln in one of the most fateful conferences of the War. And yet, there is to this day a deep mystery as to what was actually said by the four leaders. Only Sherman—the man of action—recalled with any positiveness the major parts of the conversation, and his recollections were later verified by Admiral Porter.

It was an historic meeting, there in the little cabin of the *River Queen*. With his chin resting on a hand, elbow on knee, Mr. Lincoln sat in what is now called a "captain's chair," with Porter on his left in an upholstered chair, and Grant on his right seated on the sofa built into the bulkhead of the cabin. Facing Lincoln, his arm raised in characteristic gesture, Sherman, in one of his inspired moods, told a story to which Lincoln listened intently. The painted picture—captured on a canvas now hanging in the White House—shows that all eyes are on Sherman.

And in response, his face lighting, Mr. Lincoln displayed both his optimism for a quick ending to the War and his hope for that end without a great bloody battle to mark it.

I remember well [wrote Sherman] to have said that we could not control that event; that this necessarily rested with our enemy; and I inferred that both Jeff Davis and General Lee would be forced to fight one more desperate and bloody battle. I rather supposed it would fall on me, somewhere near Raleigh, and General Grant added that, if Lee would only wait a few more days, he would have his army so disposed that if the enemy should abandon Richmond and attempt to make junction with General Jos. Johnston in North Carolina he (General Grant) would be on his heels. Mr. Lincoln more than once expressed uneasiness that I was not with my army at Goldsboro, when I again assured him that General Schofield was fully competent to command in my absence, that I was going to start back that very day, and that Admiral Porter had kindly provided for me the steamer Bat.

It was at this time that Lincoln told one of his well-known stories to bring out his point. Both Sherman and Porter wrote of the President's reiteration of his desire for charity toward the foe when their defeat came.

All he wanted of us was to defeat the opposing armies, and to get the men composing the Confederate armies back to their homes, at work on their farms, and in their shops. As to Jeff Davis he was hardly at liberty to speak his mind fully, but intimated that he ought to clear out, "escape the country," only it would not do to say so openly. As usual, he illustrated his meaning by a story:

. . . "A man once had taken a total abstinence pledge. When visiting a friend he was invited to take a drink, but declined on the score of his pledge; when his friend suggested lemonade . . . be made more palatable if he were to pour in a little brandy, his guest said, if he could do so unbeknown to him he would not object." . . .

· And Porter supported Lincoln's humanitarianism, declaring: "He wanted peace on almost any terms. . . . I do not know how far he was influenced by General Grant but I presume from their long conferences that they understood each other perfectly; and that the terms given to Lee after his surrender were authorized by Mr. Lincoln."

As for Sherman's humane terms to Johnston, upon his subsequent surrender, Porter recounted how they were also dictated by Lincoln's direction. Sherman was criticized for his· liberality but he prevented Johnston's possible juncture with Lee by the surrender terms which obviated any such desperate attempt by the Confederates.

When Lincoln and Sherman parted at the gangway of the *River Queen*, about noon on March 28, they never saw each other again. "Of all the men I ever met," stated Sherman, "he seemed to possess more of the elements of greatness, combined with goodness, than any other."

On the night of March 29, Lincoln stood alone in the darkness of the top deck of the *River Queen* and saw and heard the sounds of war. His telegram to Stanton was in itself dramatic:

It was dark as a rainy night without a moon could be. A furious cannonade, soon joined in by a heavy musketry fire, opened near Petersburg and lasted about two hours. The sound was very distinct here as also were the flashes of the guns upon the clouds.

Sheridan had taken Five Forks; the Petersburg entrenchments had been breached; Grant's army was beginning the last series of movements. After a day ashore, Lincoln returned to the *River Queen* and, according to Crook, walked the decks most of the night. Secretary Seward and Mrs. Lincoln returned to Washington aboard the *Monnohansett* and 24 hours later Lincoln telegraphed his wife the news that Petersburg was finally enveloped by Grant's army —"a magnificent success," as he later stated in his telegram of congratulations to Grant.

The next few historic days (with Lincoln's entry to Richmond as the high point of his activities) have been recounted in detail many times, and so we will return to his activities on the *River Queen*. Mrs. Lincoln and her party rejoined her husband aboard the little steamer. On that same day, April 6, word came of Secretary Seward's serious injuries upon having been thrown from his carriage. Ashore at City Point, Lincoln sent word to Grant of Seward's accident. It was a busy day for the President, as was the

next (April 7), when he conducted interviews, reviewed troops, and tired himself out shaking hands.

Returning to the *River Queen* that evening for a belated rest, he was visited by Congressmen Blaine of Maine and Washburn of Illinois. Before retiring, he sat quietly in his cabin and then sent off his famous telegram to Grant:

Gen. Sheridan says "If the thing is pressed I think Lee will surrender." Let the thing be pressed.

Lincoln now decided to return to Washington. This was sooner than he planned, and came about mainly because of the latest advices from Stanton that Secretary of State Seward's condition had worsened so that he feared for his life.

The group on board the steamer—the Presidential Party, as it may be called—consisted of Mrs.

General Lee rides away from Appomattox on his big iron-gray charger, "Traveller." The remnants of the Army of North Virginia wave farewell.

Lincoln; Senator Sumner of Massachusetts; Senator and Mrs. Harlan of Iowa, and their daughter, Mary, who was engaged to Lincoln's elder son, Robert Todd Lincoln (then on General Grant's staff); Mrs. Elizabeth Keckley; and the Marquis de Chambrun, the distinguished French observer of the Washington scene. The day (April 8) was taken up by the Presidential Party's going by special train to Petersburg, where Mr. Lincoln inspected hospital camps and conferred with various army officers. It was a day of considerable variety but to Lincoln also one of personal disappointment. He wanted to be on hand for the inevitable surrender of Lee's army; but Seward's dangerously grave condition was

bringing him back to Washington, and his loyalty to the man he had learned to trust was the decisive factor in his decision.

Unknown to the group, at one o'clock that fateful meeting of Generals Grant and Lee was taking place at Appomattox Court House, not many miles away, where terms for the surrender of the Army of Northern Virginia were being discussed. Here was where the harassed President wished most to be. As the little train chugged its way back from Petersburg, he remained quiet for some time, as if his keen perception had made him aware of the occasion.

Arriving back at the *River Queen,* following the evening meal, a military band marched down to present a farewell concert on board. Among the selections were two personally requested by Mr. Lincoln— the "Marseillaise," for the Marquis de Chambrun, and "Dixie," which

117

the President wryly remarked was now once more as much the property of the North (by capture) as that of the South.

An hour before midnight the lines holding the *River Queen* to her wharf at City Point were slipped, and with a farewell toot of her melodious whistle Mr. Lincoln's flagship began her return trip to Washington. All retired early and the steamer slowly made her way from the James to Chesapeake Bay, only the sound of her paddle wheels splashing and the steady stroke of her walking beam engine to be heard in the stillness of the night.

Up early the morning of April 9, the Presidential Party enjoyed a leisurely breakfast and then joined Mr. Lincoln in the saloon. It was an occasion long to be remembered by those few who were fortunate enough to be present. The erudite Marquis de Chambrun recalled:

That whole day the conversation turned on literary subjects. Mr. Lincoln read aloud to us for several hours passages . . . from Shakespeare. Most of these were from Macbeth . . . in particular the verses which follow Duncan's assassination.

Senator Charles Sumner also described that scene—Mr. Lincoln holding "a beautiful quarto of Shakespeare in his hand." There can be but little question as to what was weighing most on his mind. In the certain victory, so near at hand, he saw the underlying tragedy. Macbeth, having gained through the murder of Duncan the highest pinnacle of success in the throne of Scotland, now suffers the torments of mind which came with such a victory. Chambrun brings the picture to us—the gaunt Lincoln, his voice filled with the agony of the character; his listeners, caught by the feeling of their reader, intense with an interest acutely heightened beyond their comprehension, for they could not be aware of the aftermath of this day.

Mr. Lincoln paused here while reading and began to explain to us how true a description of the murderer this scene was; when, the dark deed achieved, its tortured perpetrator envied the sleep of his victim.

As if to sample to the full the darkness of the mind, which Shakespeare so eloquently described, Mr. Lincoln again read that famous passage:

Duncan is in his grave;
After life's fitful fever he sleeps well;
Treason has done his worst; nor steel, nor poison,
Malice domestic, foreign levy, nothing
Can touch him further.

Thus, ere another Sunday dawned, this great American unknowingly had anticipated the completion of his own "fitful fever," his own tragedy which was to swiftly bring him into a rest where nothing could "touch him further."

As he listened to the strong beat of the steamer's engine, and to the surge of water under her paddle wheels, he must have thought of the "Ship of State," and reflected on the analogy of no matter how staunch the hull and strong the power plant, it was the Captain, officers, and crew which made it a safe vessel.

And, too, with the final capture of Richmond he sensed the lifting of hearts of the nation with the prospect of the near ending of the war; in his own words, felt a renewed faith in that "nation, so conceived and so dedicated." He knew that this same nation had entered the War as a Union sundered and was now emerging in great strength. With his remarkable perception he saw that the bringing back of the South with charity and common sense would amalgamate a nation that would become the greatest symbol of democracy on the face of the earth.

Here, alone in the quiet of the *River Queen*'s stateroom, he sat in a remote privacy—engaged in a reverie which was never revealed. Who can say but, alone among the triumphs of the war so near at hand, Mr. Lincoln felt more at peace aboard his "flagship" than at any other time during the four long years of the Civil War. If for no other reason, this sidewheel steamer deserves its own footnote in our history.

POSTSCRIPT

As a sequel to the days when the *River Queen* was at the apex of her career in the Civil War, her subsequent use is of more than ordinary interest. Following the War she spent a few years on the Potomac and then was purchased by the Martha's Vineyard Steamboat Company to run between the mainland port of Woods Hole and the Vineyard. Shortly after, the steamer was sold for $60,000 to the Nantucket and Cape Cod Steamboat Company, running between Hyannis and Nantucket. She continued in service in Nantucket Sound (and later out of New Bedford) until 1891, when she returned to her former haunts in the Potomac River, becoming a popular excursion steamer from Washington to Mount Vernon for a quarter of a century more.

During the summer of 1874, President Ulysses S. Grant, with his family on a vacation trip in New England, heard of the *River Queen*'s new service and went to Hyannis to embark on her for a cruise to Nantucket. He stopped on that island of whaling fame for several hours, returning to the mainland on the same steamer. On the night of the return trip, as the *River Queen* ploughed the waters of Nantucket Sound, President Grant walked alone on her promenade deck, chewing a cigar. For some time he kept to himself, deep in thought. Somewhere in the gloom of the steamer's deck he must have seen again the tall, gaunt figure of Mr. Lincoln, and the memory of this man was in a measure a symbol of courage for Grant, so weighted by his own sad problems. Thus history had come to another full cycle.

"NOT EVEN GOD HIMSELF COULD SINK THIS SHIP..."

Just 58 years ago, on a night like this, the luxurious White Star liner *Titanic,* out of Southampton, reached that never-to-be-forgotten point due east of Nantucket and due south of Cape Race where there also happened to be a huge iceberg.

The White Star management was guilty of errors that would later be made illegal, and the *Titanic's* white-bearded Captain E. J. Smith and his officers seemed possessed of a recklessness uncommon among seasoned salts. Part of the reason was that the ship was built with water-tight compartments so as to be judged unsinkable. This was her maiden voyage. There was a carni-val spirit among passengers and crew alike, and even humble folk in the steerage felt pride in riding (far below) on the same ship that carried such famous people as John Jacob Astor, Isidor Straus, Major Archi-bald Butt, Sir Cosmo Duff Gordon, William T. Stead and the Countess of Rothes. White Star's president himself, J. Bruce Ismay, was aboard for the triumphal ride, and would never be the same thereafter.

Another First Class passenger was George Quincy Clifford of Bos-ton, who had taken out $50,000 in extra life insurance before the trip, not at all because of any pessimism about this glittering liner but simply because he was a conservative Yan-kee.

The *Titanic* was trying for a transatlantic record. She was steam-ing along at 22½ knots on Sunday night, April 14, 1912, into waters dotted with bergs, some small, some enormous. She should not rightly have gone so fast, with limited night visibility, especially since she was not yet equipped with a searchlight, and through some oversight her watch was not even furnished with telescopes. There had been no boat drills. Why have boat drills on an unsinkable ship?

Not far south was the Boston-bound Leyland liner *Californian,*

by W. A. Swanberg

She was, indeed, "unsinkable" unless, of course,
you tore a hole in her the length of a
football field. When that happened nothing
in heaven could keep her afloat.

The S.S. Titanic

stopped, blocked by drifting ice. Ice was a menace, and the *Titanic's* glassless watch had been warned to keep an eye out for it, but the speed record seemed more important. At 11:40 a lookout spied a big berg dead ahead, telephoned a warning to the bridge, and in half a minute the ship veered.

It wasn't soon enough. The liner's hull sideswiped the submerged part of the berg, which cut the steel like a can opener. The side of the ship grazed the white mass so that several tons of ice brushed off on the well deck.

The collision made little noise topside—only a muted thump followed by a grinding sound. Many passengers slept right through it. But down in boiler room No. 6 the crash was ear-splitting and two firemen just managed to escape through the watertight door before the sea cascaded in on them. Far above, Captain Smith (this was to be his last voyage before retiring) felt the jar and rushed out of his cabin to query First Officer William M. Murdoch, in charge of the bridge this watch.

"Mr. Murdoch, what was that?" he demanded.

"An iceberg, sir. I hard-a-starboarded and reversed the engines, but she was too close."

The report came in that two boiler rooms were flooded. A mail clerk raced up to say that the mail hold was filling. President Ismay appeared from his suite to ask if there was serious damage.

"I'm afraid there is," Captain Smith said slowly.

An investigation of the points of flooding showed that there must be a 300-foot gash—the length of a football field. The *Titanic* had 16 watertight compartments. She could float with three or even four of them filled, but it was evident that five were flooding. The unsinkable ship was going to sink. At 12:15 A.M.—

35 minutes after the collision—Captain Smith told Wireless Operator John Phillips to send out an SOS, and Phillips began working his key.

The *Californian,* only ten miles away, could have arrived within the hour. But telegraphy was young, and unfortunately the *Californian's* operator went off duty at 11:30, so she never received the call although she was close enough to see the *Titanic's* lights. · The German steamer *Frankfort,* 40 miles away, got the message but misunderstood it. The Cunarder *Carpathia,* 58 miles away,

No one worried about the poor folk in the steerage.

got the call only by merest chance. Her operator was off duty, but being a telegraph bug he put on his earphones just for fun before hitting the sack. He heard the SOS, and soon the slow *Carpathia* was steaming as fast as her lazy engines could revolve to give help.

Opposite page, above: The front page of the Boston Daily Globe *on the afternoon of April 17, 1912.*

Opposite page, below: Rescued from the lifeboats, this group of passengers has been supplied with wraps aboard the Carpathia.

Captain Smith had already ordered the boats uncovered and the passengers alerted. There was no panic as people donned life jackets and streamed out on the chill deck. The legend of the *Titanic's* invulnerability was strong. One man said, "Not even God Himself could sink this ship." The feeling was general that the damage was minor, that the ship would stay afloat, that it was foolish to take off in one of those small lifeboats in the cold night. A few men who had been playing cards in the lounge returned to their game. Since there had been no drill, there was confusion among the officers in charge of the boats, and more among the passengers. Precious time was wasted. The word was "women and children first," but some women flatly refused to get into the boats. Talk was heard that all this was ridiculous—and wouldn't the people in the boats feel silly after they rowed around for awhile, only to return aboard the unsinkable liner? Why, she was the biggest ship in the world, 882 feet long, displacing 66,000 tons, and everybody had read about those watertight compartments!

Captain Smith must have been chilled by one fact unknown to the passengers. All the boats together could hold only 1,178 people —a trifle more than half of the 2,207 aboard.

The ship's band came out and played ragtime music as the throng waited. Later, when the *Titanic* began to list, people were more willing to board the boats, but still there was vast disorganization. Boats lowered on the port side contained mostly women and children. On the starboard side, so few women wanted to leave the liner that men were admitted. Even they were so laggard that Boat No. 7—the first boat down —was lowered with only 20 people, half full. In the telegraph room Op-

The Boston Daily Globe.

To Get Results Advertise Your Wants In the Daily Globe

Advertise Your April 19th Sales In The Daily Globe

VOL LXXXI—NO 108. BOSTON. WEDNESDAY EVENING, APRIL 17, 1912—EIGHTEEN PAGES. PRICE TWO CENTS.

EVENING EDITION—7:30 O'CLOCK

CARPATHIA HAS THE 705 SAVED.

Message Sent to and From Globe Man on Franconia Calls These "Total Survivors Aboard."

MAY HAVE SOME BODIES

SS California on the Way to Boston.

Was in the Zone Where Titanic Went Down.

Shipment of 110 Coffins From Halifax to Scene of Disaster.

By JAMES T. SULLIVAN
Globe Staff Reporter.

SIGHTED 20 ICEBERGS.

Violent Electrical Storm Early Today Cut Off Communication.

HALIFAX, N S, April 17. The Globe is able to state that communication with the steamer Carpathia, en route to New York with the survivors of the Titanic disaster. The Carpathia entered the ice barrage was sighted off the banks from where the Titanic sank, but no details of the disaster were sent.

Communication with the Carpathia is greatly hampered by the mass of wireless flashes that are being sent out by the fleet of steamships nearing the scene, all working hours of the Titanic disaster. Accordingly has sent the Carpathia gets no rest of many of these ships will sending their through.

UNEXAMPLED BRAVERY.

Captain, Officers and Crew of Titanic Displayed It in Disaster.

ST JOHNS, N F, April 17, via North Sydney, N S—From an absolutely well-authenticated source comes the report that the captain, officers and crew of the Titanic displayed unexampled bravery in face of the most appalling marine catastrophe in the world's history, endeavoring to maintain order, quell the panic, launch and man boats and embark the passengers, averting all there was no immediate danger, while fully cognizant that they would soon be plunged beneath the ocean, with their fast-sinking ship.

The captain and all the principal officers heroically stuck to the

ST JOHNS STORY FALSE.

Steamer Bruce, In Harbor There, Heard Only What Cape Race Sent.

The report purporting to give details of scenes of the Titanic wreck received by the Steamer Bruce, was not published in the Globe this morning. The report was received by the Globe, in common with other papers, but was excluded from its columns as a palpable fake.

In confirmation of the Globe's judgment in refusing to print the report, the following dispatch was received by the Associated Press this morning:

ST JOHNS, N F, April 17—No details of the sinking of the White Star line steamer Titanic have been received in St Johns. The Newfoundland Government officials, wireless operators and newspaper men have maintained a constant watch for any vessel likely to have particulars of the great tragedy.

Some hope has existed that fishing vessels near the disaster might have information, but up to 10 a m today no fisherman had arrived from the vicinity of the accident. As the Titanic went down at a point 370 miles south of St Johns, there has not been sufficient time for a fishing craft to reach the harbor here.

The steamer Bruce, which arrived in St Johns Harbor at noon on Monday and remained in port until 2 yesterday afternoon, heard nothing of the tragedy except what the

Both Cabins' Lists Already Sent.

Only Steerage and Crew Remain to Send.

By WINFIELD M. THOMPSON
Globe Reporter Aboard Cunard Liner Franconia

(SPECIAL WIRELESS DISPATCH TO THE GLOBE)
S S FRANCONIA, April 17—Franconia established communication with Carpathia at 6:10 a m, New York time. Latter was then 495 miles east of Ambrose Channel, in mid sea of darkness, steaming 13 knots, should reach there at 8 Thursday evening.

Has total 705 survivors aboard. Franconia relaying personal messages from Carpathia to Sable Island.

SENT BOTH CABINS' LISTS.

Cruiser Chester Says Carpathia Has Only Third Class Yet to Send.

erator Phillips was tapping to the *Carpathia:* "Come quick, old man." Officers on the *Titanic*'s bridge could see through binoculars a motionless vessel off the port bow—the *Californian.* Why, she was almost within hailing distance! Futile efforts were made to message her with a Morse light. At 12:45 the first of many distress rockets zoomed upward from the *Titanic.* They were seen by an officer on the *Californian*'s bridge who, strangely, failed to interpret them as a call for help.

The rockets, and the steeper tilt of the deck, convinced some that perhaps the boats were not such a bad idea after all. There was more urgency now, and more error. Boat No. 5, which could take 65 people, was lowered with only 40. No. 6 (capacity 65) left with 28. No. 1, made for 40, had an even dozen. The minutes were fleeting, the *Carpathia* still hours away. Three sisters from Acton, Mass., Mrs. R. C. Cornell, Mrs. E. D. Appleton and Mrs. J. Murray Brown, got off in separate boats, not knowing where the others were. Scores of wives, some with children, kissed their husbands goodbye before taking to the boats. No one worried about the poor folk in the steerage. The concern was for first and second class people, which automatically doomed steerage passengers except those determined enough to sneak by the barriers.

By 1:30, when the band began playing "Nearer, My God, to Thee" and the list was so bad that the sea swished over the well deck, even the most optimistic knew that the *Titanic* was in real trouble. This was the moment of truth, except that it seemed to drag out forever. Some people gathered around the Rev.

Thomas Byles, who led them in prayer. A few frenzied men tried to push women aside and leap into the last boats. One man appeared in women's clothing, but was detected. Boston's George Clifford knew that his family would collect substantial insurance. President Ismay of the White Star Line, who had been noticeably nervous, suddenly climbed into Boat C before it dropped. Rich old Isidor Straus begged his wife to get into a boat but she refused and they both stayed, their arms encircling each other.

Ten miles away, watchers on the *Californian* still wondered about the meaning of those rockets.

The last boat got off the *Titanic* around 2:05, by which time her deck was a steep hill. The lifeboats, with room for almost 1,200, actually took away some 650. The night was cold and clear, and those in the nearest boats saw hundreds of left-behinds clinging to rails, to anything, some screaming, some praying, some strangely quiet. Sixteen hundred persons—150 of them women and children—were still aboard the *Titanic* at 2:20 when her bow went under, her stern rose high, and she slid almost vertically into the deep.

The water was freezing—28 degrees. Now those in the boats had a new ordeal. They heard the piteous screams of hundreds struggling in the water, grasping at debris, pleading to be saved. Most of the half-empty boats gave no aid. There was fear that frenzied swimmers would capsize the boats. Only 13 people were picked up by the 18 boats hovering nearby.

The *Carpathia* did not arrive until 4 A.M. to rescue the survivors, some with frozen feet or hands.

Meanwhile, several erroneous telegraphic reports had reached New York, one that the *Titanic* had merely been damaged and was putting into Halifax. A train was chartered in New York to meet the *Titanic* in Halifax. It rolled through Boston and was well into Maine before the real news came out and it returned.

The arrival of the rescue ship in New York with 675 survivors made one of the biggest news stories of all time. It touched off two enormous groundswells, one of admiration for the *Titanic*'s heroes, one of bitter censure of the kind of thinking that could allow a liner to carry boats for only half its passengers. A vessel went out to pick up hundreds of floating bodies. There were investigations in Washington and London. J. Bruce Ismay was so shattered that he retired his post and lived in seclusion in Ireland until his death in 1937.

But the 1,503 victims did not die entirely in vain. New international seagoing regulations were set up. Thereafter there would be lifeboats enough for all. There would be boat drills. Never again would steerage passengers be considered expendable. Never again would a ship's officer mistake a distress rocket for some sort of monkeyshine.

And never again would a liner flirt with icebergs. A direct result of the *Titanic* horror was the creation of the Coast Guard patrol operating out of Boston, one of its duties being to hunt down bergs and issue weekly charts telling mariners just where ice may be expected.

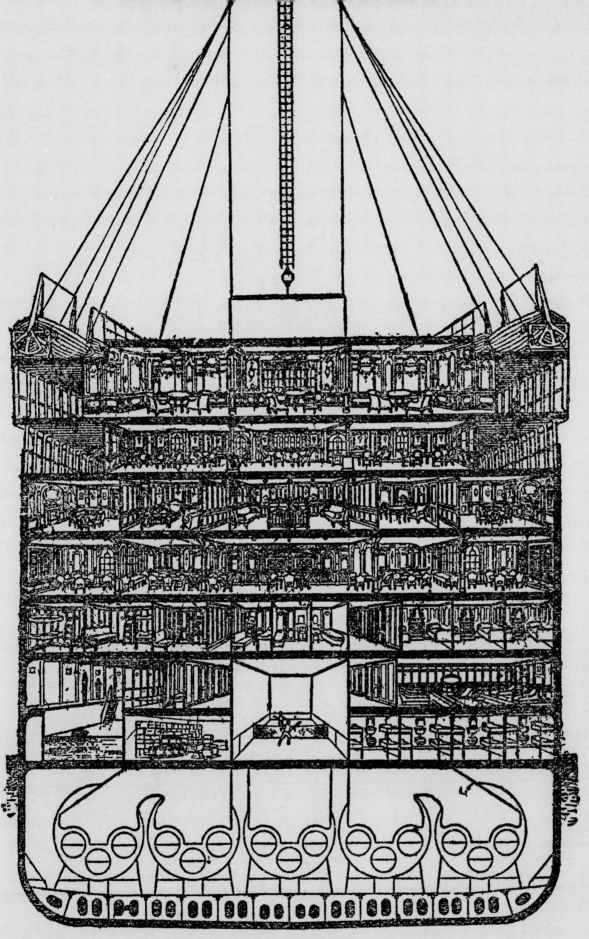

A cross section of the steamship Titanic *showing seven decks. Among her appointments were beautiful saloons, reading and lounging rooms, palm courts, Turkish baths, private baths, a gymnasium, a swimming pool, a ball-room, everything really, except enough life boats.*

125

THE
VALENTINE'S DAY IRONCLAD

by Carol W. Kimball

On February 14, 1862 a strange vessel perched on the ways in a Connecticut shipyard, the U.S. Navy's newest secret weapon in the Civil War. The gunboat about to be launched in the Mystic River represented a new breed—she was our Navy's second ironclad. The famous *Monitor* was first, but after the battle of ironclads off Hampton Roads, March 9, 1862, *Monitor* and *Merrimack* were household words, while the second ironclad, U.S.S. *Galena*, is seldom remembered.

A great crowd assembled for her launching. The ironclad on the peaceful Mystic River attracted hundreds to the Maxson, Fish & Co. shipyard at West Mystic, all curious to see the newfangled bombproof steamer which could help defeat the South.

The controversial vessel awaited full tide, her wooden frame hidden under ponderous iron, bizarre product for a yard famed for wooden ships, an alien among the river's graceful clippers. Iron-covered oak might make a formidable weapon. On the other hand, the heavy plating might sink her at once. Many thought the clumsy gunboat would founder the moment she took to the water.

Even Simeon G. Fish, 22-year-old son of shipyard owner N. G. Fish, had some doubts. Simeon had

U.S.S. Galena, *launched at West Mystic, Conn., on Valentine's Day, 1862.*

worked hard on the vessel, but grew nervous as the time for launching came. The night before he had noted in his diary, "By this time tomorrow we shall have a launch or a flummox."

Many in Mystic, predicting a flummox, rose before dawn that wintry morning to reach the river by 9:00 o'clock, and all their friends from nearby towns had joined the throng.

In 1862 iron ships were new to America, although well known in Europe. After the success of iron warships in the Crimean War, European naval powers quickly accepted them, but across the Atlantic the United States had not one ironclad

Opp. page: The photo shows the Galena's *pronounced "tumble home" to her hull. Her armor plate consisted of railroad rails to which 3" thick iron boiler plate was bolted.*

when the war began; the navy's new frigates were of wood.

However, iron ships found a champion in capable Stephen Mallory, Confederate Secretary of the Navy, who believed an invulnerable iron vessel could break through the hated blockade and make kindling wood of the North's outmoded navy. Confederates were already converting the scuttled U.S.S. *Merrimack* into the ironclad C.S.S. *Virginia*.

To counteract the Southern threat, Lincoln's Secretary of the Navy, Connecticut-born Gideon Welles, wangled money from Congress for a few experimental ironclads, one of which stood ready to launch that Valentine's Day. Her design was submitted by Cornelius S. Bushnell, president of the New Haven, New London and Stonington Railroad—a conservative wooden hull covered with iron plate to deflect cannon shot, and hopefully an ocean-going vessel.

Because it was a tricky job to make a ship both shotproof and seaworthy, the businessman went to New York to consult a leading naval architect, Swedish inventor John Ericsson, inquiring if his vessel could hold up her iron armor without disaster. It was a significant conference. After Ericsson approved Bushnell's plans, he showed the railroad man a superior model of an ironclad so im-

*Everyone has heard of the Union's first ironclad ship,
but the second is seldom mentioned in history books. Yet, for
a couple of days, both North and South alike expected
her to capture Richmond! Then came her first real test
under fire . . .*

The Galena, *accompanied by the* Monitor, *takes a pounding from the batteries at Drewry's Bluff.*

pressive that Bushnell persuaded the inventor to submit this design for government consideration.

As a result, the designs chosen for construction were the Ericsson *Monitor,* Bushnell's nameless ironclad, and a plan by Merrick and Son. And thus the second ironclad's sponsor also promoted the revolutionary *Monitor* which would soon outclass her.

On September 7, 1861, all Mystic knew that Bushnell's ironclad gunboat would be built by Maxson, Fish & Co., established in 1853 by retired packet master Capt. Nathan G. Fish and other businessmen, with William Maxson as master builder. The firm was well known, but Captain Fish, civic leader and banker, also happened to be a director of Bushnell's railroad.

Young Simeon Fish, the Captain's son, jotted down in his diary sparse summaries of his work on the strange craft. On September 17, he was "drafting and laying down the gunboat under Mr. Sam H. Pook." Samuel Hartt Pook of Boston, designer of the clipper *Red Jacket,* had already conferred with Bushnell.

The shipyard sprang to life; the Union needed this vessel. Simeon and his father scoured the countryside for timber and Pook, as government inspector, personally selected each piece for the gunboat. A hundred workmen swarmed about and Simeon even worked Sundays, knocking off now and then to attend church.

The wooden hull took shape, less radical than the *Monitor,* but with convex sides bulging oddly, a "tumble home" to reduce hull strain from rolling in rough seas. From a 36-foot width at the waterline her upper deck narrowed to 26 feet across.

As wooden construction was routine in Mystic, in seven weeks the gunboat was ready for her armor. Rolled by a new process at Winslow's Foundry, Troy, New York, the first shipment of iron reached Mystic aboard the schooner *White Rock.* The problem of fastening it to the hull was solved jointly by foundry representatives and shipyard hands.

Carefully dovetailed bars, 12 feet long, two to three inches thick and four inches wide, were bolted to the frame, fastened securely every six inches with ¾-inch bolts which went completely through the wooden hull to be held by "screw nuts." Each plate had a flange on the upper edge for the bolts. A corresponding flange

128

on the next plate covered exposed bolt heads, leaving a smooth iron surface.

With cold weather, carpenters enclosed the gunboat in a huge shed to protect the workers. Now all Mystic was busy with the war effort, but gossips loved to speculate about the ironclad's vulnerability and buoyancy. The entire Union was informed as *Harper's Weekly* followed her progress with interest, twice showing full-page illustrations of the vessel. But local newspaper editor Amos Watrous warned readers not to expect too much—he thought iron vessels too rapid a change to succeed, cautioning, "Wise persons distrust efforts made in advance of stereotyped productions."

The Mystic ironclad was certainly not stereotyped. Nothing like her had been built before, but there she was, ready for launching on Val-

Simeon G. Fish, shown here in later years, worked on the ironclad in his father's shipyard when he was 22; his brief diary tells his story of the vessel's construction.

entine's Day, 130 working days after keel laying, strong as wood and iron and hard work could make her. Like every ocean-going steamer, she had masts and rigging. Sails increased speed at sea or were used when coal gave out or engines broke down.

And when launching time arrived that Valentine's morning there was no flummox! At 9:12 A.M. the hope of the Union glided gracefully into the gray river, proud and upright, scarcely careening in spite of her heavy iron casing. The crowd cheered as she slipped from the ways, and Amos Watrous reported with surprise, "She floats like a duck!"

Simeon, delighted and relieved, wrote in his diary:

A launch and a most beautiful one too. Everything passed off in a most acceptable manner. Ship leaks somewhat from augur holes at first, but if nothing worse comes to light shall be well satisfied.

On Washington's Birthday a tug took the ironclad to the Continental Iron Works at Green Point, Long Island, where the *Monitor* was built. All this time she was nameless, but on February 25 Simeon reported tersely in his diary, "Gunboat named Galena." No one knows why this name was chosen, but she was the *Galena* all her days afloat.

While they installed her Delamater engines at Green Point, the *Monitor* defeated the *Merrimac* and all America went *Monitor*-mad. The *Galena*'s stock soared. Admiring New Yorkers on Sunday excursions flocked to see her, confident that she would be invincible, for she was larger than the *Monitor* and carried

He anchored within 600 yards of the battery
... a sitting duck for rebel guns

more guns. But engineers thought her guns were too small and her plating too thin, although they agreed she was "the fastest of this slow species of war vessel ever constructed."

She received her guns at Brooklyn Navy Yard and was commissioned April 21, 1862. She sailed the next day, officially classed as a third-rate screw steamer, 738 tons, with four 9-inch Dahlgren guns and two 100-pound Parrott rifles. The 180-foot vessel had cost the government $247,284.40, but she was ready for action, bound for Virginia to assist McClellan and the Army of the Potomac in the proposed capture of Richmond.

While McClellan dawdled and fussed on the Peninsula, Abraham Lincoln himself, on May 7, 1862, ordered the *Galena* with two gunboats to proceed up the James River. Under cool courageous Commander John Rodgers, one of the best officers in the service, she silenced a dozen guns at Rock Wharf the next day, but she could not reach the battery at Mother Tyne's Bluff. The plucky commander placed his ironclad close to the bluff, drawing enemy fire while the wooden gunboats hurried past.

Opp. page, above: The U.S.S. Galena *after rebuilding in 1878, then a wooden corvette. Iron armor was removed during the Civil War after it failed to give desired protection.*

Opp. page, below: Gundeck of the U.S.S. Galena. *Memorandum from the* Simeon Fish *diaries:* Chestnut (timber) none but best to be large and crooked suitable for futtocks and floor timbers, worth $7. White oak, large, worked with 8 or extra 9. Oak siding not less than 7 to 8 inches thick, $18. per extra $19.50 fathoms of 2¾ manilla. Copper bolts per lb. 25. Composition 22. Iron bolts 2. Oak plank per ft. 4 to 4½ cents. White pine clear 4. Black walnut 6. Copper nails per lb. 35 cents. Bushnell's G. R. $235.25

As an unexpected bonus they flushed out two rebel steamers hidden near shore.

The *Galena* struck fear in the hearts of the Confederates; they went all out to stop her. North and South alike expected her to steam all the way to Richmond, especially after Norfolk fell May 10 and the crew of the C.S.S. *Virginia* (the old *Merrimac*) blew up their vessel to prevent its capture. As a last resort to protect their capital, the Confederates established a battery at Drewry's Bluff, eight miles below the city where the river curves around 200-foot cliffs. The *Virginia*'s crew worked two days in the rain, setting underwater barricades and mounting guns atop the bluff.

On May 15 the *Galena* puffed up the James, accompanied by the *Monitor* and three small gunboats, with orders to shell Richmond into submission. At 6:30 A.M. as they sighted the bluff they were greeted by cannon and rifle fire and soon reached the river barriers, tangled masses of hastily scuttled steamers chained across the stream. They could not pass the barricades and could not remove them. Sharpshooters on the bank would pick off any who tried.

Unable to proceed, Rodgers decided to give the *Galena* a thorough testing under fire. He anchored his vessel within 600 yards of the battery, placing her as if for target practice under enemy fire, a sitting duck for rebel guns. Then he began to return the fire.

Shot from the bluff rained down on the *Galena*. She took a terrible pounding, with 28 direct hits. Eighteen times shot pierced her iron plating. Thirteen of her crew were killed and eleven wounded on the bloodstained deck. Rodgers held out more than three hours. Then, ammunition

exhausted, he withdrew down the river to write his classic statement: "We demonstrated that she is not shot-proof."

The *Galena* did not live up to expectations that day. The *Monitor* was unharmed but proved useless in the fight; her turret gun could not elevate to reach the bluff.

With all her battle damage— shot stuck in her hull at the waterline, bullet-riddled deck, and many leaks —the *Galena* could not be spared for repairs. Remaining on duty in the James, she gave valuable support during the Seven Days Battle, shelling the enemy and covering the Union retreat. Through the frantic Peninsula Campaign she performed gallantly.

Finally, in 1863, she limped to Philadelphia where her useless iron plating was removed. Larger and better Monitors were already in service and her design was never right for an ironclad. She emerged as a wooden gunboat, and in this role won Farragut's praise at Mobile Bay.

The old *Galena* was thoroughly rebuilt in 1878, lengthened 35 feet, and assigned to the European Squadron. Years later, in need of repairs, she was proceeding under tow to Portsmouth, New Hampshire, when she grounded off Gay Head, March 13, 1891, ending 29 years of service to her country after her Valentine's day launching.

This year on February 14 she is all but forgotten except at Mystic Shipyard, West Mystic, Connecticut. This firm, now in business at her launching site, uses a trim engraving of the U.S.S. *Galena* on its letterheads and advertising.

131

CYRUS
THE
GREAT

by Samuel Carter III

Could a cable be laid on the ocean floor from Newfoundland to Ireland?
"It can be done," an authority on the telegraph told young Cyrus Field of
Stockbridge, Mass., "providing there's a sea smooth enough, a wire long
enough, and a ship big enough to lay a coil of wire 1600 miles in length . . ."

A story is handed down from long ago among the descendants of the Reverend David Dudley Field of Stockbridge, Massachusetts. It concerns the Doctor's eight-year-old son, Cyrus, forced by duty to join his smaller brother and sister at their game of making dandelion chains. Young Cyrus was exasperated at this sissy occupation, inept at fitting one stem in another, irked by the taunts of the younger children when their chains outdistanced his.

"Just wait!" he told them wrathfully. "*Someday* I'll make one long enough to go around the world!"

The children, as it turned out, hadn't long to wait. They had barely reached full maturity before the prophecy came true. A hundred years ago this summer, the nations of Europe, Asia, northern Africa, the Pacific territories and the colonies of Canada, were linked by a chain of telegraph wires, thousands of miles longer than the earth's circumference, to a small house on the Stockbridge Village Green. Cyrus Field had done the impossible: laid a transatlantic cable on the bottom of the ocean, heralding a new age of communication to a long-partitioned, isolated world.

It was an extraordinary story of persistence, courage, and indomitable faith, qualities bred in him by a staunch New England heritage. He was 15 when he left his father's parsonage, with just $8.00 in his pocket, to seek his fortune in New York. He had already been outdistanced by his brothers. Three were successful lawyers, one a naval ensign, one a paper manufacturer. Even his younger brother, Henry, champion of the dandelion chains, was a freshman at Williams College at the age of 13. He, Cyrus, would have to work not only hard but fast to catch up. His youth was haunted by a sense

133

of urgency.

He got a job as clerk at A. T. Stewart's, the department store magnate whose funereal garb and manners made him the prototype of latter-day floorwalkers in the trade. His pay was $50 a year, almost the cost of room and board on Murray Street. He worked like a demon, arriving early and leaving late, and gained status with his fellow clerks by inventing a telegraphic code of signals to warn them of the boss's approach. Years later, Stewart told associates: "You know, I'm partly responsible for Field's success with the Atlantic telegraph."

After three years at Stewart's, he'd achieved the promotion he was after, and that made it time to quit. He never lingered when the goal was won. His older brother, Matthew, the paper manufacturer in Lee, required help. Cyrus went back to Massachusetts to become the company's general manager and later its field representative. In his travels around New England he made three important friends: a young landscape painter, Frederic Church; an attractive schoolteacher in Madison, Connecticut, named Mary Stone; a competitive paper manufacturer in Dalton, Zenas Crane.

Significantly for Cyrus, Matthew was no businessman. He wanted at heart to be an engineer, and shortly took off to become one. That was his younger brother's cue to take off, too. Cyrus accepted a junior partnership with Root & Company, New York paper merchants, and promptly married Mary Stone. In his world of haste and urgency, one didn't weigh decision. With stars in their eyes, the couple had barely had time to settle in an inexpensive boardinghouse before Root & Company went bankrupt.

Rightfully, Field could have walked out on a mess for which he was in no way responsible. But then, as always afterward, catastrophe was a challenge and a catalytic agent to

him. He took over the firm with all its debts, settled the latter with a partial payment, changed the name to Cyrus Field & Company. His friendship with Zenas Crane now proved a godsend. Crane & Company were among the foremost paper makers in the country. They happily made Field their representative. Crane and Cyrus formed a New York–Dalton axis, Field supplying Crane with rags and other manufacturing materials, Crane making the paper according to demand, and Cyrus marketing the finished product in New York.

It was an age in which it was difficult to fail. America was hitting its stride as a nation of unlimited resources and a booming population. The Erie Canal, the expanding railroads, the coming of steam, the sheer optimism of the Jacksonian Era promised fortunes in return for enterprising spirit. But there were sacrifices too. Field rose at dawn and breakfasted by candlelight, worked far into the night six days a week. There were children coming along, three daughters in the first half-dozen years, but he saw his family on Sundays only. "I never worked so hard

in all my life," he noted in his diary.

In 1849 his doctor ordered rest, a trip abroad. He and Mary left the children under care and sailed for Europe. But the "rest" was an illusion. He mastered only one word in the foreign languages of countries that they visited. That word was "faster!" In spite of violent revolutions blasting France and Austria and Italy, they raced from capital to capital drinking in the panorama of upheaval. It had a profound effect on Cyrus. From the insulation he had known at Stockbridge, even in New York, he saw things on a broader screen; a world beyond his previous borders, torn asunder by misunderstandings. A phrase began to haunt him: international cooperation.

Returning to New York that autumn, he plunged back into business with a raft of new ideas from overseas. He promoted many things we take for granted in that common product, writing papers: colorful hues and tinted borders, boxed or packaged stationery, tissues, even envelopes that were unknown in the early 1840's. His business prospered. Sales doubled in four years to reach

Above: This is the cable-issuing machine on the Niagara, *designed to pay out and hold five miles of suspended cable. The brake drums revolved in cold water.*

Opp. page: As the Agamemnon *neared Ireland in 1858, a sportive whale played around the cable off her stern while the ship's crew watched—with their hearts in their mouths!*

$812,267 in 1852. He was worth over a quarter-of-a-million dollars, an immense sum for that period, and built a handsome house in Gramercy Park for Mary and the children. The following year he paid off all his debts from Root & Company days, and added 6% interest to each check. It was an act of integrity that amazed hard-bitten merchants in the city.

Again he had reached his goal —a time to head off in a new direction. With his interests now more international, he had followed the writings of oceanographer Matthew Maury and editor John L. O'Sullivan in which Manifest Destiny was proffered as a catchword for the future of America. Yankee character and

ingenuity, superior commercial and political institutions, gave the new, exploding nation the right, if not indeed the obligation, to expand beyond its borders. Some looked north to Canada, some south to Mexico and Cuba. Field followed Matthew Maury's eyes to the Valley of the Amazon. Maury had described it as the future Eden of mankind, ripe for cultivation and development.

With dreams of empire, Cyrus organized an expedition to that country. Chandler White, a prosperous retired merchant, listened and subscribed. Frederic Church, now well known as a painter, was enlisted to portray this South American land to his compatriots. In April of 1853 they sailed to New Granada, went

by horses, mules, boats, anything available, to Bogota, the highlands of Colombia, and on to Ecuador, losing Chandler White somewhere along the way. They climbed mountains to visit emerald mines, gold mines, and silver mines; stood on the high Cordilleras to survey the fertile Valley of the Amazon.

Whatever Field had in mind for South America (and he never revealed this to Matthew Maury or his fellow travellers) was pre-empted by a new and unexpected vision. His brother Matthew was visiting New York and noted, "I never knew Cyrus so restless as when he's trying to sit still." Like Cyrus, Matthew too was looking for new fields to conquer, having finished with building

giant bridges in the South. In the lobby of the Astor House he met a lanky, raw-boned engineer from Canada named Frederick Gisborne. Gisborne had been building a telegraph line across Newfoundland to connect, by boat or carrier pigeon, with the mainland and New York. He'd run out of money, couldn't meet his payroll, was all but a fugitive from justice.

Matthew took Gisborne to Gramercy Park to talk with his restive brother. Would Cyrus advance the money to complete the job? To Cyrus it looked like small potatoes. But that night, studying the globe, he had a brainstorm. Newfoundland was a third of the way to Ireland from New York! Why not a submarine cable to complete the circuit? He quickly asked of Matthew: Is it possible? Years later Matthew's son related the outcome of that interview to his schoolmates: "My pa told Uncle Cyrus he could do it, and he done it!"

Tons of water struck the dec

It would take money, mints of it. And two questions sprang to mind: could an electric current travel through so long a wire, and was the ocean bottom a salutary environment for such a cable? He sought the answers from two foremost authorities: Samuel Finley Morse, inventor of the telegraph, and Matthew Maury. Morse told him he himself had projected the idea as feasible. Maury likewise said it could be done, provided there was a "sea smooth enough, a wire long enough, or a ship big enough, to lay a coil of wire 1,600 miles in length."

Now to raise capital. Field figured that ten wealthy financiers would do. He called first and wisely on his neighbor, Peter Cooper. Cooper had a religious as well as business side to his nature. He saw in this project a mystical chance to spread the word of God throughout the world. He contributed himself, and helped bring in two other capi-

talists, Moses Taylor and Marshall Roberts. To these Field added poor Chandler White, who wanted only to be left alone but couldn't resist Field's earnest salesmanship. Cyrus wanted more backers, but at this point Cooper told him, "If five of us can handle it, why get ten?"

They met for the next six evenings at Field's house in Gramercy Park, with David Dudley Field as legal adviser; bought out Gisborne's company with all its debts and landing rights; and changed the name to the New York, Newfoundland, *and London* Telegraph Company. To complete the first link, across the St. Lawrence Gulf from Newfoundland to Nova Scotia, Field went to England to get the necessary cable, which no manufacturer in the United States could supply. It was shipped over by bark, ready to be

laid. Field chartered a luxury steamer to tow the bark, invited his friends along for the excursion, and sailed for St. John's in midsummer, 1855.

Recorded by dramatist-reporter Bayard Taylor, it was a farcical introduction to the cable business. On arrival, the passengers fell in love with the Newfoundland dogs that came to greet them. They purchased 40 of them, and kept others who swam out and climbed aboard, until the dogs outnumbered passengers. They then sailed to Cape Ray, the landing area for the cable, with lumber to build a telegraph house. But the steamer couldn't get close enough to unload the lumber. It was tossed overboard, and the Newfoundlands swam it ashore in their jaws, plank by plank. "Noble beasts, noble sight!" wrote Taylor.

nd plunged down the hatchways

From then on the expedition was a comic opera. The steamer's captain, assigned to tow the cable vessel, was miffed at being seated below the pastor in the dining saloon. He rammed the bark and all but wrecked her. When the damage was repaired and the captain warned to keep a straight course, he deliberately sailed in circles, tangling up the wire. By the time they'd traveled 30 miles they were only seven miles from shore—at which point a rising tempest forced them to cut the cable to save the ships. It was total disaster; and of the captain who had largely caused it, Peter Cooper later wrote with secret satisfaction: "Poor fellow, he was shot at Shiloh."

The Niagara *and* Agamemnon *in the 10-day storm of 1858. Both ships, overloaded with cable, ran the risk of having their sides bashed out.*

It taught Field that this was serious business. He left Samuel Canning, his engineer, with Chandler White, to work on the line across the Gulf (completed in 1856), and sailed to England on the bigger project of the ocean cable. It was another of more than 60 voyages he would make in promoting the Atlantic cable, suffering from seasickness every time. In London he introduced himself to two invaluable supporters, John Brett and Charles Bright, who had laid the Dover-Calais cable in the Channel. With them he formed the Atlantic Telegraph Company, English counterpart of the firm he'd organized with Peter Cooper. He realized he would need capital from both sides of the ocean. He could get it better in England with a British company behind him.

Field called on Lord Clarendon, the British Foreign Secretary, for ships to help lay the cable and a subsidy to underwrite it. Obtaining both, he approached the United States government with the same proposition. It was regarded with suspicion. The projected cable lay between British territories; let the English supply all the ships and subsidies required. But with Secretary Seward's help, a bill of support was pushed through Congress, passed precariously by a one-vote margin.

It was estimated that 350,000 pounds of capital, or roughly $1,750,000, would be needed. In maritime-minded England, where the cable's value to a far-flung empire was apparent, this wasn't hard to raise. All was subscribed except for 88 shares, at a thousand pounds a share, which Cyrus purchased in his name to sell in the United States. He was overly optimistic. Only 21 shares were bought by skeptical compatriots, leaving him by far the leading American investor, with British capital dominating the affair by ten to one.

It took six months for a London firm to make the 2,500 miles of cable: a copper core with gutta percha insulation, wrapped in rope, with an outer armament of iron wire. Its bulk and weight were enormous; one mile weighed a ton; no single ship could carry it. The *Great Eastern,* largest vessel in history, was being built at Millwall. Its designer, Isambard Kingdom Brunel, told Field: "*There* is the ship to lay your cable." But the *Eastern* wouldn't be finished for a year or so. They would have to split the job between the government-commissioned ships. The American frigate *Niagara* would carry half the cable half way across. The British warship *Agamemnon* would follow with the other half. The line would be spliced in mid-ocean, then carried on to Trinity Bay in Newfoundland.

The Telegraph Fleet—two cable ships, two escorts—assembled at Valentia in southwest Ireland on the 4th of August, 1857. A raucous carnival-minded crowd had come from miles around to see them off. Small boats bedecked with bunting jammed the harbor, sightseers lined the shore. Such dignitaries as Fitzgerald, Knight of Kerry, and the Earl of Carlisle gave a royal flavor to the gathering. Speeches were made, toasts drunk, and hundreds of over-eager volunteers helped drag the cable's landing end to shore.

The following morning they got under weigh, delayed by a break in the shore end of the cable that required splicing. Aboard the *Niagara* were Cyrus Field, who was seasick but wouldn't leave the bridge, Samuel Morse, who was also sick and wouldn't leave his cabin, Charles Bright, as supervising engineer, and Charles de Sauty, an electrician who was someday to become a myth. The first few days and nights were uneventful. Signals passed from ship to shore along the extending cable, indicating all was well. Yet all aboard were in a state of anxious tension, talking in whispers, moving softly, as if anything untoward might snap the wire. Wrote Cyrus' brother Henry Field, in his *History of the Atlantic Cable*, "So much had they grown to feel for the enterprise, that the cable seemed to them like a human creature, on whose fate they hung, as if it were to decide their own destiny."

Four days out, the cable suddenly went dead. Morse and de Sauty could find nothing wrong. But the depth was measured at 2,000 fathoms, and the pressure might have been too much. Then just as suddenly the signals started up again; some underwater gremlin had knocked off. But to Cyrus the incident "cast ominous conjecture" on the expedition. Were there unknown factors in the deep sea stacked against them? He didn't have much time to worry. The following dawn,

a brakeman checked the outflowing cable too abruptly, and the line snapped like a cracking whip. Down plunged half-a-million dollars to the bottom of the ocean.

There was nothing to do but return defeated. Yet they had some consolation. Over 300 miles of cable had been laid, some of it in deepest water, and the signals had been perfect till the accident. On the way back, Cyrus wrote his family in Stockbridge:

"My confidence was never so strong as at the present time, and I feel sure, that with God's blessing,

The cable used on the expeditions of 1857 and 1858 had a seven-strand copper core covered by three layers of gutta-percha, a tarred yarn sheath, and a protective layer of 18 seven-strand iron wires.

Courtesy of "The Atlantic Cable" by Bern Dibner, published by the Burndy Library, Inc., Norwalk, Connecticut.

After the successful (temporarily) laying in 1858, Tiffany and Co., N.Y., sold sections of surplus cable as souvenirs.

we shall connect Europe and America with the electric cord . . . Do not think that I feel discouraged, or am low in spirits, for I am not."

There were no recriminations when they landed, and no real despair. The directors agreed to raise the money for more cable, and to try again next summer. Leaving for home, Field received a letter from the Knight of Kerry expressing gratitude at hearing "that you were indeed, as I might have judged from your character, plucky and well. It is a great comfort to think that the experience obtained in this, the first attempt, must immensely improve the chances of success on the next occasion."

He arrived at New York in the middle of the 1857 panic. His paper firm had suspended payments, owing $600,000. He had been through all this before, and, as always, substituted action for despondency. He called his creditors together, and settled with them for notes paying 7%. As one historian says: "Given any kind of a chance, Field had quick powers of recuperation, and his firm enjoyed much good will despite his wasting time on a wild-goose chase across the Atlantic."

But more and more he left the paper business to associates, and concentrated on the cable. What had they learned from that first expedition? A clue seemed to lie in a ditty popular with the *Niagara* cable crew:

Pay it out, oh pay it out,
  As long as you are able;
For if you put the darned brakes on,
  Pop goes the cable!

It was indeed the paying-out machinery that needed fixing. He got hold of a naval engineer to redesign it. A self-releasing "jockey" brake was adapted from apparatus used in English jails "to regulate the amount of labor in proportion to the prisoner's strength." It adjusted to strain without snapping the line.

In late May of 1858, the cable squadron reconvened in the Bay of Biscay, and this time, on Field's insistence, went through a complete rehearsal of the operation—testing the cable for conductivity, checking the new paying-out machinery, practicing splicing and retrieving. There was no crowd later at Valentia, no exuberant send-off. But Cyrus' younger brother, now the Reverend Henry Martyn Field, had come from America to bless the fleet, somewhat as Ulysses' men had invoked the Greek gods before setting sail. Henry was concerned, as others were, with Cyrus' overtaxed strength. "He was working (wrote Henry) with an activity that was unnatural, and which involved the most serious danger. The strain on the man was more than the strain on the cable, and we were in fear that both would break together."

Field and Bright had settled on a new procedure for this expedition. Instead of laying the cable in tandem, the two ships would meet in mid-ocean, make the splice, then move in opposite directions. If the cable broke within a radius of 100 miles, they'd return and try again.

Fair weather blessed their departure; but within three days the worst storm in memory struck the North Atlantic. Mountainous seas and gale winds scattered the escorting vessels. The cable ships, *Niagara* and *Agamemnon,* tried to keep in sight of one another; but the smaller British vessel, overloaded with cable that might at any moment bash her sides out, finally disappeared—possibly to the bottom, for all Cyrus knew.

Day and night the lone *Niagara* battled seemingly unconquerable seas. Tons of water struck the deck, plunged down the hatchways. Spars broke, stays snapped, rigging crashed from overhead. The American Eagle figurehead sent one wing flying into space. Field shuddered with each glance at the barometer. Falling! And the next day—falling! The entries in his log grew repetitious: "Strong gales, high seas, ship straining dangerously." Yet it wasn't the ship that worried him, but the cable. Come what might, he wouldn't allow it to be jettisoned.

After ten tempestuous days, when the ship seemed beaten and could take no more, the storm miraculously lifted. Groggily they noted they were almost at the point of rendezvous! Even more remarkable, the *Agamemnon* shortly limped toward them, almost mortally wounded by the storm. Her decks were awash with black coal, broken timber, shattered spars, and rigging.

Forty-five men were in sick bay, one driven mad by the ordeal. The cable was still intact, though a less dedicated captain would have thrown it overboard for safety. But much of it was strewn on deck in a writhing, tangled mess. It took a day to unravel it, another day to make the splice; and then—as if nothing untoward had happened—the *Niagara* headed toward Newfoundland as planned, the *Agamemnon* toward Ireland.

Both ships, of course, could keep in contact with each other by the cable. Signals flowed back and

The enthusiasm and celebrations that followed the apparently successful laying of the cable in August, 1858, seemed to know no bounds. So intense and widespread were the fireworks that the cupola of New York's City Hall, shown here, burned and the building was almost destroyed.

forth continuously, giving each an idea of the other's progress. But they'd gone just three miles when the cable snarled and broke from the *Niagara*'s stern. The ships returned by prearrangement, respliced the line, and headed off again. This time they were 80 miles apart before the cable snapped again—for reasons exasperatingly unclear. They reassembled, made another splice, and moved apart.

The gloom of repeated failures lifted as a hundred miles of cable were paid smoothly out . . . then a hundred and fifty . . . then two hundred. And then—silence! Somewhere, somehow, the line had snapped again. They were past the

hundred-mile limit; had lost contact. It was the point of no return.

It was a grim body of directors that awaited Field in London. What had they to show for two years' effort? The chairman proposed selling the remaining cable and abandoning the project. The vice-chairman went further, and resigned in protest of the "hopeless undertaking." But Field, with his eloquent sincerity, went to work on those remaining. To give up was unthinkable! They still had the ships, the crews, enough line left to try again. Given a verbal green light, they could take on fuel and start within a week.

Of Cyrus Field's father, David Dudley Field, it was said that he preached to the waves for practice, and they all but listened. The directors not only listened, but hypnotically agreed.

Off sailed the fleet again from Ireland, July 17. The crews were weary, disillusioned. They began to think the young American was chasing dreams, and destined for a rude awakening. Reaching mid-ocean they spliced the line, and again moved east and west. Only Field "expressed his usual confidence to his companions." Yet the first day . . . the second . . . the third and fourth passed uneventfully, with only minor incidents to mar the voyage. Before they knew it, they were in their second week. Then suddenly they sighted icebergs! Porpoises! Gulls! They had left the deep abyss and were climbing up the Grand Banks! Incredibly, they could almost smell the land, the pines, the kelp, the woodsmoke. . . .

On August 4 they sighted Trinity Bay, its arms wide open to them. It was two the next morning when they finally dropped anchor. Field ordered a boat put overside and rowed ashore. He groped through the underbrush to the telegraph shack and roused the startled occupants. He had two telegrams to send —to Stockbridge, Massachusetts, and New York. They read, to Mary and his father:

"Arrived here yesterday. All well. The Atlantic telegraph cable successfully laid. Please telegraph me immediately."

The cable was landed from the *Niagara* shortly after sunrise. Installed in the telegraph shack, de Sauty heard from the *Agamemnon,* some fourteen hundred miles across the ocean. She had had a harder fight to reach Valentia. A sportive whale had played around the cable off her stern; ships threatening her course were driven off by gunfire; faults in the insulation had had to be repaired while running. But the final link was on its way from ship to shore.

At Trinity Bay, while Cyrus waited to see de Sauty settled with his instruments, the wires sang with laudatory messages—from President Buchanan ("I congratulate you with all my heart upon the success of the great enterprise with which your name is so honorably connected"), ambassadors, governors and mayors. And one that he welcomed most, perhaps, from his senior brother, David:

"Your family is all at Stockbridge and well. The joyful news arrived here Thursday, and almost overwhelmed your wife. Father rejoiced like a boy. Bells were rung; children let out of school, shouted, 'The cable is laid! The cable is laid!' The village was in a tumult of joy. My dear brother, I congratulate you. God bless you."

The message was sent from the small stone house of another brother, Jonathan. The building, equipped as the telegraph office for the village, still stands in modest memory of a glorious day when it was once the center of the world.

On August 18 Field returned to New York and a celebration the like of which America had never seen, and hardly ever would again.

The city almost literally exploded. Guns thundered, fireworks shelled the sky, bells pealed and whistles shrieked. People swarmed the streets with pyrotechnical enthusiasm. Newspapers broke out banner headlines hailing "Cyrus the Great" . . . "King Cyrus" . . . "The Columbus of America!" Henry Ward Beecher preached a sermon on the "sublime wire"; and the poet-editor William Cullen Bryant wrote: "Tomorrow the hearts of the civilized world will beat to a single pulse, and from that time forth forevermore the continental divisions of the earth will in a measure lose their conditions of time and distance. . . ."

The fervor was echoed from across the ocean, where the staid London *Times* told its readers: "Since the discovery of Columbus, nothing has been done in any degree comparable to the vast enlargement which has thus been given to the sphere of human activity. . . . The Atlantic Telegraph has half undone the declaration of 1776, and has gone far to make us once again, in spite of ourselves, one people."

After some delay in opening the cable, Queen Victoria and the President exchanged formal, florid greetings which high-spirited wags translated as:

"Dear Buchanan: I send this by my rope."

"Dear Victoria: I send this by *Europe.*"
These salutations sparked another round of celebration, an uninhibited free-wheeling binge. All normal work gave way to pandemonium. Stores, hotels, and business houses displayed banners and transparencies with such legends as: "Married, August 1858, by CYRUS W. FIELD, Old Ireland and Miss Young America." Under not unwelcome pressure, Field sold the remainder of the cable to Tiffany & Company, jewellers, to be cut up and offered to a public clamoring for souvenirs. Songs were composed

and ballads sung, couples danced the "Cable Polka," and *Harper's Weekly* displayed a poem that would later find its way to grade school readers—of which one verse is an adequate example:

Bold Cyrus Field he said, says he,
"I have a pretty notion,
That I can run a telegraph
Across the Atlantic Ocean."

The carnival lasted for all of two weeks, culminating in a victory parade from the Battery to the Crystal Palace, with crowds so dense it took the marchers six hours to reach their destination. There, a reception to Cyrus was followed by a torchlight procession that set fire to the City Hall. The next evening a more exclusive reception, attended by 600 dignitaries, featured a seven-course dinner washed down by repeated toasts, the first of which was "To Cyrus W. Field: To his exertions, energy, courage and perseverance are we indebted for the Ocean Telegraph; we claim, but Immortality owns him."

It was during this banquet, a pinnacle of his career, that Cyrus was handed a telegram from de Sauty in Trinity Bay:

"C. W. Field, New York: Please inform . . . government we are now in position to do best to forward—"

The rest was blank. For the cable, as the world would shortly know, had failed. At this heartbreaking moment, Field's clouded eyes could focus only on the last word, "forward."

When the cable which Cyrus Field had laid from Ireland to Newfoundland in August, 1858, failed at the height of celebrations honoring its success, there was endless speculation as to what had caused the failure. It was variously attributed to an electrical storm in the North Atlantic, a too-powerful current that had burned the wire, exposure that had rotted the insulation. But once the dismal fact leaked out, the cry of "Fraud" was heard across the land. The press asked: "Was the Atlantic Cable a Humbug?" Detractors came forward with "eyewitness proof" that the line had been lost or had never been laid; the messages between the Queen and President had been a prefabricated hoax. One newspaper humorist challenged even the existence of de Sauty, whose name had been a typographer's nightmare:

Thou seperator, silent, glum,
*   Shut up there in your shanty,*
Do tell us what your name is—come!
*   De Sauty or De Santy?*

Field was stung most by charges that the pretense of success was engineered so that he could dump $750,000 of stock on a gullible market. One financial commentator demanded to know: "How many shares of stock did Mr. Field sell during the month of August?" The answer, which nobody saw fit to learn, was *one* share—at a loss! No one human is a saint, and to whitewash Field of every failing is to deny him the warm humanity he had. But dishonest he was not. His sometimes dubious association with the so-called Robber Barons came from his naive belief in the rectitude of others.

But it was no time to revivify the cable project. The public had lost faith, and he himself had dropped from hero to pariah. Practically all his personal fortune had gone to the bottom with the cable. To stay afloat, and keep the project alive, he mortgaged everything he owned—his home, his stock in the company, all the household furnishings, even the portraits of his family. He was virtually bankrupt.

On top of these catastrophes came the War Between the States. England looked for a Confederate victory, and would make no move until the issue was decided. The Un-

ion was too involved to think of cables. Field himself threw his energies into the Union cause.

He approached Lincoln and McClellan with a plan to strangle the South with a girdle of cables, purveying military information, from Norfolk to Key West to Galveston. McClellan generally approved. But the war emphasized the need for his Atlantic cable. When the "Trent Affair," involving the Union's interception of a British vessel, led to grave misunderstandings due to lack of quick communication, the London *Times* noted: "We nearly went to war with America because we had not a telegraph across the Atlantic."

Field seized this opportunity. He wrote to Secretary Seward urging quick completion of the cable to avoid further dangerous misunderstandings: "I have no doubt that the English government has expended more money during the last thirty days in preparation for war with this country than the whole cost of manufacturing and laying a good cable between Newfoundland and Ireland."

He could get nowhere in either country until peace came. But he never gave up. He spent so much time racing between New York and Washington that the Secret Service started trailing him. With that honest face, what could he be but a spy? When they arrested him, they found his satchel filled with sample bits of wire. That was all right, but his cheerful attitude exasperated the arresting agent. "Mr. Field thought the incident was *funny!*" he complained to Washington.

The war was over in 1865, but the bitter feeling between England and America remained. Neither government could be counted on for help in another try at the Atlantic cable. Only extraordinary luck put Cyrus back in business. Two British financiers, Thomas Brassey and John Pender, advanced a large part

of the necessary capital; and a British cable manufacturing firm contracted to do the entire job at cost, in return for shares of stock upon completion *if* the cable worked. In addition the owners of the *Great Eastern,* which had proved too large for other profitable use, offered the vessel on the same terms—payment only if the project was successful. The cumbersome two-ship operation would no longer be required.

From that point on, things steamed ahead at full speed. New cable was manufactured, improved from past experience and "as nearly perfect as human skill could make it." In June of 1865 it was stowed, all 5,000 tons of it, in tanks on the *Great Eastern,* and a barnyard of cargo was taken aboard, including a herd of cattle, cows and pigs, flocks of hens and gaggles of geese —enough to feed Nelson's entire fleet at the battle of Trafalgar.

Cyrus Field was the only American on this expedition, the only American now physically dedicated to the effort. He became an endearing figure of resolution in his adopted battle dress of Inverness cape, deerstalker cap, and spectacles. He got on well with the "black hands," as the cable crew were called; they referred to him as "Our Sister of Mercy" because of his genuine interest in their welfare. A captain in the Royal Navy wrote that his "indefatigable energy and perseverance . . . inspired every officer and man of the British Navy employed in laying the Atlantic Cable with the most profound admiration and respect." More than faint praise for a Yankee landlubber from the Berkshire Hills.

Once again the shores of Valentia Bay were bright with flags and gaily dressed sightseers; booths and tents sold gypsy fortunes and illicit whiskey, couples danced Irish jigs while fiddlers played, the harbor swarmed with bunting-bedecked boats. On Sunday, July 23, with the land end of the cable brought ashore, the *Great Eastern* headed majestically toward Trinity Bay in Newfoundland, where Field had selected a more favorable landing spot with the intriguing name of Heart's Content.

"Happy is the cable laying that has no history," wrote the London *Times* reporter aboard ship, noting the even operation of the paying-out machinery, the black line of cable slipping smoothly from the stern, the signals traveling from shore to ship and back without a flaw. But they had gone only 84 miles before a leak in the current was detected. Since they knew the resistance of each mile of cable, it was possible to trace just where the fault lay.

They reeled in the line on special picking-up machinery installed for such a mishap, and discovered the disturbing cause. A small bit of wire like a needle had been driven through the outer wrapping, allowing the current to escape. "Flagrant evidence of mischief," wrote the *Times* reporter. But it could have been a freakish accident. The damaged section was cut out, the cable spliced, and the ship was on its way again.

Day after sunny day passed uneventfully; and when a heavy sea developed in mid-ocean, the *Great Eastern* cleaved it like a millpond. For the first time on an ocean voyage, Field's stomach rode in comfort. He himself was filled with optimism. He wrote in his diary:

There was a wonderful sense of power in the Great Ship and in her work; it was gratifying to feel that man was mastering space, and triumphing over the wind and waves; that from his hands down into the eternal night of waters there was trailing a slender chan-

Above: The interior of one of the tanks on board the Great Eastern. *She carried 5000 tons of cable.*

Opp. page: Built to sail to Australia and return without refueling, and to carry 10,000 troops, this sea giant, the Great Eastern, *bankrupted three corporate owners before being used to lay the Atlantic Cable. She's shown here releasing cable as she leaves Valentia on her way out to open sea.*

nel through which obedient lightning would flash forever instinct with the sympathies, passions and interests of two mighty nations.

No one now doubted the successful outcome of the expedition. They had passed the point where the *Niagara* and *Agamemnon* had met in tragic rendezvous. The ship's official bulletin reported: "The *Great Eastern* speeds nobly on her mission of towing the islands of Great Britain and Ireland to America. In less than ten days it is expected that a splice will be effected between the two countries, and long, long may it last!"

Such optimism was an invitation to catastrophe. On the seventh day, with 800 miles of cable laid, blank went the signals. Again the line was reeled in for examination, when (wrote the *Times* observer) "an exclamation literally of horror escaped our lips!" There, driven through the cable, was another needle. It dawned on everyone aboard that the same crew had been on duty as before. Was it sabotage by a disgruntled crewman? The evil work of a competing cable manufacturer? Or an attempt to devalue the company's stock so someone in London or New York could make a fortune?

From then on, a watchful guard was posted over each shift in the cable tank. Field, having no specific assignment, volunteered for this unpleasant duty—inspiring a sailor-poet to pen the quatrain:

No useless sentry within the tank,
Not in slumber or sleep we found him;
But he sat like a warrior stiff on his plank,
With his Inverness cloak around him.

"*There was a wonderful sense of power in the Great Ship and in her work . . .*"

He was thus sitting when there were only 600 miles to go to Heart's Content. The same crew was on duty as at the previous times of accident. A wicked flash of silver caught his eye. Before he could shout a warning, the black snake of cable swooped up through the canvas funnel. He raced to the top deck in time to see it plunge into the sea. From the telegraph cabin, de Sauty reported the signals stuttering.

Bitterly they started winding in again. The damaged section with its sinister needle reached the top deck. Then came a sound like a pistol shot as the balance of the cable snapped and whipped into the ocean. "Gone, gone forever," wrote the *Times* reporter, "down in that fearful depth! It was enough to move one to tears."

This was catastrophe they had not anticipated, and were ill-equipped to handle. But Field and Canning, his engineer, were fighters, not inclined to giving up. A five-pronged iron was attached to several miles of pieced-together rope. They would fish for the sunken cable on the ocean bottom. The *Great Eastern* stood up-wind, the tackle was cast overboard (it took two hours to reach the bottom), and the idling ship drifted down across the cable's estimated path.

Back and forth, hour after anxious hour, they grappled for the missing line. Twice they hooked it, brought it almost to the surface, when the rope broke from the rising weight. They had one anchor left and barely enough rope to try again. But try they did—snagging the cable and getting it almost to the surface, only to see it snap back as the rope again broke. That was the death blow. They were out of fuel, food, fishing tackle; they were out of patience—all except Field. As they steamed back to England, Cyrus went below to draft his proposal for another expedition the next summer.

Surprisingly, even following this defeat, England gave him a tri-umphant welcome. He had become the man who couldn't be beaten, affectionately known as "Sir Cyrus" and "Lord Cable." The *Great Eastern* too had come into her own, after an equally up-and-down career. James Dugan writes: "In the hour of her deepest failure, the big ship was a heroine. And Cyrus Field was the hero. He had eclipsed the biblical Job, who had endured only seven years of misery. Field had survived eight years of knockouts, and still had some time to go."

There was no talk now of abandoning the project. The cable had been laid beyond dispute, and made to work for two-thirds of the distance to America. The "sabotage needles" were found, on analysis, to be part of the casing that had grown too brittle during storage, splintered off, and pierced the insulation of their own accord. Otherwise all had functioned well. The manufacturers agreed to supply additional line on the same favorable terms; the *Great Eastern* was available again, too. A new company was formed to raise £600,000 of further capital. They would not only lay another cable, but try to retrieve the one they'd lost.

In July of 1866, the extra cable was completed, stowed aboard along with the barnyard fowl and cattle; and as a coast guard band played "Goodbye, Sweetheart, Goodbye!" the *Great Eastern* steamed to Valentia for the count down. They were ready to sail for Heart's Content on Friday the 13th. Not a good luck date; but Field observed that Columbus had sailed on a Friday the 13th, and fetched the New World on a Friday, so the omens were auspicious.

Every precaution had been taken against past reverses. The cable crew were encased from head to toe in canvas—no boots containing nails, no pockets for secreting tools of sabotage. They hovered like silent ghosts around the iron coils.

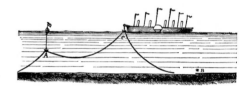

With the loss of the 1865 cable 2½ miles down, the swiveled rope method for grappling it, shown in the top drawing, was found inadequate. The next year, it was recovered by raising the end section in several places, buoying a length near the surface, and finally lifting one bight above the surface—see illustration.

The newly polished hull of the *Great Eastern* moved so smoothly that they disengaged the stern propeller to reduce speed. The only discordant note aboard that silent and majestic ship was the cackle of hens and honking geese, the grunting of pigs and lowing of the cattle.

Field's diary, day by day, grew repetitious: "Weather fine, signals perfect" . . . "Still everything going well, sea like a millpond." Four days out, he sent a message to Valentia:

Please write Mrs. Field today and tell her, "all in good health and spirits aboard this ship, and confident of success." Machinery works perfectly, and the cable pays out splendidly.

After another six days of "delightful monotony," Cyrus signaled

Valentia for European news to send from land when they arrived. On Tuesday, July 24, he wired: "We are within four hundred miles of Heart's Content, and expect to be there Friday. When shall the Atlantic cable be open for public business?" Field's daughter Isabella writes of these messages: "Nothing is so remarkable and characteristic as the tone of absolute confidence while the issue of the voyage was still in doubt. It was this confidence that not only sustained the projectors of the enterprise through all its mutations, but that infected his associates."

On Friday, July 27, heavy fog enveloped the *Great Eastern* as it inched into Trinity Bay. Suddenly it lifted like a curtain on the gentle scene of Heart's Content! With no

fanfare or public greeting, Cyrus went ashore to wire Mary:

All well. Thank God the cable has been successfully laid and is in perfect working order. I am sure that no one will be as thankful to God as you and our dear children. Now we shall be a united family. We leave in about a week to recover the cable of last year.

The contradiction of the last two sentences must have been heart-breaking to his wife. But Field could never leave the job with a loose end in the bottom of the ocean. Back the *Great Eastern* sailed to grapple for the cable lost the year before—going windward of its estimated lie,

drifting down time after time to snare it. "I often went to the bow," wrote Cyrus in his diary, "and sat on the rope, and could tell by the quiver that the grapnel was dragging on the bottom two miles under us."

It was a long, frustrating operation. Two hours to drop the tackle, hours more to reel it in. Time and again they brought the cable almost to the surface, and then lost it. By the end of August they were running low on food, the men were exhausted, they had grappled day and night without a let-up. Twenty-seven . . . twenty-eight . . . twenty-nine attempts had failed. Approaching from a different angle, they snagged the line on the thirtieth try and, hearts in five hundred mouths, lifted the squirming snake aboard and lashed it fast.

145

But would this year-old cable work as well as the one just completed? A wire was rushed to the telegraph room to hook up with the instruments, and a signal sent to the operator in Valentia. Field noted in his diary:

Never shall I forget that eventful moment when . . . in an instant came back those six memorable letters, "Both O.K." I left the room, I went to my cabin, I locked the door; I could no longer restrain my tears, crying like a child . . .

The honors that were heaped on Field with this dual victory were far more enduring, less hysterical, than those of 1858. Congress voted him a gold medal as its highest tribute from the nation; Queen Victoria wrote through her Prime Minister, Lord Derby, that only Field's American citizenship withheld the Knighthood she would like to offer; the French and Italian governments both gave him honorary medals. Yet none of these could have meant to Field as much as the knowledge of his own accomplishment, so personal in meaning. The New England country boy, who had run fast all his life to catch up, had arrived. He wrote his own summation of that victory:

It has been a long, hard struggle. Nearly thirteen years of anxious watching and ceaseless toil. Often my heart has been ready to sink. Many times, when wandering in the forests of Newfoundland, in the pelting rain, or on the deck of ships, on dark, stormy nights—alone, far from home—I have almost accused myself of madness and folly to sacrifice the peace of my family, and all the hopes of life, for what might prove after all but a dream. I have seen my companions one and another falling by my side, and feared that I too might not live to see the end. And yet one hope has led me on, and I have prayed that I might not taste of death till this work was accomplished. That prayer is answered; and now, beyond all acknowledgements to men, is the feeling of gratitude to Almighty God.

One could well ring down the curtain on Field's life story at this point. He had achieved his goal; established a high niche in history. But he himself could never settle down.

A popular Currier & Ives print of this period shows a telegraph operator at his instruments, with a printing press and locomotive in the background. It suggests the two logical concomitants of ocean cables: newspapers and railroads. It was into these two areas he next moved—becoming owner and publisher of the combined New York *Evening Express* and *Daily Mail,* and organizer of the Manhattan Elevated Railroad into a well-run, coordinated system. The elevated railways are no more; but for a while they dominated New York transportation, changing the pattern of urban living in the nation's greatest city.

But Field's monument lies mostly underwater: in the proliferation of cables that link every nation, every major island, on the globe. If knowledge is the handmaiden of truth, and truth is the hope of mankind, then those glowing wires are a mighty promise for the future. And Cyrus Field, the unschooled, untrained country lad from Stockbridge, with nothing working for him but a vision and sheer courage, has given the world a lot for which to thank him.

laid and is in perfect working order . . ."

The arrival of the steamship **Great** Eastern, *with the Atlantic Cable at Heart's Content, Newfoundland.*

A chromolithograph illustrating the destruction of the U.S. Battleship Maine *in Havana Harbor, February 15, 1898.*

To this day no one knows for sure what happened.
The mystery lies buried with the ship itself in 600 fathoms of the
Caribbean. But at the time we thought we knew and
the cry, "Remember the Maine, To hell with Spain!"
swept over the country....

REMEMBER THE MAINE

by Samuel Carter III

The air was heavy and still as death. Sprawled in his hammock, Marine Corporal Frank G. Thompson of Charlestown found it hard to believe that this was the middle of February. Unable to sleep from the heat, he longed for some of the frigid weather blanketing New England in that winter of 1898 . . . longed to be anywhere but on the *U.S.S. Maine* anchored in Havana Harbor.

In seconds his wish was singularly granted. On what he described as "a hurricane of flame" he was hurled through the overhead awning, hung in midair for a fraction of a second—long enough, he remembered, to see the superstructure of the battleship—and then lost consciousness before his body struck the water.

At that same moment Lt. John J. Blandin, lately graduated from the Newport Naval Training Station, was standing watch at the starboard rail. The night was still . . . too still, he thought. Suddenly (his report ran in the Boston *Herald*) "there came a dull sullen roar. Would to God I could blot out the sound and scenes that followed . . . a perfect rain of missiles, from huge pieces of cement to blocks of wood, steel railings, fragments of grating and debris . . . I was struck on the head by a piece of cement, but was not hurt."

Not hurt? Hospitalized at Key West, Blandin died there of his injuries.

On the bridge, Quartermaster Millard Harris of Boothbay Harbor, Maine, was waiting for his coffee. He had found that if he sent an obliging shipmate to the engine room with a stewpan (smuggled from the galley), an equally obliging fireman would heat some water on the coals. Harris needed that coffee; night watches were hard on the morale. Then—something split the air like gunshot, the deck trembled, the forward section of the ship rose, and . . .

Quartermaster Harris never felt the mighty blast, the heat and flame which followed that first detonation and which few survived to tell of. He was one of the 258 killed instantly, out of the total of 267 officers and men who lost their lives in a naval disaster which had greater long-range consequences for the nation than the blasting of Pearl Harbor by the Japanese in 1941.

To this day no one knows for sure what happened. The mystery lies buried with the ship itself in 600 fathoms of the Caribbean. But at the time it seemed no mystery. With feeling high against Spain's persecution of the Cuban rebels, and Spanish acts of provocation toward our vessels on the high seas, there was no doubt who the villain was. The cry, "Remember the *Maine!* To hell with Spain!" swept over the country as "Carthage must be destroyed" had once swept Rome.

The *Maine* catastrophe had special meaning for New England.

Whether from sentiment for the vessel's name or by sheer accident, a larger proportion of its crew came from the New England states than from any other section of the country, more than half of these from Maine and Massachusetts. Many of its 26 officers had been trained at the Naval War College in Rhode Island, and were fondly recalled by Newport residents. And in New England the inevitable consequences of that tragedy, the threat of war and the moral issues war involved, were more keenly felt and thoroughly discussed than anywhere else in the United States.

There is little in the background story of the *Maine* to foreshadow her role in history. She was launched at the New York Navy Yard in November 1890, and commissioned almost five years later in September 1895. On her shakedown cruise she visited, first, Newport, and then Portland, Maine, where she was passed by a board of inspection headed by a Vermont naval officer named George B. Dewey. A sort of dedication ceremony followed at the Portland City Building, where a group of distinguished citizens presented the ship with a silver table service. It was minus drinking goblets; Maine was a prohibition state.

For her day, the *Maine* was a formidable answer to the threat of growing naval might abroad. She was an early step in President Chester Arthur's program for "a thorough rehabilitation of the Navy." Costing $2.5 million, she was 325 feet long, 27 feet abeam, with a displacement of 6650 tons. True, the *Maine* would be dwarfed by a modern battleship (though battleships today are obsolete). The *Wisconsin,* for example, built in the 1940s, cost $110 million, was 887 feet long, 108 feet wide, and displaced 45,000 tons. The *Maine* carried a varying complement of around 370 men, the *Wisconsin* 2700.

Still, she was a beautiful ship, her hull a glittering white, her superstructure ochre. First of her class, she had been conceived as a flagship, with an admiral's cabin adjoining that of Capt. Charles D. Sigsbee, who assumed command in the spring of 1897. Sigsbee, who looked like a college professor, had a strangely prophetic personal creed. "A naval officer," he wrote, "should pour ice water over his personal feelings in time of an emergency, to postpone nervous prostration to a proper moment." It would later serve him well.

The story of the *Maine* leading up to her explosion might begin off the New England coast in the summer of 1897. There she joined the ships of the North Atlantic Squadron which assembled for maneuvers and (if the itinerary is an indication) a good amount of social life ashore. Under Rear Admiral Montgomery Sicard, they spent a week each at Newport, Portland, and Bar Harbor, with four days at Portsmouth, and the festivities were anything but martial.

But sinister forces were building in the Caribbean, where the Cuban rebellion and the island's status were becoming critical. American sympathy went out to the insurgents, along with smuggled arms and ammunition, which led to fre-

quent clashes with the Spanish navy. On top of this, Spain's Ambassador to Washington chose this moment to write an inflammatory letter (accidentally brought to light) insulting President McKinley and Americans in general. Admiral Sicard was ordered to leave off parading, and repair to the Southern Drill Grounds for preparatory target practice.

It was off Cape Charles at midnight of October 8 that a sleek little vessel of destiny approached the squadron. She was the torpedo boat *DuPont,* built at Bristol, Rhode Island, by the Herreshoffs, who up to now had been known for their America's Cup defenders. (Ironically, the Herreshoffs had also built vessels for the Spanish navy to help suppress the Cuban rebels.) The secret orders which the *DuPont* carried were that the *Maine* should proceed to Port Royal for conditioning, and then to Key West.

To be dispatched to Key West, 90 miles from Cuba, told Sigsbee there was trouble brewing. In fact, his presence at Key West had been requested by America's Consul General in Havana, Fitzhugh Lee, who saw the Cuban crisis growing more acute, and American involvement likely. A private code was arranged between Lee and Sigsbee. If the former cabled a message containing the words "two dollars" the *Maine* was to stand by for action. A following message would give specific battle orders.

For almost a month Lee and Sigsbee kept in touch. Their exchange of cables discussed the cost of bullfight tickets, the dollar market for Cuban sugar, the price of palm fans in Havana. None contained the fateful words "two dollars." Christmas and New Year's came and went, with the battleship's

superstructure strung with green and red electric lights. "One of the finest displays of electricity ever witnessed in this city," reported the Key West *Citizen.*

Apart from the bars on Duval Street, there was little amusement for the Yankee crew at Key West. The men explored the tiny island, on the highest point of which so many of them would be buried. Seaman John H. Bloomer of East Deering, Maine, led his ship's baseball team in games against the local competition. But the contest scheduled for January 18 was abruptly called. Sigsbee received an innocent-seeming cablegram from General Lee. The words "two dollars" leaped like rockets from the text.

The *Maine* was stripped for action and put out to sea. No further word arrived from Lee, but orders from Washington sent the warship to the Dry Tortugas to await the balance of the North Atlantic Squadron. There, on the night of January 23, Sigsbee saw red and green rockets bursting in the east. They signalled the approach of a swift-moving courier vessel. Again it was the fateful *DuPont* headed for Admiral Sicard's flagship. Sigsbee didn't wait to get the message from the admiral. He knew already what it was. He ordered a full head of steam. The *Maine* was going to Havana.

On the morning of January 25, 1898, the white-and-buff warship steamed into Havana Harbor past the guns of Morro Castle. There was a moment of tense apprehension. Would the Spanish battery open fire? If so, gunner's mates Clarence Safford of Taunton, Massachusetts, and Charles Nolan of Boston had had their orders—"to clear away ob-

throughout the nation.

structions from the guns and make the ship ready for fighting." All men were at their battle stations, some concealed inside the turrets. Captain Sigsbee later belittled this warlike preparation, writing: "The *Maine* was merely in such a state of readiness that she could not have been taken at much disadvantage had she been attacked."

No untoward incident occurred. A Spanish pilot came aboard, as customary, and guided the vessel to buoy number four. It later developed that this was not the mooring first selected for the *Maine,* but no one gave it much thought. Salutes were exchanged with the Spanish batteries on land, after which Captain Sigsbee went ashore for the traditional official visits. Everything was, on the surface, coldly cordial and correct.

It was while ashore that Sigsbee was handed, surreptitiously, a handbill being circulated in Havana. It was a vicious document, one paragraph referring to the *Maine* and to "these Yankee pigs who meddle in our affairs, humiliating us to the last degree and, for still greater taunt, order to us a man of war of their rotten squadron." The next ended with the war cry, "Death to the Americans! . . . Long live Spain!"

There were further disturbing revelations when Sigsbee talked with General Lee. In spite of the "two dollar" message he had wired from Havana, Lee had *not* sent for the *Maine.* He had dispatched the coded message merely as a warning. The order to sail for Havana—to protect American citizens there—had come from the State Department, and Lee, having heard about it, urged that it be rescinded. The Spaniards did not want the *Maine.* They might well resent her presence in the harbor.

Not surprisingly, no shore leave

was allowed the crew, and a double watch, with sentries posted all around the ship, was maintained day and night. Seaman Bloomer, who had enlisted that summer when the ship was in Portland Harbor, wrote home on January 30 that he feared the ship would be blown up, and added with some exaggeration, "We cannot go ashore here, as the Spaniards would kill us."

Bloomer's fear of the vessel's being blown up was shared by others of the crew. Circulated as gospel was the firm belief of one Yankee sailor that "We'll never get out of here in one piece." Even Sigsbee was infected with alarm. The Boston *Herald* later noted that "Captain Sigsbee was keenly alive to the possibility of an infernal machine being taken aboard and took every precaution to prevent it, even going so far as to make a careful inspection of the water and provisions brought from shore."

As a matter of fact, Sigsbee refused to take on coal in Havana. "It would be too risky. Not that I suspect anyone in authority, but there is such an impossible rabble in Havana that it would be an easy matter to get a couple of sticks of dynamite in the coal bunkers without knowing it." Sigsbee was voicing a fear that 10 years later plagued the Great White Fleet of Teddy Roose-

velt in its epoch-making voyage around the world.

January passed to February, and the *Maine* chafed at her tether like an anxious watchdog. Her only neighbors within a hundred yards were the Ward Line's *City of Washington* and the Spanish flagship *Alfonso XII.* In fact, on the fateful day of February 15 the whole harbor seemed deserted, strangely devoid of any maritime activity.

Hindsight often lends wings to suspicion. Cadet W. T. Cluverius of Worcester, Massachusetts, remembered seeing an empty, unmarked barge towed purposefully back and forth across their mooring; while Corporal Thompson, later to be catapulted through the awning, noted "the presence of a strange small black boat which entered the harbor and circled the *Maine* several times during the evening." Quartermaster Harris, who never heard the blast that killed him, "hailed this mysterious boat twice . . . but got no response."

Night and a deadly stillness had descended on Havana Harbor. In his cabin aft, where all of the officers' cabins were, Sigsbee was composing a letter to his wife. At ten after nine he heard Fifer Newton sounding taps, and "laid down my pen to listen to the notes of the bugle, which were singularly beautiful in the op-

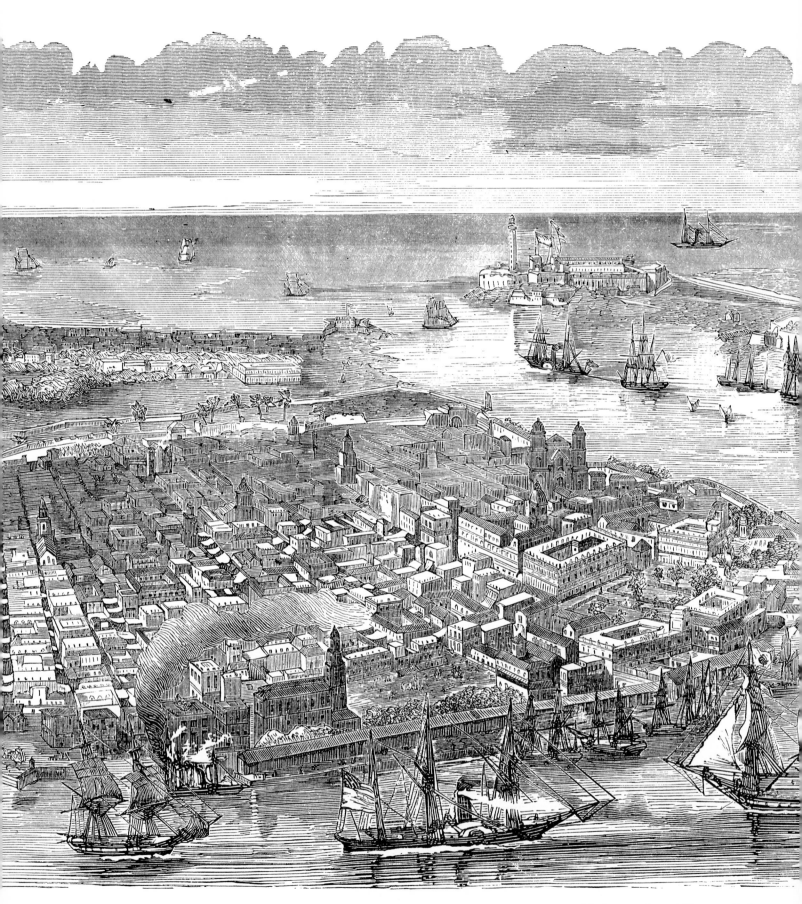

Bird's-eye view of Havana, Cuba

pressive stillness of the night." The notes faded, and Sigsbee continued writing for another 30 minutes. Then the lights went out, the cabin trembled, and he was lying on the floor —in his ears "a bursting, rending, crashing roar."

He heard cries for help and knew, he later testified, that the ship had been mined or torpedoed. Others thought that they'd been shelled by Spanish batteries; but all knew that the ship was sinking. Sigsbee groped his way to the slanting deck where he found his executive officer, Newport-trained Commander Richard Wainwright, directing rescue operations. Dazed but recovering from shock, he ordered Wainwright to flood the magazines. "That won't be necessary, sir," said Wainwright, "they're already underwater."

Only three of the lifeboats were intact; but gigs from the *City of Washington* and the *Alfonso XII* were picking up survivors. There were pitifully few. Corporal Thompson was plucked from the water and survived, along with Joseph Kane of Worcester, Massachusetts, who had been trapped by wreckage below deck until a "second explosion" blew him free. In 15 minutes all was over. Two-thirds of the crew were dead or missing. The tangled, smoking wreckage of the *Maine*, still shaken by exploding ammunition, barely hovered on the surface. To the officers with him on the tilted poop deck, Sigsbee gave the order to "Abandon ship." He looked, said one survivor, "ten years older."

Rowing to the *City of Washington,* Sigsbee flashed the news to his superiors. He might have colored his message with inflammatory charges or heroics, but he didn't. His cable read simply: "*Maine* blown up in Havana at nine-forty tonight and destroyed." He then thoughtfully added: "Public opinion should be suspended until further report."

But public opinion cannot be suspended. The following day the Boston *Herald,* misgauging the importance of the news, devoted its feature story to the opening of the New England K.C. Dog Show. Buried in a single column, one inch deep, was a 12-line item on the *Maine.* Reporting time and place, it ended simply: "As yet the cause of the explosion is not apparent. The wounded sailors of the *Maine* cannot explain it. It is believed that the ship is totally destroyed."

That reticent bit of news was dynamite. Author and journalist Gregory Mason, then only eight years old, recalled that winter morning when the *Herald* reached his home in Milton, Massachusetts. His father pointed to the single paragraph, and told him, "This means war." It meant war to almost everybody in New England and throughout the nation. And the enemy was self-revealed. In spite of Sigsbee's caution to suspend opinion, and in spite of sober reason, America chose to believe that Spanish perfidy had done the deed. *Remember the Maine! To hell with Spain!*

There had, of course, to be an investigation—if only as a matter of formality. Secretary of the Navy John L. Long, a former Governor of Massachusetts, appointed a Naval Board of Inquiry which arrived in Havana on February 21, just six days after the explosion. Long was a wise and temperate man. He believed with Sigsbee that the explosion *could* have been an accident, and if caused by a mine it was probably the work of a fanatic. Sigsbee wrote that "the anti-American rabble [in Havana] . . . would not stop at any kind of crime, but they lacked the means of execution. You cannot blow up a 7000 ton man-of-war and escape detection. . . ."

Spain made its own investigation. It concluded that the *Maine*

153

had been destroyed by spontaneous combustion of the coal dust in its bunkers. It hinted that Yankee negligence had been responsible, and pointed to the lack of dead fish in the harbor as an indication that no mine had been exploded. American testimony noted that the forward bunkers (in the area of the explosion) had been empty. As for the dead fish, there were *no* fish in Havana Harbor—they couldn't survive the putrid water.

Much was made of the piece of cement that had mortally wounded Lieutenant Blandin. The only cement aboard the ship was between the seams at the very bottom of the hull. An internal explosion would have blown it downward, not up into the air. Divers had also noted that the hull plates in the wreckage generally bent inward; and the entire keel had been forced up almost to the surface, as if lifted there by some tremendous force below.

Marine Private Edward McKay of Hartford, a key witness, offered

The battleship Maine *was 318 feet long by 57 feet beam and weighed 6,682 tons. She was armed with four 10-inch, six 6-inch and fifteen smaller guns.*

the only argument contesting the assumption of a mine. Had a mine exploded, the water of the harbor would have been disturbed. McKay had been on deck at the time, and was asked by the American court: "Did you feel any water thrown up into the air?" "No sir," replied McKay, "none at all." Blandin, before he died, was also questioned about the water, and replied, "None fell on me, and I saw none fall around me."

Such negative testimony was disparaged in the news that reached America. While much had been said of the part that yellow journalism played in whipping up sentiment for war, most of it is true. James Gordon Bennett and William Randolph Hearst competed in building circulation for their papers. It was not enough to report the news; one had to make it—and making war was making news. Even the prize-endow-

ing Joseph Pulitzer confessed after 1898 that he "rather liked the idea of war—not a big one—but one that would arouse interest and reflect in circulation figures." Hearst's rebuke to his staff artist Frederic Remington, who complained a lack of military subject matter, is a classic: "You furnish the pictures, and I'll furnish the war."

Spanish authorities in Cuba did their best to keep inflammatory information from reaching the United States. The cable to Key West was under tight control, and news concerning the *Maine* was strictly censored. Reporters did their ingenious best to get past the restrictions. Following the catastrophe, one correspondent cabled home a description of Havana, the beauty of the scenery, the sunlight gleaming on the harbor, and "buzzards roosting on the keel of the *Maine.*" His editor winced at the reporter's boner. How could buzzards roost on the keel of a battleship riding upright in the harbor? He crossed the line out.

"Preparations for war go on apace at all defensible points in Boston Harbor."

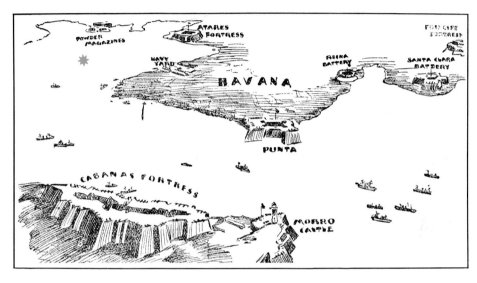

Captain Charles D. Sigsbee of the Maine *believed that "a naval officer should pour ice water over his personal feelings in time of emergency . . .*

The harbor of Havana, showing the arrangement of defenses. The Maine *was positioned opposite the powder magazine when she was blown up.*

Another correspondent, however, scooped the verdict of the Board of Inquiry. He received a tip that evidence pointed to destruction by a mine. But how to get such critical information past the censor? He dispatched an innocent story on the Yankee sailor's love of poetry, of Rudyard Kipling in particular, and inserted a Kipling passage that contained the lines, *The doom-bolt in the darkness freed, / The mine that splits the main.* The censor shrugged his shoulders at this literary twaddle and okayed the story. In another hour "the mine that split the *Maine*" made headline news throughout America.

This was indeed the conclusion of the court of inquiry as released officially March 21, just one month after starting the proceedings. No one was surprised by the verdict that "the *Maine* was destroyed by

the explosion of a submarine mine" (an opinion supported by further investigation when the hull was raised in 1911). But, added the report, there was nothing to connect the Spanish government with this atrocity.

Few paid attention to the latter observation. The cry for justice and revenge was loud across America. On March 21, before the report was published, the cautious Boston *Herald* assured its readers that "there is no warlike significance to be attached to activity now noted at our forts and seacoast defenses." Two days later it announced: "Preparations for war go on apace at all defensible points in Boston Harbor." Similar preparations were observed at Portland, Portsmouth, and New Bedford. The Watertown Arsenal went on a round-the-clock alert, Fort Winthrop was reactivated, while

"never in the history of the Newport Naval Training Station was more activity apparent."

Nowhere in the United States was the fate of the *Maine* and its significance more hotly debated than throughout New England. Hawks and Doves were almost equally divided. Calling for war, Boston's youthful fiery Henry Cabot Lodge told Congress: "I have no more doubt than that I am now standing in the Senate of the United States that that ship was blown up by a government mine, fired by, or with the connivance of, Spanish Socials." To which Senators Hoar of Massachusetts, Frye of Maine, and Gallinger of New Hampshire added their vigorous endorsement.

Opposing the Hawks were the weighty voices of Senator Thomas Reed of Maine and that "topmost oak" of New England, Charles William Eliot of Cambridge, who denounced America's "battleship diplomacy" and referred to warmongers Theodore Roosevelt and Lodge

as "degenerate sons of Harvard." Professor Elliot Norton of that university advised his students to resist involvement. Gamaliel Bradford, descendant of the first Governor of Plymouth Colony, helped organize a league of "Anti-Imperialists" in Massachusetts (from which so many of the *Maine*'s crew came), with Brookline's George S. Boutwell, former Secretary of the Treasury, as its president.

But the clincher came from Senator Redfield Proctor of Vermont, who perhaps more than any other individual swayed American opinion toward war. Returning from a tour of Cuba, he delivered on March 17 "one of the most influential speeches in the history of the United States." Describing the desperate plight of Cubans under Spanish rule, he had Congress all but clamoring for war with Spain; and only Thomas Reed opposed him.

The wreck of the Maine *lay in Havana Harbor for fourteen years before she was raised. The 64 bodies imprisoned in her hull were buried in Washington's Arlington Cemetery. On March 16, 1912 the twisted wreck of the* Maine *was towed out to sea and sunk with impressive ceremony.*

Noting that Proctor owned marble quarries in Vermont, Reed dryly observed that Proctor's position might have been expected, since "war will make a large market for gravestones."

But as Reed himself said, trying to stem the martial tide was like trying to harness a tornado. Even Boston's philosopher William James saw no retreat from the fighting spirit that possessed the country. Americans rushed to war, wrote Richard Harding Davis, like college undergraduates participating in a cane spree. "Remember the *Maine!*" was their declaration of intent; but their spirit was better reflected in a song

now wildly popular from Maine to California: *There'll Be a Hot Time in the Old Town Tonight.*

Spanish officials worked hard to avert the conflict, even offering autonomy to Cuba; but America's ultimatum, calling for complete evacuation of the island, was rejected. War was declared on April 25, and the first shot was fired at a Spanish merchantman off Florida, who thought he was being honored by a courteous salute.

Considering how many had advocated war with Spain, a surprising amount of panic gripped the six New England states. Rumors were rampant that the Spanish Admiral Cervera with a mighty fleet was planning to bombard the open seacoast with its unprotected bathing beaches. Wrote Gregory Mason, of that summer at Cape Cod, "I found that the annual sea-serpent scare in Buzzards Bay had been supplanted by the much more vivid fear of 'Spanish cruiser.'" The Navy Department was so "bedevilled" (wrote Assistant Secretary Roosevelt) with pleas for protection that the North Atlantic fleet was split, one squadron being sent to Cuba, the other to guard Nahant and other Boston Brahmin colonies.

Actually, the opposing forces were peculiarly uneven. Spain had a standing army of half a million men, with 200,000 in Cuba alone. America's standing army numbered only 28,000 plus an ill-trained National Guard (some units of which refused to serve for reasons of social snobbery). But this was to be a naval war; and although the Spanish navy ranked numerically above our own, it had suffered serious neglect, while the "New Navy" of the United States was fast, smart, and efficient. The surprises were to come at sea.

Some months previous, in his home town of Montpelier, Vermont, George B. Dewey had told a friend: "There will be no war before I retire from the Navy, and I will be known in history only by the records of the Naval Department." In the month of May, Dewey joined the ranks of the immortals. Entering the Philippine harbor of Manila with his six-ship squadron headed by the *Boston* and *Concord,* Dewey made history with the command, "You may fire when ready, Gridley." In less than seven hours superior Yankee gunnery "reduced the Spanish fleet to junk" (quoting Samuel Eliot Morison) without the loss of a single man in battle.

But it was at Cuba that the *Maine* was most decisively "remembered." The much-feared fleet of Admiral Cervera had not attacked the bathing beaches of New England. Against Cervera's better judgment, it had been ordered to Santiago, and was bottled up in that harbor by Admiral Sampson's Atlantic Squadron, including the *Gloucester,* captained by Commander Wainwright of the *Maine,* the battleship *Massachusetts,* and the swift and mighty *Oregon,* which had steamed 14,000 miles around Cape Horn to join the fray.

Cervera was a gallant man. As American troops closed in on Santiago, sparked by Roosevelt's Rough Riders, he knew his fleet was doomed. But he preferred to go down fighting. Steaming deliberately into the mouth of the trap, he met the American fleet head on, and lost his entire force of seven ships in less than 240 minutes. The *Maine* had been avenged; the outcome of the war was settled.

What happened subsequently—in the Philippines, in Cuba, and in Puerto Rico—has little bearing on the story of the *Maine,* and some of it reflects no credit on the valiant sacrifice of those aboard her. But long before the autumn leaves had fallen in New England, Spain had been vanquished as a New World empire. In a war that had lasted just 115 days, the United States had usurped her place and risen to a first-rate power, a position it would never lose.

The cost in human life was slight for so significant a victory. Total casualties for the Americans on land and sea were 4023, but only 385 of these were lost in battle (yellow fever took a 13 times more deadly toll). In the Navy alone, only 17 had perished. Fifteen times that number died aboard the *Maine* before hostilities had even started.

What of the few who did not go down with that memorable ship? A letter dated July 11, 1967, from Adjutant General James H. McElroy of the United Spanish War Veterans reads: "There are no survivors of the *Maine* left. The last one we knew of was Admiral Cluverius of Worcester, Massachusetts, who died several years ago."

And what of the *Maine* itself, or what was left of her? Even before the war began, Senator Eugene Hale of the state of Maine pressed a measure on Congress for funds to raise the sunken ship and recover the 64 bodies still imprisoned in her hull. This was not done until 1911–12, when the hulk was raised and the remains of the seamen transported to Washington's Arlington Cemetery (many others had been buried at Key West after the catastrophe). Then the twisted wreck, garlanded with flowers and escorted by a naval cortege, was towed out to sea.

Boston-born John O'Brien, of the Havana pilots corps, was chosen to ride the hull and guide the towed ship to her burial ground. He remembered later: "I looked across that desolate deck, and there rose in my mind a picture of it bristling with cannon and crowded with strong sailormen. I never felt so much like crying in my life."

Beyond the three-mile limit, the petcocks were opened. The ship seemed at first to resist her fate, and then accepted it. O'Brien wrote: "Down she went, smoothly and with almost incredible velocity, her decks exploding under the pressure and hurling masses of flowers and clouds of spray into the air. In a moment she was gone."

It is doubtful if the "splendid little war" with Spain is much recalled in this day of greater power struggles. Is there any reason in 1968 to resurrect the story of a single battleship, or "remember the *Maine*" as more than a dying echo in the halls of history? Captain Sigsbee offered a reason, 70 years ago, in writing: "In the way that the men of the *Maine* died and suffered there was enough of the heroic to provide a sound foundation for the motto . . ." He was speaking also of a sound foundation for the future of America.

Commercial lines served all New England. Section V records their moments of prosperity and failure . . .

. . . Some of these GREAT YANKEE LINES are still in existence.

The "Dionis," first locomotive of the Nantucket Railroad. She made her inaugural run on July 4, 1881.

ACTIVE *and* DIONIS

Without a railroad, "all spirit of improvement will depart from our borders, the town will become a waste, a howling wilderness; rats and mud turtles will crawl over our streets, and owls and bats will sit in our high places." And with this as the alternative, so began the story of two colorful and all-but-forgotten island railroads.

by John H. Ackerman

The locomotive "Active" of the Martha's Vineyard Railroad. This photograph was taken in Oak Bluffs.

A century ago, railroad fever was very much with us. Like any affliction, it was democratic. It attacked rich and poor alike; it was known in the crowded cities and in rural hamlets drowsing in green shade. It drove shining rails westward to the Sierras and the Golden Gate; and it sent lightly laid track curling up Vermont swales and along the beaches of Martha's Vineyard and Nantucket.

Two more unlikely victims of railroad fever cannot be found. Both islands had prospered on a mix of agriculture, whaling, and fishing; both had suffered declines after the Civil War as whale oil gave way to petroleum from Pennsylvania. Neither island had then or has now any physical connection with the main-

land save the steamboat and, in these latter times, the plane. Both had sniffed the breezes of possible economic salvation in the post-Civil War travel and resort trade.

Martha's Vineyard succumbed first and with virulence to railroad fever.

"We want a railroad and we are going to have it," thundered Edgar Marchant, editor of the *Vineyard Gazette,* at an 1874 Edgartown meeting called to debate the merits of investing $15,000 of town money in the proposed railroad.

"Manufactures will come with some of the men this road will cause to come here. Build this road and manufactures will come along . . . and we shall be a very Vineyard indeed. Refuse to encourage and lend

our aid to this enterprise, and this town will disappear into the darkness of oblivion. All spirit of improvement will depart from our borders, men of brains will go where they can use them, and for aught I see to the contrary, the town will become a waste, a howling wilderness; rats and mud turtles will crawl over our streets, and owls and bats sit in our high places."

Neither owls, bats, rats nor mud turtles deterred critics at the same meeting from speaking up and out. Typical of those who disagreed with Mr. Marchant's prophecy was Ichabod N. Luce—boatbuilder, California goldseeker, Massachusetts Legislator, Abolitionist, Free Soiler, keeper of the Gay Head Light and customs inspector. "It is in my inter-

161

est, personally," he said, "to play second fiddle for this road, to electioneer for it, to vote for it, and all that, but my conscience will not allow it."

A two-thirds vote in favor was required for approval; when the silences came, the measure passed with a one-vote margin.

Possibly Editor Marchant had been unwise in mentioning bats and owls, two creatures frequently regarded as ill omens. For the Martha's Vineyard Railroad, from the very start, was embarrassingly rich in ill omens.

To take the ill omens in order: trouble erupted immediately over the route of the proposed narrow-gauge line. One faction demanded an inland route from Oak Bluffs south and east to Edgartown and beyond to Katama and South Beach, the sandy southern margin of the Vineyard. The other faction wanted a cheaper, easier-to-build line running between the Beach Road and the water and linking the same communities. The sea captains who were quick to invest their money in the railroad seemed curiously blind to the fact the chosen route along the beach was vulnerable to high tides and storms. Washouts and the subsequent repairs proved grievously costly in later years.

Construction was barely under way when the workmen struck; they were getting $1.75 a day and wanted $2.00. Replacement of the disgruntled navvies took time.

At Sengekontacket Inlet, an island builder pushed the railroad bridge out from one shore, a mainland builder from the other. When they met, the elevations of the two sections differed by two inches. With some pride, Henry Beetle Hough, editor of the *Vineyard Gazette,* points out the error was made by the off-islander.

Optimism over the completion of the line in that summer of 1874 proved unwarranted. A newspaper prophecy predicting its completion by June 20 was in error; completion by July 2 declared sure; the arrival of the necessary rails and ties on July 17 duly noted. By July 24, failure to complete and operate the railroad was estimated to be causing a loss of $250 a day and there was no rolling stock yet at hand.

That rolling stock had been ordered. A Vineyard committee had been sent ashore with a purse of $9,000. For this sum, the committee procured one coach brave in brass and red plush; one excursion coach with seats running lengthwise; one boxcar that doubled in brass as a coach and could seat 22 persons, and a dummy coach-locomotive combination that could accommodate 24.

Dummy engines were so called because they were designed to mislead apprehensive horses. Their

wheels, side rods, valve gear, and boiler were all shrouded in sheet metal or, as in the case of the Vineyard model, enclosed at the front end of an ordinary appearing coach. Dummy engines were used, before the advent of the electric trolley car, to haul trailers on city street railways and along short resort pikes.

Builder of the Vineyard dummy was Jerome Wheelock of Worcester who guaranteed a speed of 25 miles an hour pulling 150 persons, and 320 miles per ton of coal. He made no statements as to the dummy's ability to take curves—which was just as well: on its inaugural run, August 7, the dummy proceeded down the track to the first curve and stopped. Its sprocket-driven rigid front truck was unable to go around the curve.

The whole matter ended in opprobrium of a high order. Like much Yankee opprobrium of a high order, it ended up in court, with Wheelock losing the case to the chagrined Vineyarders who said his dummy suffered from "general debility" and made other unkind remarks.

Apparently, after some tinkering, the dummy did go into service after a fashion. It proved too frail to pull the other two coaches and the boxcar, suffered from hotboxes and utterly failed to deceive Vineyard horses, who were prone to try and climb beach plums when the dummy panted into view.

With the best part of the summer well past and the receipts of their railroad virtually invisible, the desperate islanders shopped around hastily for a locomotive and found one named "Active" built by the respected firm of H. K. Porter of Pittsburgh, Pennsylvania. Hopes had soared by August 21; Active and her tender had arrived at Woods Hole on Cape Cod, closest port to the Vineyard. But the ill omens lingered; a couple of freight cars being switched about the yards nudged the hapless Active and her tender into Woods Hole Harbor. Rescued by a crane, Active proved to be congested with seaweed and suffering from a damaged cowcatcher. A trip to the shops of the Old Colony Railroad near Boston for surgery was necessary.

On August 28, the restored Active was gently lowered to the wharf at Oak Bluffs and went into service immediately, hauling delighted islanders, bemused magnates, and summer visitors along the nine-mile right-of-way. But it was an all-too-short triumph. Hasty jury-rigging of the line's finances was demanded after the sheriff attached the rolling stock for debts in November of 1874. In 1875, matters brightened a bit; the little line hauled 28,911 passengers some 12,554 miles and earned $5,002.62.

The road was hardly a gold

Above: The Martha's Vineyard Railroad ran from Oak Bluffs to Edgartown and beyond to Katama Lodge on South Beach (shown in the photograph on the opposite page). Crowds came to the Vineyard aboard steamboats and rode the railroad to Katama.

Vineyard horses were prone to climb beach plums when the dummy panted into view

mine though. By 1877, disillusioned Edgartown voters sold the town's interest in the railroad for the meager sum of $315; owls and bats could hold no terrors for sufferers from railroad fever. And yet, the little pike survived . . . somehow. For one thing, the Vineyarders who built it proved quite accurate in their assessment of their island's charm for mainlanders. Despite the financial losses suffered by Edgartown, Editor Hough opines the railroad was well worth the cost. It did make of Edgartown and Oak Bluffs two popular summer resorts. Trains of the Old Colony Railroad, 30 cars long and pulled by three engines, deposited Vineyard-bound excursionists at the Woods Hole dock where they boarded the steamer for Oak Bluffs and the cars of the Martha's Vineyard Railroad waiting for them. Clambakes and picnics drew thousands to the island; their descendants have been returning ever since.

The 1890s saw hopes rise even higher; the Old Colony bought the Vineyard railroad. But the depression of the early 1890s offset the Old Colony move. Summer business fell off. The hotel at the line's Oak Bluffs Terminal burned; with the hotel perished the line's terminal and its turning wye. In 1894, the railroad halted all service south of Edgartown, but the cutback failed to help. In 1896, the little train ran for the last time.

Little is left on the Vineyard today to recall the railroad's days of glory. But Edgartown is crowded with summer residents, its harbor stuffed with expensive yachts, and its streets with expensive cars—and neither bats nor rats, owls nor mud turtles are to be seen.

Sole reminder, in fact, is a service station located on the site of the old Edgartown depot. A very large very outgoing railroad buff named Jesse Morgan has perpetuated the

---

Below: The "Active" of the Martha's Vineyard Railroad was built by the H. K. Porter Company of Pittsburgh, Pa., long-time locomotive builders. "Active" boasted a cowcatcher and headlight that was rather overpowering for a 3-foot-gauge engine.

Right: Locomotive "Active" and three cars of the Martha's Vineyard Railroad wait on the wharf at Oak Bluffs. The sidewheeler steamer *Martha's Vineyard* is at dock. Note the diminutive station with the Old Colony baggage room at this end, New Bedford-bound baggage room at the other.

The "Sconset" of the Nantucket Railroad. The engine drive wheels could swivel beneath the boiler for sharp curves.

memory of the little railroad by naming his place of business the Depot Corner Service Station; by naming his service truck, Active; by installing a train arrival-and-departure board with his hours of business chalked upon it; and by decorating his gasoline pumps with a handsome wooden cutout of an old diamond-stacked locomotive and coach.

Railroad fever did not assume a virulent form on Nantucket until 1880, perhaps because it is farther out to sea than the Vineyard. To a contemporary newcomer to the island, arriving by air and seeing, far below, a piece of land so small as to lead him to wonder if the stewardess will give him a parachute and a friendly shove, the notion of a railroad on Nantucket may seem ludicrous and most unlikely.

But it seemed quite likely in 1880. The prosperity of the whaling era had gone decades before, but the sharp-eyed descendants of generations of whalemen discerned the attractions their island home had for summer visitors. Perhaps because the Nantucket line was privately fi-

nanced, its birth pangs were not a matter of acrimonious public record and its beginnings were seemly and decorous. Philip H. Folger organized the company; it received a charter in 1880 and made its inaugural run on July 4, 1881. Like the Vineyard railroad, the Nantucket line was a narrow-gauge line with the rails just three feet apart.

Its downtown depot was at Main and Candle Streets, handy to the steamboat wharf; its ultimate terminal was at Surfside on the southern edge of the island, conceived as a resort area for concerts and clambakes a few years earlier. There were flag stops here and there along the line.

On July 4, 1881, Engineer C. M. Stansbury helped himself to a handful of throttle and the locomotive "Dionis," named after the wife of Tristram Coffin, puffed away hauling two former Long Island Railroad coaches crammed with

dignitaries, summer visitors, island railroad magnates, and islanders.

Dionis was a classic American-type locomotive built by the Baldwin Locomotive Works with a four-wheel leading truck and four driving wheels. Like most Nantucket Railroad stock then and later, Dionis was second-hand. She came from the Danville, Olney and Ohio River Railroad in deepest Illinois. As Dionis rolled out of town, passengers saw their island in a new light; familiar scenes whirled by . . . the harbor, the flats, Goose Pond, the clay pits, pine groves, and moors.

Surfside was popular and the 25-ton Dionis kept busy hauling trainload after trainload of pleasure-seekers to band concerts and Saturday night dances at the beach resort. In that first year, the railroad carried 30,135 passengers without an accident. Encouraged, the promoters laid more track east to Siasconset at Nantucket's eastern edge. More motive power was called for and Dionis was joined by another second-hand engine, this one built by William Mason in Taunton and purchased from the Boston, Revere

Beach and Lynn. Christened " 'Sconset," the new engine was a so-called Mason bogie, a tank engine whose drive wheels, beneath the boiler, were designed to swivel like an ordinary truck to permit the engine to take sharp curves.

Despite their seafaring background, the dangers of a beachfront right-of-way were no more apparent to Nantucket railroaders than they had been to their Vineyard counterparts. In 1883, pounding surf nearly removed the roadbed and the tracks were moved inland for safety's sake. In 1884, a storm washed out part of the track, and an 1893 gale saw much of the railroad under water and little Dionis unexpectedly taking a salt-water bath.

Other problems also arose. Surfside's charms waned and so did the railroad's passenger business. The railroad beat a strategic retreat, abandoned its Surfside trackage and laid a new, shorter line of track to 'Sconset in 1895. At the time, 'Sconset was just starting its rise to its present costly elevation as an enclave for the very rich. But there was enough stirring there in 1895 to encourage the railroad's new owner, Francis B. Keene, who had picked it up in 1894 for just $10,800. But the railroad was hardly a bargain. Its right-of-way was so casually built that passengers, engine, and cars pitched like a dragger in a gale on the way to 'Sconset. Every spring, the entire line had to be virtually rebuilt.

By 1906, business was so slack the railroad rested, unmoving, for the entire summer season. A stagecoach ran between Nantucket and 'Sconset, though, and its ride, even worse than the trains, belatedly won friends for the railroad. The Macy family of Nantucket lured some New York investors to the scene and persuaded them to take over the little line.

In an effort to economize, the New Yorkers introduced the island to the "Bug." A large box with a gasoline motor, the "Bug" could carry six to eight people plus baggage and additional riders in a sort of wheeled birdcage towed behind. Resembling a child's wooden block atop a roller skate, the four-wheeled "Bug" and its lacy trailer swooped and leaped along the track like a pair of neurotic beetles, frightening riders and amusing spectators.

The "Bug's" failure to win friends saw it exiled, but the New Yorkers, still economy-bent, tried out a sort of Toonerville Trolley with a gasoline engine.' It carried 30 passengers, vibrated like a fulling mill, and was returned to the mainland in disgrace.

In 1910, Nantucketers were heartened: the New Yorkers purchased the road's first brand-new locomotive, two new coaches, and saw to it the roadbed was improved. But the new equipment failed to bolster the line's ebbing revenues.

True, the line did possess an endearing familiarity. Did a passenger's hat blow off? The train politely stopped and waited. Did blueberries beckon? Pickers were deposited amid the laden bushes and retrieved on the return trip. But such personal service, even with new rolling stock, could not overcome the problems inherent in a railroad that ran in warm weather and lay idle in cold. A 1906 Nantucket ban on autos probably boosted the line's revenues, but the island's mood changed a decade later and autos were invited back. It was a final blow to the tottering pike; with a warring Europe hungry for scrap, the railroad was bought by a Boston scrap firm in 1918 and the rails and rolling stock shipped to Bordeaux, France, to do their bit for the AEF.

The passing of the little line was mourned by many Nantucketers who found the idea of selling THEIR railroad for scrap distasteful. Summing up the island's mood of nostalgic regret was a poem quoted on Nantucket:

O, flagman by the Goose-Pond
  shore
Your banner waves in vain;
For you shall greet O never-
  more,
Dionis and her train!

STEAM BOAT   MASSACHUSETS

BOSTON & SALEM

Kneass, Young & Co. Philad.

ADMIT
The Bearer

Politics, prejudice, the financial problems plagued the Boston & Hingham Steamboat Company from the beginning; but prosperity, perseverance, and the popularity of the fabulous seaside resorts helped pioneer the beginning of . . .

THE OLDEST STEAMBOAT LINE

It was warm that June day in Salem 153 years ago. A light breeze hardly ruffled the blue waters of the bay and a sailing packet bound for Nahant and Boston was having difficulty making any headway against the flooding tide. It was a peaceful scene except for the fact that an eager crowd had gathered on Crowningshield's Wharf, drawn there by the news arriving by stage that morning from Boston: the steamboat *Massachusetts* was on its way up to Salem.

There was nothing particularly exciting to Salemites about the arrival of another ship—that was a daily occurrence since Salem was one of the leading maritime ports in America—but these watchers were agog with excitement, for not one of them had ever seen a steamboat—that is, until now.

The *Massachusetts* had been built for some adventurous Salem businessmen in Philadelphia in 1816. On the 25th of April, 1817, she set sail on her maiden voyage north. The engine had broken down in heavy weather off the Jersey coast, and two schooners had towed her up off Atlantic Highlands where the hawsers broke and she was cast adrift. Then a stiff easterly sprang up and the *Massachusetts* was able to make New York under sail.

After temporary repairs to the engine, the steamboat proceeded up the East River with a favorable tide and through Long Island Sound to Newport, where further repairs had to be made to the temperamental power plant; then on round the Cape to Salem, where she was arriving five weeks after her departure from Philadelphia.

When the boat appeared off the entrance to Salem Harbor, she presented a strange sight to the enthralled spectators on the wharves. The shape of the hull was familiar enough to the seafaring Salemites; it was that of a typical sailing vessel of the period, with bluff bows, billet headed, a single mast stepped well forward, and with an overhang transom stern. But with that, all similarity with anything afloat at that time ended. Rising amid-ships from the deck just aft the mast was a great iron-tapered stovepipe almost as tall as the mast with the top bent back at right angles. From the opening the flames and smoke were spitting out so that the whole effect was that of a fiery dragon. Behind the stack were the paddle boxes with a huge wooden beam above, rising and falling slowly as the boat proceeded at about five miles an hour up the harbor. Instead of paddle wheels familiar to us, she was propelled by two sets of oars fastened to a rotating shaft.

The purpose of the owners was to run a daily service between Salem and Boston in competition with the sailing packets and the stage line, but another three weeks went by while the engine was being repaired again. Crowds gathered on the dock to watch the work in progress. There was much speculation about the safety of the new mode of transportation. What would happen when the engine broke down at sea, and how about a boiler explosion or fire breaking out? Then too, how could the boat be operated at a profit considering the cost of fuel (wood, of course) and the high wages they'd

have to pay the engineer?

The proprietors of the *Massachusetts*—sensing the prejudice against the vessel—must have inspired a reassuring article in the Salem Register, the local newspaper of that period, which pointed out that the boiler was made of copper, not wood; that it had been tested for four times the pressure needed to propel the boat and that to render it still more safe, there were two safety valves, one in the control of the Captain, and the other in the control of the Engineer, and that if the boiler did blow up, it was so located that it would not injure the passengers! And furthermore, the article went on, "there was an apparatus attached to the engine capable of discharging fifteen barrels of water a minute from the bilge so that if twenty holes, each one inch in diameter, were bored in her bottom the engine would discharge the water as fast as it came in." What could be safer!

Finally the repairs were completed and the *Massachusetts* paddled off to Boston on her first and last trip with a passenger list of adventurous souls who paid one dollar fare for a three-hour trip.

The prophets of gloom were right; the *Massachusetts* was not a success and it would hardly deserve mention in the history of steamboating if it had not been for one trip she made that pioneered the starting of the oldest steamboat line in continuous service in the Western Hemisphere—the Boston and Hingham Steamboat Company.

That momentous trip occurred on July 15, 1817 when the *Massa-*

IN THE WESTERN HEMISPHERE

by Thomas P. Smith

chusetts churned her way down Boston Harbor and into the quiet waters of Hingham Bay. One of the passengers was a famous diarist of his time, the Rev. William Bently of Salem. Let him tell of his experience on that historic voyage in his own words:

"Agreed with A. Dunlop Esq. to go with him in a chaise and then from Boston to take passage with him to Hingham in the Steamboat *Massachusetts*. We reached Boston between 7 and 8, but the boat was not ready until 11. We had a pleasant company and moved from Center Wharf. The motion was easy and regular throughout the passage. It so happened that the tide was flood and against us. We passed round the *74 Independence* and were saluted with the music of the ship lying between the town and Noddle's Island. We took our course between Fort Independence and Dorchester point over the flats at full tide, passing between Thompson and Spectacle Island, then between Moon Islets and Long Island, and between Hangman's and Sunk Island and between Nut Island and Puttock's Island, north of Sheep Island, south of Pumpkin Island, and near the point of land running west from Hingham Beach on the way to Nantasket, called World's End, and into a little basin where are the wharves of Hingham. We went to the Rev. Mr. Richardson's where we were hospitably entertained. After dinner, to get our passage up, we passed to Crow Point about 4 miles from our landing in the road and 2 minutes west. We passed around Otis Hill and then left on our right or E, the inlet in which lay Ragged and Button and Sara Islets, and after several risings we reached the top of the beautiful hill near Crow Point, from which we had a beautiful view of the surrounding country and islands and then descended suddenly to the point at which our boat was anchored. On our return we passed between Grass and Sheep Islands and kept our course so as to pass between Spectacle and Cattle Islands and up ship Channel to the Town. Both passages were performed in about two hours without any particular trial to the force of the steam engines.

"The direct distance ten statute miles and about fourteen miles in our course giving us between six and seven miles an hour without any exertion whatever. The boat answered every expectation and when an accommodation is given for landing at every tide, will find this cruise a safe and pleasant one."

In spite of the Rev. Bently's persuasive propaganda about the trip, the *Massachusetts* never came

again. She was sold to parties in Mobile, Alabama, and ran aground on her trip south at Little Egg Harbor in New Jersey and was lost. Seafaring New Englanders preferred sail to steam.

There were two rival packet lines serving Hingham then, the Republican Line and the Federalist Line, named respectively for the two political parties struggling for power in the country. Acrimonious political debates in Congress found their echoes on the wharves in Hingham. If you were a staunch Republican, you wouldn't step foot over the rail of a Federalist packet. Both lines maintained vociferous barkers at Broad Bridge where Main Street crossed the Town Brook, ballyhooing the virtues of their respective ships. You couldn't cross the Bridge on a sailing day without being buttonholed by these insistent salesmen. To be able to list your occupation as "Packet-Master" in the town records was a mark of distinction.

It remained for the *Eagle*—the next steamboat to appear in Hingham Harbor—to break through the crust of prejudice against steamboating. She was only ninety-two feet long, but the advertising poster described her as having palatial accommodations for 200 people. Hingham took the *Eagle* to its heart. Perhaps her greatest asset was her Captain Barnabus Lincoln, Hingham-born and a blue-water sailor. His schooner *Emily* had been captured and burned off Boston Light by the British during the War of 1812. He acted as agent, ticket collector and skipper of the *Eagle* and everyone knew and trusted him.

The *Eagle* began more or less regular service between Boston and Hingham in 1819, and continued until 1821. Even under the skillful navigation of Captain Barney Lincoln, the trip occasionally had its exciting moments. Hingham Harbor, then as now, was pretty shallow, and sometimes when the wind was across the course, the little boat would nose into the mud and go hard and fast aground. Thereupon the men would roll up their pants, pick up the lady passengers and in spite of their squeals step over-board and wade ashore with their breathless burdens. Then with his lightened ship, Skipper Barney would be able to back up and proceed to the wharf. This happened so often that the bullfrogs in the marshes along World's End learned to intone in monotonous chorus, "Backup—Backup—Backup." You can hear them to this day.

As a dashing sea captain, Barney had many female admirers. One young lady in particular pursued him assiduously, making frequent trips as a passenger on the *Eagle* so that she could be near her idol, somewhat to the embarrassment of Lincoln, who was happily married and had two children. One day the *Eagle* ran aground while the young lady was on board. She insisted that only the skipper could carry her ashore. So in spite of the tradition that a captain never abandons his ship, Barney picked her up and started for the beach. Half way to the land he gently disengaged her loving arms from round his neck and dropped her in the mud to let her make her own way ashore. That ended the romance.

After the *Eagle* discontinued her Hingham run in 1821, Captain Barney Lincoln took to sail on the high seas again. He left Boston in November in command of the trading schooner *Exertion* bound for Trinidad. When less than 150 miles from its destination, the schooner was captured by pirates. After humiliating and barbarous treatment by the pirates, Barney and four of his crew were abandoned on a small key in the West Indies, there to die of hunger and thirst. And that would have been the fate of the castaways, had it not been for one of the band of cutthroats called "Nichola." In spite of his name and occupation, Nichola wasn't a Mexican bandit like his pals, but a redheaded Scotsman named Nicholas Jamieson. He had been captured by the pirates sometime before and offered the choice of joining with them or walking the plank. Being Scot, he chose the former course. Through some secret grip, he recognized Captain Lincoln as a fellow Mason and from that time on began to plan how he could rescue the captives and himself escape from the pirate band. One night when his shipmates were deep in their cups, he seized the ship's pinnace, sailed over to the key, picked up Captain Barney and his four companions, and with them set sail for the Florida Coast where they finally landed. Captain Lincoln was so grateful to his rescuer that he promised to help him if he ever decided to settle in America.

Sure enough, Nicholas sent word to Captain Barney later that he had reached New York and needed help. So the good Captain had Nichola come to Hingham, where he promptly settled in with the Lincolns. He went to sea as mate for Captain Lincoln several times and finally started a school in Hingham where he taught navigation to young men anxious to go to sea, until he himself was unable to navigate due to too close addiction to the bottle.

Following the *Eagle* on the Boston to Hingham run came the *Lafayette,* a crude little craft smaller than the *Eagle.* She had been built originally with a wooden boiler, which blew up on her trial trip in the Sound with fifty passengers

aboard. She was rebuilt and named the *Lafayette* in honor of the Marquis de Lafayette, who made his triumphal visit to the United States in the year she was built. The poor little *Lafayette* only lasted a season or two. It took her two hours to make the trip to Boston, and often if there was a strong head wind she'd have to turn around and come back. She was finally sold for duty on the St. Crois River in Maine.

So far, steamboating had not been a financial success. There were sporadic attempts to organize a line to run between New Bedford and Nantucket, but the steamboats were so underpowered that the trip took at least eight hours in fair weather and had to be abandoned entirely when there was a head wind or a rough sea. The attempts had always ended in financial disaster. It didn't look like a profitable field for investment.

It was not until 1831 that any serious attempt was made in America to organize a stock company to operate a steamboat line. The moving spirit behind this venture was David Whiton who owned a hay, grain and feed store at the harbor in Hingham.

Whiton was a versatile man. He had, five years earlier, been one of the organizers of the Hingham Mutual Fire Insurance Company, serving that Company as its first treasurer. Then in 1831, he was one of the incorporators and a director of the Hingham Bank (now the National Bank of Plymouth County). And in 1834, he was one of the "corporators" of the Hingham Institution for Savings, acting as its president until he died in 1843. He was also an active member of the "Mutual Aid Society for the Detection of Thieves in Hingham"—the only police force the town had for many years. How he found time to handle sacks of grain in his store must remain a mystery.

Whiton, whose brother and an uncle were both swashbuckling "packet-masters," must have been alive to the risks of steamboating. Yet he proceeded to raise $20,000 by selling 80 shares of stock in the new venture at $250 each to his fellow townsmen. In spite of the gamble these investors took, no purchaser ever had occasion to regret his investment. For many years the stock never paid less than 10% a year and at least once it paid 50%.

The new Boston and Hingham Steam Boat Company, as it was called, purchased the *General Lincoln* for service on their line. She had two walking beam engines and two smoke stacks with sufficient power to make the run between the two towns in an hour and a half.

The new Company left no stone unturned to make its new venture a success. To attract passengers,

To be among the elite in Boston you had to have a summer home along the shore

the Company built a luxurious summer hotel on Neck Gate Hill (now Old Colony Hill) in Hingham called the Old Colony House, just above its dock at the harbor. To stay there as a guest cost real money. The rate per diem including meals (four of them) was $1.50. If you could afford to stay a week the rate was seven dollars. There were, to be sure, certain restrictions. You couldn't smoke above the ground floor and you were forbidden to deface the white columns that supported the piazza by carving or writing on them. And if you wanted breakfast you had to be in the dining room by 7 A.M.

As an added attraction to the trip down the harbor, the "Boston Brigade Band" was frequently employed to entertain the passengers. The captain of the *General Lincoln* was George Beal who served the Company for more than fifty years both as captain and pilot.

The Steamboat Company was faced at the start by the problem of docking in Hingham Harbor at all tides. Its first dock was built on Mr. Burr's land on the north side of Mansfield's Cove on the spit of land known as World's End. Here was erected a windmill to supply the ship with water and a huge wood pile for fuel. The only approach to the wharf by land was by way of Martin's Lane, so foot passengers had a long walk to get to town. To overcome this handicap, the Company built a floating bridge across the mouth of the Cove to Captain Laban Hersey's land on the other side. But Captain Laban Hersey was a "packet-master" and he had no use for the steamboat, and he served notice that no one was to cross his land. The boat Company posted guards night and day to protect the bridge, but one night it was cut loose and floated off. It never was replaced. The Company then built a new pier at Barnes Rocks to overcome the difficulty.

The new steamboat line still had to overcome the feeling of many people that traveling on the water in a boat with a boiler and a fire under it was dangerous. Many people hesitated to try this new method of transportation just as many today feel that flying is too risky. George Beal, the skipper of the *General Lincoln,* like Barney Lincoln in the old *Eagle,* had a lot to do with giving timorous people confidence. It is said that prospective passengers would arrive on the dock, look over the rail and if Beal was in his pilot house, all was well with their world.

Actually, the steamboat company started operations at an auspicious time. The only means of travel to Boston were by Wilder's stage which took three hours for the trip, or the rather uncertain sailings of the packets which were dependent on wind and tide. The South Shore Railroad connecting Hingham with the Old Colony Railroad in Braintree was still seventeen years in the future.

Then, too, resort hotels were beginning to spring up along the coast and the steamboat was the comfortable way to reach them. The wharf on Beach Street in Hingham would become alive when the evening boat from Boston was due, with stages for Nantasket, Scituate and Marshfield, and with horses and carriages of summer residents along the South Shore. On one such summer afternoon a young Hingham lad had been fishing in the harbor and got back to the dock with his catch just as the steamer was discharging its passengers. An impressive passenger dressed in a blue long-tailed coat with brass buttons, a cream-colored waistcoat and buff trousers tucked into shiny black shoes, stepped up to the youngster and said, "I'd like to buy those fish from you." "I'm sorry," the lad replied, "but I'm taking these fish home to my mother for her supper." The immaculate gentleman nodded and turned away. A bystander, who had watched the whole proceedings, turned to the boy and said, "Do you know who that man was who wanted to buy your fish?" "No Sir," the boy replied. "Well," said the bystander, "that man was Daniel Webster and if you live to be a hundred, don't you ever forget this day." The boy did live to be over ninety and to become president of the steamboat line, and he never did forget the story. Nor have his grandchildren.

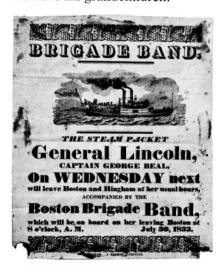

A typical handbill of the period. The General Lincoln *was purchased by the "new" Boston and Hingham Company about 1831.*

Right: The Eagle *was in more or less regular service between Boston and Hingham from the years 1819 to 1821. She was captained by Barney Lincoln, who had more female admirers than a happily married man would want.*

172

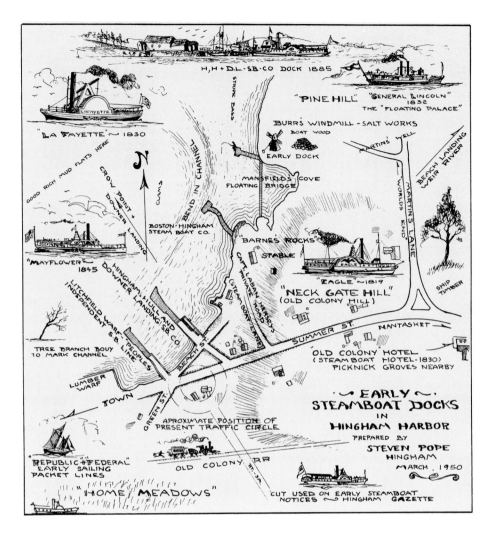

Left: The first dock in Hingham Harbor was built on Mr. Burr's land on the north side of Mansfield's Cove known as World's End. The approach by sea was shallow and sometimes complicated by wind. When the wind's direction was across the course, small steamboats would nose into the mud. According to legend, this happened so often that the bullfrogs in the marshes learned to intone in monotonous chorus, "Back up—back up—back up." Eventually the Company built a new pier at Barnes' Rocks.

The *General Lincoln* continued in service until 1844 when she was sold to be used as a towboat in Boston Harbor, and the next year she helped pull the Cunarder *Cambria* off the beach at Truro where she had run aground.

In 1854 the *Mayflower,* especially built for the Boston and Hingham Steam Boat Company, was put in service. She was much larger than the *General Lincoln* and could accommodate 800 passengers. Each succeeding boat through the years was larger and more luxurious than its predecessors and almost without exception they were named after some local hero or figure or place in colonial history. There were two *General Lincoln*s, three *Nantasket*s, two *Rose Standish*es, and one *Governor Andrew* named after our famous Civil War governor. He had been a regular commuter during the summers he lived in Hingham.

From the beginning all the boats were kept in top condition. During the years when Charles B. Barnes, who lived above the pier in Hingham, was president of the line and commuted regularly to his office in Boston, all hands on board from the skipper to the stoker knew that

nothing out of order would escape his eagle eye or caustic (and fearful) tongue.

Every Sunday morning during the summer season, Barnes would stand on the knoll in front of his house with his eye glued to a telescope to watch for the morning boat on its trip down from Boston. When it came through Hull Gut, if it didn't have a full complement of passengers on board, his language would be so vitriolic that Mother Barnes would have to hurry the children out of ear shot.

Every morning when Barnes appeared at his front door in his business suit, a Prince Albert, striped trousers, square-toed Congress boots, and a top hat firmly set on his head with his business papers stashed in the crown, the skipper would know that it was time to cast off. No need to look at his chronometer!

The story goes that one day when President Barnes was looking

---

The Mayflower *was especially built for the Boston and Hingham Steamboat Company. She eventually collided with a United Fruit boat in the channel. She is presently berthed in a mud bank at Nantasket.*

over the rail on his trip to Boston, a gust of wind blew his hat off into the water with all his precious papers in it. A deckhand seeing the accident promptly dove overboard, rescued the hat and the papers, and presented them with a flourish to Mr. Barnes, who reached into his pocket and presented the sailor with a dime as a reward for his bravery.

Until after the Civil War, the Boston and Hingham Steam Boat Company was able to take care of its traffic with one steamboat in commission each summer. During the war the United States Government took over two of its ships—first the *Nantasket* and a year later the *Rose Standish*—for use as supply ships in southern waters. The line chartered two vessels to replace them, the *Gilpin* and later on the *Halifax,* the latter a stern-wheeler. Then in 1867 a competing line was established called the People's Line. A rate war ensued, fares on both lines dropped from 25¢ to 15¢ and then 10¢ and for at least one month the Boston-Hingham Steam Boat Company carried passengers free. The People's Line finally abandoned Hingham in favor of Strawberry Hill as a terminus and eventually the

older company absorbed its competitor.

By 1870 a great change had begun to take place in the economic and social life of New England. Cotton and woolen factories along its many rivers; mills and machine shops of all kinds were pouring wealth into the pockets of their Boston owners. In Boston, the noisome swamp known as the "Back Bay" was being filled in and stately brownstone mansions were being built on the newly made land.

To be among the elite in Boston, you had to have a summer home along the shore, or spend the summer in the White Mountains or at one of the fashionable beach hotels, like the Atlantic House or Pacific House in Nantasket, or the Hotel Pemberton on Wind Mill Point in Hull. You never left your winter home for your summer vacation, regardless of the weather, until after Harvard Class Day. Then the hegira began. If you were going to the shore your coachman would load a huge pile of horse-hide trunks filled with feminine furbelows and cart them down to the Boston and Hingham Steam Boat at Rowe's Wharf. The family would follow later in a car-

riage. Maybe you were bound for a summer's stay at the Hotel Pemberton in Hull (where only "nice" Bostonians were welcome!) The Pemberton was perhaps the most fabulous (and fastastic) hotel of its era. It was a three-story wooden building with 100 rooms, entirely surrounded by triple deck, wide piazzas. The rooms on the first two floors were luxuriously furnished with black walnut and Brussels carpet. On the top floor the rooms had straw matting and golden ash furniture. The roof had steep gables, towers and minarets. The hotel had wine vaults, its own gas works for lighting, and "a bar of generous proportions." No mention was made of any bathrooms in the contemporary advertising. Every afternoon and evening the guests were entertained by band concerts from an adjoining bandstand. And in the evening you could stroll in a grove lighted with flickering incandescent lamps. The five o'clock boat from Boston would

---

The Addison E. Andrews *was named for the Civil War Governor of Massachusetts. Most of the boats belonging to the Boston and Hingham Steamboat Company were named after some local hero or place in colonial history.*

bring the pater familias down from town at the close of the day.

All of this meant increasing traffic for the steamboat line, but another factor contributed even more.

During this period, a man named Samuel Downer of Boston bought a large tract of land in Hingham, including Crow Point and Otis Hill. He had originally intended to build an oil refinery there, but the beauty of the site, plus the fact that there wasn't enough water to float tankers, led him to turn the area into a pleasure park which he named Melville Gardens, after his wife.

Downer was an altruist. He had refused to join forces with a young bookkeeper in Cleveland named John D. Rockefeller in the oil business because he did not approve of Rockefeller's ruthless methods. He developed Melville Gardens as a summer playground, easily accessible by boat, largely for families from Boston. The Gardens had all kinds of entertainments—a bear pit, a monkey cage, a lagoon, a dancing pavilion, a bowling green, and clambakes at regular intervals to feed the hungry. Not the least of the attractions in the Gardens were twenty

The boats were the finest excursion steamers operating
anywhere in the inland waters in this country

electric lights, a startling innovation in those days. For his friends he built a luxurious summer hotel—the Rose Standish House—on the point and three wharves, one to accommodate freighters and the other two to handle the steamers of the People's Line and the Boston and Hingham Steam Boat Company.

Nantasket Beach, too, was gaining in popularity, although it was not for nearly twenty years that the Weir River was dredged deep enough to reach the present dock. It created quite a bit of talk at the time, but daring women, dressed of course in black bathing suits from head to toe, could be seen taking a dip at the beach on hot Saturday afternoons!

By 1870 the line had two boats in commission, the *Rose Standish* and the *John Romer,* each capable of carrying 1000 passengers. In the succeeding twenty-five years, six boats were added to the fleet, each more luxurious than its predecessor. In 1890 the name of the Boston and Hingham Steam Boat Co. was changed to the Nantasket Beach Steamboat Company and the beach resort became the principal port of call. The steamers, however, continued landing at Hingham until the great storm of November 1898 destroyed the wharf there and badly damaged two steamers, the *General Lincoln* and the *Hingham* that were tied up there. The docks were never repaired and the steamers never came into Hingham again. They continued touching at Downers Landing

on Crow Point until 1928.

The boats that were added to the line during its heyday in the forty years from 1870 on, were the finest excursion steamers operating anywhere in the inland waters in this country. The salons were decorated with oil paintings, the ship's paint was kept spotless, the brass well shined and the decks holy-stoned every morning. They were taut ships. Some of the later boats had "Directors' Rooms" where if you were a director or a friend of a director you could make the trip isolated from the common folk. On the regular commuting boats, certain chairs were tacitly reserved for some of the more distinguished passengers and woe be to the unwitting stranger who happened to sit in one of these sacrosanct chairs. When the regular commuters came aboard at night, each had tucked under his arm a copy of the *Boston Evening Transcript.*

One of the new ships during this period, the *Hingham* built in 1895, was christened in a novel ceremony as befitted the launching of the only boat in the fleet to be named *Hingham.* The sponsor was a young girl, Ruth Cushing, the daughter of the manager of the company. It didn't seem fitting to the straight-laced management that so attractive a young lady should use champagne for the christening, so she was provided with a wreath of the famous English forget-me-nots out of the Hingham town brook. Old salts will tell you that any ship not christened with champagne is a hoodoo ship, which accounts for the fact that the *Hingham* was badly damaged in the storm of '98.

All through these years the line carried hundreds of thousands of passengers without loss of a single life, but not without a swarm of lawsuits. Among the regular commuters

was a ferret-eyed lawyer, a kind of marine ambulance chaser, who made a practice of circulating among the passengers when the weather looked as though there might be a thunderstorm or a fog, handing out his card and saying to each recipient, "Just keep this card and call on me to protect your rights when anything happens."

One cause for trouble for the old side-wheelers was the fact that they were not too maneuverable. It was hard to get them started and once started hard to control the speed. Starting the engine at the dock was accomplished by a process called "barring." The engineer would drop a long eight foot steel bar through a slot in the deck to the engine below. Then he would surge forward on the bar until the engine said "whish," upon which he would pull the bar back until the patient engine said "whish" again. By repeating this process, he would get the paddle wheels turning until they were able to pick up steam from the engine.

By the late 1920's, the halcyon days of the excursion steamers were on the wane. The automobiles were taking their place in the family outing. In a disastrous fire at the wharf in Nantasket, the steamboat company lost six vessels, practically its whole fleet. Boats were chartered to replace those lost, but a large part of the glamour of the century-old company had gone up in smoke. Through the years the line continued operating one company after another succeeding to the franchises and the original wharf privileges in Boston, Pemberton and Nantasket. Today, the Wilson Excursion Line has succeeded to the right of way and docks of the original Boston and Hingham Steam Boat Company—the oldest steamboat line in the Western Hemisphere.

West Point graduate, designer, inventor
and pioneer in the Age of Steam—whoever heard of . . .

WHISTLER'S FATHER

by H. F. Thomas

We have heard a great deal about "Whistler's Mother," a painting of Mrs. George Washington Whistler made famous by her artist son, James Abbott McNeill Whistler. Yet the father, undistinguished as he is in not being remembered in a painting by his son, perhaps deserves a greater fame than either his good wife or his son.

Born during a lull between Indian wars within the stockade of the frontier post at Wayne, Illinois,

May 19, 1800—son and heir of the founder of Chicago—he progressed quickly through early schooling to enter, at age 14, West Point. After graduation, his first important work was that of establishing the northern boundary of the United States.

Railroading, however, was to be his greatest field. By 1832 his

Above: One of the earliest iron bridges in the country was on the Baltimore & Ohio Railroad 21 miles from Baltimore, near Elysville.

fame had spread around the world. In that year, Vanderbilt, then supporter of the Stonington Railroad (chartered as the New York, Providence, & Boston) took on Whistler as his Managing Director. His chief problem here was the great Kingston swamp. This Whistler mattressed, Indian style, as he had done for the Erie some years before in New Jersey.

In between the ups and downs of the Stonington, he took time off

Photo from Railroadians of America

Above: This daguerreotype of the *Bristol* (taken around 1840) portrays the earliest engine in America to be recorded by camera. The engine was one of nine designed by Major Whistler. Note the little steam whistle, atop the steam dome, close to the cab. It was probably the first in America.

Below: The Locomotive "Massachusetts" was designed by Major Whistler and built by the Locks and Canals Company of Lowell, Massachusetts in 1840. This engine was purchased by the Western Railroad of Massachusetts (now the Boston and Albany).

Early sailing cars were tried by the Baltimore & Ohio Railroad in the early 1830's.

In 1842 Russia's Czar Nicholas I selected Whistler to build a 500-mile railroad

in 1834 to run not only the Locks & Canals Company of Lowell, Massachusetts—one of America's earliest successful locomotive shops—but also in 1840 to build the Western Railroad of Massachusetts. This road is now that part of the Boston & Albany between Worcester and Albany. In that day it was supposed a railroad could not be built over the Berkshire Ridge. It was the first trunk line, the longest, and most costly railroad up to that time. Passengers will not be amazed when we inform them no change of line so far has been necessary. Whistler's experience with the B & O—his first railroad employment—was of great value to him on the B & A. It was for the B & O that he calculated his

famous elevations (standard tables today) for the outside rails on curves and also developed the realization that steam locomotives would ascend the B & O's grades. The little locomotive Tom Thumb made by Peter Cooper proved Whistler's contention by doing just this on August 25th, 1830.

Late in 1837, he laid down the Concord Railroad, now part of the Boston & Maine. It was during this decade, one notes, that the first six little 8½ to 10-ton locomotives came out of Whistler's Locks and Canals Company at Lowell, one of which, the little Apponaug, hauled on November 10, 1837 the first regular

passenger train to operate in Connecticut.

In 1842 Russia's Czar selected Whistler to build bridges, fortifications, arsenals, and docks, as well as his 500-mile railroad (the greatest project of the century) from St. Petersburg to Moscow. Whistler died there April 9, 1849. His funeral was conducted September 13th of that year in the little Episcopal Church in Stonington near which he is buried.

At his death, his famous son, James Abbott McNeill Whistler, was about fifteen years old. He had been born in 1834 at Lowell by George Whistler's second wife, Mathilda McNeill, sister of William Gibbs McNeill, a former B & O associate.

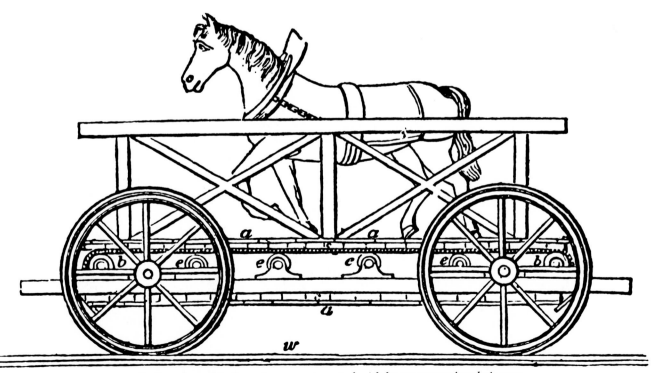

Railroads at this time also experimented with horse power for their cars.

The Bar Harbor Express at Mount Desert Ferry around 1880.

the BAR HARBOR EXPRESS

by Roger B. Buettell

*In 1901 it was possible to step aboard a Bar Harbor Express
Pullman in New York City, and leave it the next morning at Mount Desert Ferry.
For a dollar you could have dinner in the diner and enjoy the company
of passengers whose names, when listed, read like the pages of* Who's Who.
Where was the train headed? To the "Promised Land."

There's something about a train, —especially in these days when we see few of them. There was certainly a special something about this one in particular. Even its name was glamorous. When you spoke of riding the Bar Harbor Express, you had the distinct feeling that you belonged to a very select coterie, to be found only in an equally select location. And you were right on both counts.

Mount Desert Island and the adjoining coastal area, and its desirability for recreation and summer vacations, had begun to attract attention even before the Civil War. The war, of course, had slowed down this trend; but in the years that followed the growth of the area had kept pace with the phenomenal industrial and cultural expansion of

the reunited country. It was inevitable that there should come into being one best way to reach this fabulous area, unless you didn't mind risking a rough passage at sea in one of the coastal steamboats that served the Island. There was train service from Bangor into the coastal region to the south and east; but this was year-round service, not tailored to the interests and needs of a particular area or a special clientele.

From left to right: A distinguished gathering at the Bar Harbor home of Secretary of State James G. Blaine, Jr. Mrs. Henry Cabot Lodge, President Benjamin Harrison, Mrs. James G. Blaine, Secretary James G. Blaine, Miss Margaret Blaine (later Mrs. Walter Damrosch). Top row: Henry Cabot Lodge, Walker Blaine, Mr. Halford (unidentified).

That was how and why the Bar Harbor Express was born. The first Express made its first run on June 29, 1885, between Boston and Bangor. The Boston and Maine brought it to Portland, and turned it over there to the Maine Central for the remainder of its journey to Bangor. To reach Bar Harbor, its passengers boarded the Mount Desert branch at Bangor, and after a 42-mile ride to the head of Frenchman Bay, they transferred again to a Maine Central steam ferry boat for the last eight miles across the bay to Bar Harbor.

The Bar Harbor Express was a summer train only. It ran from about the middle of June to the end of September. Northbound trains ran on Monday, Wednesday, and Friday; southbound trains on Tuesday, Thursday, and Sunday. No

Right: Ferry wharf was the scene of the tragedy (August 6, 1899) in which the gangway to the steamer collapsed under the weight of passengers and 20 were drowned in the water below.

Below: The Bar Harbor Express leaving Mount Desert Ferry around 1925.

trains were scheduled for Saturday; if you were not already on the Island, you'd better wait a week, and arrange a full weekend; if you were there, you certainly wouldn't want to start for home on Saturday. During its first two summers, the performance of the Bar Harbor Express was closely watched by the Maine Central's Board of Directors, who made the following year-end report in 1886 to their stockholders: "Our travel, particularly to and from Bar Harbor, shows a large increase over previous years, and to properly care for this travel a Limited Express Train should be put on another season, running from Boston and Bar Harbor."

The "limited" feature which the Directors so greatly desired meant that the number of stops would have to be reduced, and the train's running speed also increased. Accordingly, on June 27, 1887, the Maine Central gave the Bar Harbor Express a companion, which was named the Bar Harbor Limited. Stops were reduced by using track water pans at three points, so that the train's steam engines could take water "on the run." In addition, new, fast engines were bought for this run, and lighter Pullman cars were used. With these improvements, the Bar Harbor Limited was the fastest express train in the country. But it had been primarily an ex-

perimental train; and since the same improvements were equally available to the Express, and since two trains of such speed could not then be justified, the Limited was discontinued after the 1889 season, and the improved Bar Harbor Express was again without a challenge to her superiority.

Then followed, over the ensuing years, a unique and highly successful venture in promotion, by the two partners in it, each of whom promoted the other as much as it promoted itself, thereby assuring the success of both. The Mount Desert people promoted the Express as the best way of reaching their fabulous island; and the Maine Central peo-

The train crew scattered in all directions, and the car bounced an

ple promoted Mount Desert as the beautiful destination of their increasingly popular train. As a result, the convenience afforded by the Express was extended in 1892 by moving its eastern terminus from Bangor to Mount Desert Ferry, so that its passengers were not required to change trains at Bangor but left the train at the ferry wharf. This was the wharf which, on August 6, 1899, was the scene of the tragedy in which the gangway to the steamer collapsed under the rush of passengers from another train, not the Express, and 20 were drowned in the water below.

In 1901 it became possible to step aboard a Bar Harbor Express Pullman in New York City, and leave it the next morning at the ferry wharf, since, in that year, New York cars were attached to the Express at Portland. In 1905 the western terminus of the Express was moved to New York City, and cars from Boston were attached at Portland. This made the Express a truly metropolitan train. One year later the final touch was added: in July of 1906 the Maine Central put its first diner into service on the Bar Harbor Express between Portland and Mt. Desert Ferry. Going east, breakfast and luncheon were served, and going west, luncheon and dinner. From 1906 through the 1916 season, you could get dinner in a diner for a dollar on the Express. Breakfast was also a dollar, and this price was for *a la carte* meals. In 1917 the dinner charge had to be raised to $1.25, and in 1921 to $1.50; and in 1922, for the first time, the $1.00 breakfast and the $1.50 dinner was *table d'hote*. Passengers for Mt. Desert on the Bar Harbor Express must have been convinced that the Maine Central intended its dining car should

also contribute in every way to their enjoyment of their holiday.

In 1917 the Hell Gate Bridge across the East River in New York City was opened, offering new and fast extensions of service to the south. This made it possible to reach Mt. Desert Ferry from as far away as Washington in one long overnight run, from early afternoon of one day to mid-morning of the next. To meet the immediate demand for this service, Pullman cars were run directly to the ferry from Washington, Baltimore, and Philadelphia, so that the western (and southern) terminus of the Express had in reality been moved to the nation's capital.

If sleeping cars and parlor cars and diners had guest books, many interesting signatures might have been preserved, and many intriguing bits of history could have been recorded during the years when the Bar Harbor Express was at the peak of its economic and social life, carrying the owners of the summer colony "cottages" on the Island. But even in the absence of such guest books, we can still guess with reasonable accuracy at the names of some of its nationally known passengers. A listing would read like the pages of *Who's Who,* or like New York's 400. Among them we find Mr. and Mrs. J. Pierpont Morgan; President Charles W. Eliot of Harvard; John S. Kennedy, E. T. Stotesbury, and Schuyler Schieffelin of New York City; Potter Palmer of the famous Chicago family; Edsel Ford of Detroit; A. Atwater Kent, the radio manufacturer; T. DeWitt Cuyler of Philadelphia; Mr. and Mrs. John D. Rockefeller, Jr.; Mr. and Mrs. Joseph Pulitzer; Mary Roberts Rinehart; Mr. and Mrs. Damrosch, of the New York Symphony and Metropolitan Opera; Mr.

and Mrs. Leopold Stokowski, of the Philadelphia Orchestra; Mr. and Mrs. Robert A. Taft of Cincinnati; James G. Blaine, Secretary of State under President Benjamin Harrison; and many others equally well known. Probably not all of these people used the Bar Harbor Express exclusively to reach Mount Desert Island, but it must have been the major means of reaching the Island for their families and their friends; and the Express usually carried the private cars of those who had them. It would be no exaggeration to say that the Express made a significant contribution to the fame of Mount Desert and Bar Harbor, since in the year 1916 a book was published in New England which was entitled *Who's Who in Bar Harbor and Newport.* To have reached Newport's level so soon after 1900, though hundreds of miles more distant from the top financial and social centers, was no mean achievement. There must have been a highly acceptable means of bridging those hundreds of miles. That means was the Bar Harbor Express.

While the fame of the Express was continuing to spread year after year, a new rival had raised its head, hesitantly at first but with increasing strength and with rapid public approval. This rival was the motor vehicle. In the form of the passenger automobile, it threatened every railroad's passenger business. It ran on highways built and improved with public funds. It was subject to regulatory laws, but only in the interest of safety; and it was not concerned with matters of revenue or labor costs, as the railroads were. The railroads, in fact, had none of the freedom of the automobile in transporting passengers. They were now faced at every turn with one or more of three "facts of life": government

ureened off the pier and into Frenchman Bay

Thoroughly posed, this photograph was taken at Mount Desert Ferry during the 1880's. The last run of the Bar Harbor Express was in 1960.

regulation of their revenues; diminishing control of their labor costs; and the motor vehicle. In providing passenger service, they might have withstood any two of these at the same time, possibly all three for a limited time in a limited area. But they couldn't withstand all of these factors all of the time in all of their operations.

During the summer months in particular, when the Bar Harbor Express operated, the competition of the motor vehicle reached its greatest intensity. The pressure finally became too great as the number of automobiles mushroomed and more and more tourists and vacationers came to Maine in their own cars. In 1931 the eastern terminus of the Express was moved back to

Ellsworth, and the use of Mount Desert Ferry and its steamers was abandoned. From Ellsworth its passengers reached Bar Harbor by Maine Central busses. As time went on, the handwriting on the wall became all too plain. At the end of the 1960 season, the last Bar Harbor Express pulled out of Ellsworth for New York.

Before this last trip, however, this writer was privileged to enjoy a well-remembered ride on the Express. I boarded it one hot July afternoon in Wilmington, Delaware. The comfort of the air-cooled cars kept reminding me of the comfort of my destination. I awoke the next morning, after a night's sleep under a blanket, to find that I was on a 15-

car train. I hurried to the diner, but it was full so I sat down in the parlor car. In my business travels, I had been in many parlor cars, and the faces I had seen there, behind newspapers and magazines, were sometimes haggard, often troubled, always sober. But the people who occupied these chairs were happy people, smiling or laughing, full of animation. And well they might be, for they were riding into a "Promised Land."

There will be for many people many other memories of the Bar Harbor Express for a long time to come, and some of these memories are amusing. There was the day, for example, recalled by Robert W. Fenlason, a former engineer on the Express now retired and living in Charleston, Maine. On that day one of the passengers was a lady who was enjoying her first ride to Bar Harbor, and who had apparently been told by her friends that she would get off the train at Mount Desert Ferry. The conductor that day was Charles Whitehouse, who Mr. Fenlason describes as "quite a character." The lady approached Mr. Whitehouse near the end of the journey, and said to him: "Conductor, does this train stop at Mount Desert Ferry?" "Lady," said Charley Whitehouse, "I certainly hope it does, because if it doesn't, we will all get one hell of a ducking!"

Then there was the experience of the late William G. Marston, as related by his son Donald Marston of Lewiston, Maine, which is not only amusing, but could be symbolic as well. One day in 1915, Mr. Marston, who was conductor on the Express, stepped from his train

on its arrival at Mount Desert Ferry, and saw on the pier a small swarm of Maxwell automobiles, all roadsters, that had just been unloaded from box cars. They were destined for Sullivan and Sorrento, where buyers awaited them (they were at that time not permitted on Mount Desert Island). The train crew started to look them over, and Mr. Marston playfully seized the crank handle of one of them, and gave it a turn. The motor came to life, and the car instantly began to move, as it had been left in gear. The train crew scattered in all directions, and the car bounced and careened off the pier and into Frenchman Bay. It was later recovered at some expense to the train crew; but in retrospect, it would almost seem that Mr. Marston and his crew had recognized their deadly rivals, and had promptly consigned one of them to a place where they wished all of them were—the bottom of Frenchman Bay.

Since that day in 1960 when the Bar Harbor Express made her last run, the rival whose onrush, like a monstrous wave, swept everything before it, has been found to be much less than a perfect blessing. The motor car has come to a day of reckoning, and its makers and its owners are learning many things about its contribution to the growing evil of air pollution. We may be closer than we think to a determination of what national restrictions in its use we must adopt to keep this evil within proper bounds. Fortunately, we in Maine are still free from its effects; but that does not mean that we shall never have to deal with it. Writing in the *Maine Central Messenger* for February, 1967, President E. Spencer Miller of the Maine Central puts it this way:

"In common with many others who look into the future, I see a time when, in large sections of this country, the highways are going to become glutted and the great attraction of moving freight over them in single vehicles, or moving passengers over them with one or two people being carried in a vehicle powered by an internal combustion engine, is going to become non-existent and may even become limited by imposition of law.

"One of our freight trains carrying 80 loads would supplant 150 trucks on the highway and all of the pollution, as well as congestion, they involve. One train operating into a metropolitan area could easily accommodate 800 to 1,000 people and therefore supplant somewhere between 500 and 1,000 automobiles, eliminating all of the congestion and all of the air pollution which they cause.

"We of the Maine Central believe that those things are going to happen and our state of mind is simply this: we are preparing for them in the planning stage and thinking about them.

"We went out of the passenger business pursuant to public desire as evidenced by the fact that each of our trains by 1960 was handling less than half a bus load. We are willing and anxious to get back into that business when the pendulum swings to such an extent that it will be the desire of the people once again to have the comforts and reliability of passenger train service, in addition to the great public need to eliminate the uneconomic expense of super highways, the congestion on existing highways, and the pollution of the air which a multiplication of vehicles on them necessarily produces."

Who knows?—there may some day be another Bar Harbor Express of 15 Pullmans and a diner, and the steps already taken in 1970 to restore railroad passenger service may bring that day back sooner than we think. When it arrives, you might not be able to get a dinner in the diner for a dollar, but you would be certain to get all you wanted of laughter, animation, and good spirits—all that goes with a carefree summer in a blessed land, and all for free.

THE MAGNIFICENT FAILURE

*Captain John Collins, partner in
the Collins Steamship Company*

*From the start, the Collins Steamship Company
suffered from want of capital, and bad timing. And when
it finally failed, it sounded the death knell of
American ocean steam navigation for a full half century.*

by E. Milburn Carver

Speaking a Collins Steamer.

High up, on the "lower" Cape Cod peninsula, a few miles south of Provincetown, is a place called Truro. It is a very old town which dates its incorporation as a townsite well back into the 18th Century.

In summer, this is truly a paradise, a veritable cornucopia of pleasure to the senses as it spills forth its abundance of climbing roses, creeping cranberry, and bathing—from the surf at Nauset, on the ocean side, to the warm small shallows of Pamet Harbor on Cape Cod Bay.

But this changes with the waning of Indian Summer, for as the days shorten and the last roses die, Aeolus looks toward the Cape and unties his bag of winds to send them hurtling against the peninsula. It is then one learns that the sea can be ugly.

The old-timers, who built their homes upon the sandy hills, were not niggardly with either the dimensions of the buildings nor of the material which went into their making, for well they knew what havoc winter storms brought to this land.

One such home is near the end of Depot Street; it lies a little way off the paved road, but is accessible to it by a sandy lane. It sits high upon a bluff overlooking the salt

marshes and the Pamet River which meanders through them to eventually join Cape Cod Bay in a welter of sand bars, a mile or so to the west. This square-topped, strong old house was once the Collins homestead.

The progenitor of this family was one Captain Mark Collins, who was called "Mark Antony." That distinguished appellation seems to have kept him separated from other Collinses in and about Truro. His sons, Israel and John, were also ship captains, both of whom will claim some further attention.

Captain Israel Gross Collins married an English gentlewoman named Mary Ann Knight. Their son, Edward Knight Collins, with whom we shall be mostly concerned, was born in 1802.

Edward's sea-going career seems to have been limited to a few voyages with his father. He then came shoreside to the busy New York waterfront—and stayed. Had he chosen to follow the family precedent and become a shipmaster, his membership in the Marine Society of New York would have been of Active status, as was that of his grandfather, father, and uncle, rather than Honorary (admitted June 14, 1853).

With the 1830's under way, young Collins was associated with

his father in operating a fleet of commercial packets between New York and Vera Cruz, Mexico. In 1832 Edward became the New York agent for a larger fleet of coasting vessels which ran to New Orleans via way ports en route to their terminus. The line soon became known as the "Collins Line," and under the gifted touch of its youthful manager did rather well financially. Collins bought his own first ship in 1835 —the 750-ton *Shakespeare*—and Captain John Young, Edward Collins' uncle, was put in command of it.

A few of the so-called Collins ships were good sailers. But as a group, all coasters were referred to as "droghers" by deep-water men, and this was partly in derision and partly in truth. Their best sailing qualities were sadly impaired by first loading them down to their deadeyes with cargo and then as an afterthought piling on deck cargoes of families, livestock, and household goods.

It was E. K. Collins who started an avalanche of ship design changes, but he did not do this alone; his helper and advisor was Captain N. B. Palmer, who hailed from Stonington, Connecticut.

According to Palmer, a flat-

The Adriatic—*Collins thought she'd be the answer to his problems.*

bottomed hull—indigenous to coasters for negotiating river bars—could and would sail well. He had proved this by driving the *Huntsville* from New York to New Orleans in only nine days. And Mr. Collins listened to his captain, for he accordingly dispatched the *Shakespeare* to Liverpool as a deep-sea packet.

David Brown built three packets of the radically new design for Mr. Collins in 1836–37. Brown was, perhaps, the most distinguished of all early American shipwrights. His yard in New York faced the upper East River at 134 Goerck Street. The ships which Brown constructed were massive great vessels of nearly 900 tons apiece, and they were named for famous actors; viz., *Garrick, Sheridan,* and *Siddons.*

Officially, the Collins packets were identified as the "Dramatic Line," and, unofficially, as the "Actor's Fleet," which may have been a jibe at Collins personally. In any event, they hoisted a new flag, a double-barred blue and white square with twin L's in the center to denote them as Liverpool ships.

Old shellbacks dubiously regarded the building of these new full-rigged ships, with the weird design which Palmer had worked into execution. They marvelled at the elongated and elevated poop, so reminiscent of the by-gone galleon, incarnated again into a practical and relatively comfortable passenger accommodation. They questioned the aberration, however, of building any ocean-going vessel with a shallow dead-rise to its flooring, arguing that a bottom should rise steeply as in the letter "V," the better to cleave the water.

The new Dramatic liners handled well and performed admirably. Their western transit from England, against the prevailing westerlies, averaged 30% better than those of their closest rivals, and they came scudding into New York with bunting and burgee all a-flying in just under a month's time.

Knowing that his South Street neighbors in the shipping business would soon equal his temporary success with make-weight new ships of their own, Edward Collins now contracted with David Brown to build a super liner. This one was called the *Roscius* (for a Roman actor), and the vessel was launched by 1839. Her burden of 1,009 tons was another milestone in progress, for the *Roscius* was the first merchantman in the world to surpass the 1,000-ton figure.

The dimensions of the ship stir one's admiration for Collins's daring and Palmer's genius. She cost $100,-000 to build, or 40% more than any other contemporary ship afloat at the time. Part of this expense was accountable in size and the remainder in a lavish stock of heavy timbering, fine-grained cabin woods, and tons of copper sheathing and fastenings. She crossed a main yard of 75 feet in length, representing a sail power almost comparable to that of the famous *Flying Cloud,* a sharp clipper and much larger ship of a much later date. But the *Roscius* was not a clipper—far from it. She was bluff-bowed, wall-sided, and a very heavy vessel which favored a gale of wind in order to sail well.

Captain John Collins was skipper of the *Roscius* for a few years, until his retirement from the sea about 1845. When he did come shoreside it was to join his nephew as a business partner. Their family ties were distinctly more fraternal than otherwise, for there was only a six-year gap between them.

The heyday of the Dramatic

The magnificent 4000-ton screw steamer
Adriatic was launched by the Steers Brothers,
builders of the cup-winning yacht America

Casting of the bed plate of the Adriatic.

His steamers carried 70% of all the Atlantic passengers but little or no cargo

Line was relatively short, for with the enormous tide of emigration from Europe to this country during the 40's, more and more packets were built to handle it. By 1852 there were 24 lines serving Liverpool alone, while others went to London, LeHavre, and Hamburg.

Who knows the exact date when Edward Collins first conceived the idea of becoming a tycoon of steam? Perhaps he foresaw the eventual decline of sail; or perhaps he was only emulous of Cunard's success with four little paddle boats, called the *Asia, Africa, Europa,* and *Niagara.*

After a long period of negotia-

tions for a subsidy from the United States Government, the Collins Steamship Company became a reality. Its home berth was located at the foot of Canal Street, on the Hudson River.

Four 2,855-ton, wooden sidewheelers, the world's largest, made their debuts upon the Atlantic between 1849 and 1851. The pioneer vessel of this fleet was called the *Atlantic,* and she was quickly fol-

Above: The grand dining room on the main deck of the Adriatic. *It was seventy-five feet long.*

Right: The steamship Atlantic

lowed by the *Pacific, Baltic,* and *Arctic.*

In most respects these vessels were so much alike in mold and tonnage that they may be treated as sister ships. They were originally painted black with a red band circumscribing the hull and a likeness of the United States Seal decorating the center of the paddle-wheel box.

Two side-lever, 1,000 H/P engines drove the paddlewheels. Their 95-inch cylinders developed a 12–13 knot speed—with some slight assistance from auxiliary sail—under favorable weather conditions. Their coal consumption was enormous since it amounted to approximately 87 tons a day, or an amount almost equal to the ship's tonnage per round trip!

The length, on deck, was 280 feet, beam at midships 45 feet, depth from keel to deck 31 feet. Each of the paddle wheels contained 36 floats and they measured 36 feet from tip to tip. A crew of 170 operated the ship, whose passenger-car-rying capacity amounted to 250, less than double the crew complement.

A long deck house extended from the stern to a point just abaft the foremast. This edifice housed the passenger cabins, saloon, officers' quarters, bakery, and barber shop.

From the start, the Collins Steamship Co. suffered from want of capital. It began its steamboating operations with a debt of nearly two million dollars, which was scarcely offset by the $878,000 annual subsidy. Income and subsidy were both quickly exhausted by 7% interest rates, maintenance, general depreciation, and frequent but costly engine repairs. But the line's inevitable collapse was due more to circumstance and misfortune than to mismanagement, as sometimes alleged.

The circumstances involved dealt with a coincidence in time, for it was certainly a coincidence that Collins should undertake such a vast-scale project of operation during the same decade as the appearance of the American clipper ship.

Frustratingly enough, his steamers carried 70% of all the Atlantic passengers but little or no cargo. They were, in fact, short-haul oddities in contrast to the practical sailing ship which bore its cargo over long distances, free of all water and bunkering problems.

On October 27, 1854 the steamer *Arctic,* Captain Luce, eight days from Liverpool and 50 miles off Cape Race, collided with the French propeller bark *Vesta* while steaming at 11 knots in a dense fog. The shock to the *Arctic* stove in her bow, put out her fires, and created a panic while the *Vesta* slipped off into the fog.

Five lifeboats were launched from the *Arctic* amid wild confusion, disorder, and wholesale desertion of the crew; two boats immediately capsized, dumping their human freight into frigid water. The remaining three cleared the stricken vessel in a partly loaded state. They were never heard from again.

The after part of the ladies' saloon, steamship Adriatic.

Under the direction of Captain Luce and Third Mate Dolan, the only officer who stayed behind, a raft was made by the passengers from the topgallant spars.

Seventy-two people climbed aboard this contrivance when it was launched, while another 32 squeezed into the one remaining lifeboat. Two days later, one survivor was removed from the raft; he was a Mr. McCabe from Philadelphia and his graphic account of the *Arctic*'s sinking was widely publicized.

At 5 P.M. the *Arctic* sank. Amongst the many victims to go down with her were A. M. Comstock, brother of the *Baltic*'s commander, and Mrs. Edward Collins with the two Collins children.

James Luce, the Captain, stayed with the *Arctic* until the ship started her last roll. He then tried to jump clear while holding his small son in his arms. The two of them

were pulled under by the suction set up as the *Arctic* plunged below the sea. Luce and the child became separated. When the former managed to surface, he saw the boy clinging to a broken paddle box; then the box crumpled and crushed the child. Luce clung to a fragment of this box for two days before he was picked up.

Four hundred people perished in this disaster. The survivors included only those left in the last lifeboat and a dozen others who, like the captain, clung to bits of wreckage long enough to be saved by passing vessels.

Captain Asa Eldridge commanded the ill-fated *Pacific*. He followed John Collins aboard the *Roscius* when the latter retired, and he had taken the S/S *Pacific* when Captain Ezra Nye, of Sandwich, Massachusetts, had retired.

Everyone connected with, or

interested in the sea, knew about Asa Eldridge, for this cold-eyed, black-bearded captain from Yarmouth Port had become the sultan of sail. In January 1854, Eldridge had taken the extreme clipper *Red Jacket* across the Atlantic, from dock to dock, in the unprecedented time of 13 days and one hour. He had established a sailing record which has never been broken.

Eldridge had become the toast of society—a society, incidentally, which loved these "driver" captains —and fortunate indeed were the passengers whose tickets permitted them to sail with this man!

On January 25, 1856, the S/S *Pacific* cleared Liverpool with 145 passengers and 140 crew. She thrashed her way out into St. George's Channel, passed Tuskar Light, and was never seen again!

Even to this day no one knows what happened to the *Pacific*. It is assumed that she was caught up in the Arctic icepack and frozen in—this is only a hypothesis—but no wreckage or debris from the steamer was ever found to provide a better theory.

Meanwhile, Collins had stretched his credit almost beyond the breaking point upon a new vessel intended to replace the *Arctic*. The magnificent 4,000-ton screw-steamer *Adriatic* was launched in September 1856 by the Steers Brothers, builders of the famous cup-winning-yacht *America*.

The *Adriatic* was to be a floating lighthouse with illumination provided by the "open-type" arc lamp. Vessels, icebergs, and other navigational obstructions in the ship's track would be seen in time to prevent another collision course. But these wonders never materialized for Collins.

Since the mail contract could not be fulfilled by the Collins Line with only the *Baltic* and *Atlantic*, the government withdrew its subsidy. It was impossible to censure this act, or even gain an extension of terms, for the government was in trouble too, and amongst those troubles was a strong Southern opposition in Congress to the support of any Yankee shipowner.

Collins was bankrupt—he was bankrupt both financially and spiritually. John Collins died in 1857, and with both John and Mary gone there was no use in trying to carry on. But the failure of the Collins Line was the death knell to American ocean steam navigation for the next half century.

Edward Collins died at his Madison Avenue home in New York City on Tuesday, January 22, 1878. He was buried in Woodlawn Cemetery in the Bronx. The coroner's report simply stated that the deceased had died of "old age," but perhaps he (the coroner) considered this statement more ethical than saying that the victim had died of a "broken heart."

Let us suppose that Edward Collins returned to Truro sometime before his death, or sometime after the Civil War when he would have had plenty of company in terms of shipping failures.

He would have probably trudged across this narrow land, by the Pamet Roads, in about an hour. Climbing the Nauset Bluffs would not have been easy, for Collins was reputedly a heavy-set man. But once on top of the bluffs, it would have been worth his effort, for here he

could see the whole vista of the broad Atlantic unrolled, stretching out and away towards England.

Perhaps he would muse a bit, as old men so often do, and in musing he would recall that this point upon which he stood is the first and closest landfall in the United States that a New York-bound packet raises before coming about on a southerly tack so as to swing the Monomoy Bar off Chatham.

And now his memory is no longer hazy, or sad, for it is galvanized into action as he visualizes his Dramatic fleet as though it were only yesterday. Here they come, one by one, all his canvas liners: the *Shakespeare, Garrick, Siddons, Sheridan,* and *Roscius,* with lee rails almost awash as they lean beneath their terrific press of sail. And after them come the paddlers, belching smoke and churning the water white, raising a wake that can be seen for miles, their names fluttering and snapping upon the long pennants which stream out from each main mast truck: the *Atlantic,* his first steamer; the *Arctic,* fastest of the lot, indeed the fastest ship in the world; the *Baltic,* another first, the first ship to cross the ocean in under 10 days; and last, but by no means least, the great *Pacific,* famous for her "driver" captains.

The steamship Atlantic *wrecked on Mars Head on the morning of April 1, 1873.*

With a
HOOT, TOOT
and a
WHISTLE,

by Roger Bowen

... four New England railroads are back on the black ink side of the ledger, thanks to 1968's version of a "railroad tycoon" who started some 30 years ago with a little money "and a heck of a lot of nerve."

While railroads continue to decline all across the country, the Hoot, Toot & Whistle goes hooting and tooting along the black-ink side of the ledger over in southwestern Vermont. Farther up the state the once abandoned Montpelier and Barre Railroad is now financially sound. And in northern Vermont the St. Johnsbury and Lamoille County Railroad has made an impressive comeback after extensive renovation which has increased its revenue as well as its prestige. (Local residents no longer refer to it as the "St. J. and Lazy Cuss!")

All three lines, as well as the Claremont and Concord Railroad in New Hampshire and a couple of

A St. J. and L. C. freight near Hardwick, Vermont, on its way from Morrisville to St. Johnsbury.

southern shortline railroads, are the personal property of a canny New Englander who likes to turn losers into winners. Samuel M. Pinsly owns these six railroads, lock, stock, and barrel, and they have made him a modest fortune. He controls his $6 million collection of shortline railroads from his Boston offices on Causeway Street, next to the North Station, effecting numerous economies through centralized purchasing, billing, and bookkeeping. It might be romantic to say that Pinsly, nearing 70, has fulfilled a boyhood dream of becoming a railroad tycoon. But he says the only dreaming he did as a youth was of not having to get up at five in the morning to milk cows.

Born in Cambridge, Massachusetts, Pinsly was two years old when his family moved to a farm in Medway. He grew up on the farm, he says, without having any interest in railroading at all. At the age of 19, he was called into service during World War I, but never served overseas. After the war he entered Northeastern University, having decided that he might be interested in engineering. He studied law at the same time, in night school. Before graduation he quit school to play drums in a Boston band. Pinsly is noticeably reluctant to talk about his early years. He became an automobile salesman in Boston for awhile in the '20s, but apparently was not spectacularly successful and soon drifted to New York to become a $35-a-week novice salesman for a railroad equipment company. He sold locomotives, cars, and rails, and during the course of visiting many railroads found that he was acquiring a liking for railroading. Though he had little money of his own, he decided that he was going to buy a railroad.

In 1936 Pinsly found what he wanted: the ailing Hoosac Tunnel & Wilmington Railroad which had 31 miles of track stretching from the east end of the Hoosac Tunnel along

197

Right: In modernizing the S.J.&L.C. R.R., Pinsley had to replace several of Vermont's old covered bridges. But he was able to save this one by supporting it with steel beams. It is now the last wooden, covered, railroad bridge in Vermont.

In the bottom photo, brakeman R. A. Young takes time out for a cigarette on the morning run to St. Johnsbury. The photo below shows an engine of the same line back in 1871.

"*A railroad never deserts*

198

ipper, the shipper deserts the railroad . . ."

the Deerfield River to Wilmington, Vermont. The price was $75,000, a fair sum in depression years for a business running in the red. "I had a little money, and a heck of a lot of nerve," says Pinsly. "I got the railroad on my name, really."

Pinsly rebuilt the road, managing to get liberal credit from suppliers and untiring devotion from his employees. The 20-mile stretch from Readsboro, Vermont, to Wilmington was not in operation due to a bridge washout and Pinsly abandoned it—"there's no business in Wilmington, anyway." The 11-mile stretch from Readsboro to the Hoosac Tunnel became very profitable. The 1938 hurricane all but finished Pinsly's railroad. The line suffered

106 washouts and lost three bridges. Again Pinsly was able to get credit from suppliers and depend upon the loyalty of his employees. The damage was repaired, with men working day and night to get the railroad back in operation. In two years' time Pinsly had paid off his debts and the railroad was making money.

The Hoosac Tunnel and Wilmington Railroad, known throughout the area as the "Hoot, Toot & Whistle," has done even better in recent years with the coming of the Yankee Atomic Power Plant at Rowe, Massachusetts, which the line supplies. It also transports paper products from Monroe, Massachusetts.

The second railroad Pinsly

bought is no longer part of his holdings, having been liquidated about ten years after he bought it. The Sanford Eastern Railroad is no more; but while Pinsly owned it, it made money. The Sanford Eastern ran from Rochester, New Hampshire, to Portland, Maine. Its main customer was the Goodall Sanford Mills which manufactured Palm Beach cloth and automobile upholstery. When Pinsly acquired the railroad in 1947, the mill employed some 3,400 people and provided the railroad with most of its business. When labor problems developed and the mill finally closed down, Pinsly decided to liquidate the railroad. Some of the smaller shippers protested and Pinsly told them:

199

"A railroad never deserts a shipper, the shipper deserts the railroad."

Pinsly is a realist, operating his railroads to make a profit, and is quick to abandon a section or service of any railroad which does not produce revenue. At one time Pinsly's third acquisition, the Claremont and Concord Railroad, carried passengers, but it is today, like all of the other Pinsly roads, purely a freight line. Says Pinsly:

"I didn't want to give up passenger service, but I can't run a railroad on love or sentiment. In Claremont, for instance, the train would be crowded on a rainy or snowy day. When the sun was out I might have three passengers, maybe four or five, on the whole train. That wouldn't pay the cost of one of my employees. As long as we carried the government mail, we could subsidize the passenger service. The government took the mail away and gave it to the trucks. We had to suspend passenger service and today the government has to pay twice as much to send the mail by truck as it did by rail."

Pinsly's Claremont and Concord Railroad is made up of two roads—The Claremont Railway, a small city line, and the main line from Claremont to Concord. When the government built the Hopkinton-Everett Dam, Pinsly found his main line cut in two, and had to abandon the track on the Concord side.

"Of course we lost some customers," Pinsly says, "but we run today between Newport and Claremont and West Claremont and it makes a good operation. There was compensation from the government, naturally."

The same year (1954) that Pinsly bought the Claremont and Concord Railroad, he moved south and acquired the 21-mile-long Greenville and Northern Railroad in South Carolina.

"It's a good little road," says Pinsly. "It has three connections: with the Piedmont Northern, with the Seacoast, and with the Southern Railroad. There are many food brokers and warehouses on the line and we do a big scrap metal business."

In 1956 Pinsly bought the Montpelier and Barre Railroad. Ac-

Engine 1494 and plow, early equipment of the St. Johnsbury and Lamoille County Railroad.

tually, he bought two roads and merged them into one. The original Barre and Montpelier line went to Wells River over very mountainous country. The entire road had been abandoned when Pinsly bought it. A competing railroad into Barre from Montpelier Junction was also purchased by Pinsly from the Central Vermont Line. Pinsly used parts of both tracks to reinstate service between Barre and Montpelier. Most of Pinsly's business on this line is Barre granite, but there is also quite a lot of shipping of grain and beer. Pinsly also owns Granite Central Delivery, a truck line which operates in the Barre area, bringing granite in from the quarries to plants in the area to be loaded on Central Vermont cars.

As at Barre, Pinsley looks for customers before he buys a railroad. If the shippers are there, then a railroad ought to be able to make money if it is run right, Pinsly believes. In 1959 he bought the 51-mile Frankfort and Cincinnati Railroad in Kentucky because it serviced several distilleries. Bourbon makes a compact and valuable freight cargo.

Pinsly's latest and biggest—in terms of mileage—purchase was the St. Johnsbury and Lamoille County Railroad which runs all the way across Vermont, from St. Johnsbury to Swanton, a distance of 96 miles—100, now that Pinsly has added a four-mile connecting link at Swanton. Like other Pinsly purchases, this road was in deplorable condition, lacking adequate repair shops and other basic facilities, with scenic wooden bridges which could not carry the weight of modern "jumbo" freight cars; locomotives of inadequate size and power, and a road bed limiting them to 20-mile-an-hour speed. Pinsly paid a reported million dollars for the road, and by his own statement has spent $2 million in improvements in the two years he has

owned it. He has built new general offices in Morrisville with modern facilities for maintenance and repair of locomotives and cars. He has bought four more powerful locomotives. He has replaced three bridges, including a couple of tourist-attraction covered bridges. He has, however, retained one wooden covered bridge after promising The Vermont Historical Society and the Governor that he would save it if he could. At a cost of somewhat more than a new bridge, Pinsly had supporting steel beams built into the old wooden bridge where they wouldn't show but would support the 100-ton jumbo cars which a modern railroad now has to handle. The going hasn't been easy—a recent derailment cost the road heavily in time and money. But Pinsly expects this railroad to make money in time, as do all the others.

The St. Johnsbury and Lamoille County Railroad connects the Maine Central Railroad with the Central Vermont (part of the Canadian National System). It has some large businesses along its length, including the Ruberoid Company, Johnson & Johnson, Eastern Magnesia Talc and Ralston Purina, and there is shipment of grain and limestone. The road is a shortcut across the state of Vermont for certain shippers like the Maine paper manufacturers, but more important, says Pinsly, "we provide more competition, and the more competition there is in transportation, the better off a shipper is. You take the merger of the New York Central and Pennsylvania Railroads—that brings together two giants, and why the government allowed it I'll never know. It's bad enough to do business with one of them, without the combination. Yes, it affects small railroads,

No. 3 of the St. Johnsbury & Lake Champlain R.R.

too, as well as the shippers."

Pinsly keeps tight control of his railroads. Each is run by a general manager who calls him every morning in his Boston office. Each railroad has a foreman of maintenance and ways, a foreman of the shop, and a freight man. Pinsly does all bill handling, purchasing, making out of payrolls, and buying of insurance in the Boston office, and charges each railroad a percentage of the cost of the office. But each railroad is a separate business entity, wholly owned by Pinsly; there is no overall organization or business structure despite the centralized office.

Though he is an owner and operator of shortlines only, Pinsly has definite ideas as to what is wrong with some of the bigger railroads like the bankrupt New Haven. He has built his own success on two factors: service to the customer and employee loyalty, so he says; but it is evident that he is a shrewd businessman with a sharp eye on cost factors. He is willing to invest money in modernization for both reasons, because it is a service to the customer and be-

cause it leads to reduced costs of operation. He believes that the New Haven Railroad has been bucking odds with its passenger service, but he thinks it could be profitable in the future. He told me:

"I read yesterday that the Boston Red Sox took a train to New York for the first time in years. Now if you had good, fast service, good clean cars, a lounge and good food, and you could read and enjoy yourself and be in New York in two and three-quarters hours . . . who would want to fly? I believe transcontinental train passenger service is finished. Absolutely. But between nearby cities—Boston to New York, New York to Washington—the future of rail passenger service is bright. There is no more room on highways, or in cities, for cars. Traffic will double in the next few years. Airplanes land outside the cities, and it takes too much time getting to and from the airports on short flights. Mass transportation *has* to come back, and the only way I can see that it can be handled economically is by rail. Railroads have only begun to be appreciated for what they can do."

All that's left are memories. In Section VI we find them strong and vivid . . .

. . . so here's some PURE NOSTALGIA for your indulgence.

I REMEMBER FIRE HORSES

It was long, long ago when the fire horses were on the American scene. I remember them. They are among the few brightest memories of my childhood. Those handsome and intelligent horses, always so eagerly responsive to their work, were regarded in a heroic light by everyone who watched them galloping with all their spirit and vigor to a fire scene. People stopped and gazed after them; everyone glowed with admiration. I remember, too, the tradition: once a fire horse, always a fire horse. To explain this:

When one of them left his or her fire station home, no longer able to keep up the speedy pace, it didn't always mean that the old faithful would be retired to green pastures of some farm. Often they would continue working—as grocery wagon, milk wagon or even (sadly enough) junk wagon horses.

But it seemed their ears and spirit were always alert to the old, familiar clanging of the bells and the rhythmic pounding beat of hooves of their erstwhile comrades plunging on to another fire. The old, so well-loved excitement would sometimes come to them several blocks away. So, one of these old-timers not infrequently would forget his or her humble role and go racing off with a crazily careening grocery, milk or junk wagon, to join his former comrades in the dash to the fire. They might start out from the curb unattended or if the driver was in the seat they would take the bit in their teeth and the driver would be helpless. A wagon would topple over at a wild corner turn, or a policeman would jump out into the street, waving his arms to stop the runaway.

Of course people loved all this. There was the lasting love of one's old job besides the humour in it that they appreciated. I remember the many times the newspapers printed stories about the fire horse veteran craving to return to his old role. Once a fire horse, always a fire horse.

The firemen, too, loved their horses even though they expected of the brave animals a fine, consistent discipline. The horses themselves seemed to understand this for most of the time they filled their roles without a flaw. Like humans, they would lag at times or show a bit of temperament, but there would be a sharp word or two and then they would promptly be back in line. The fire horses had fast-speaking names

"1908—Answering Alarm 18—Lowery driving" is the caption we found on this rare old photo of a horsedrawn steam engine pumper in action.

A vignette of bright memories by Jack Johnson   (Complete on this spread)

like Jim, Duke, Ned, Dolly and Nell. No doubt that was to save time when there was need for haste in an emergency.

What I remember with special fondness was the evening drill at the fire station. This was after supper time in our neighborhood in Providence when I was a little boy, and in New York, too, perhaps Greenwich Village. Children would gather beside the wide-open doors of the station to watch the horses getting into harness just as though they were about to get off to a real fire. What a thrill! (No movies or television then: the smaller delights sufficed for us little ones.)

When the bars of his stall were raised, a fire horse took his place beneath the suspended harness in front of the steam engine.

Firemen would come zipping from their living quarters aloft, sliding down the shiny brass pole. At the same instant the bars to the stalls would raise- and the beautiful horses would come clopping out at a brisk trot. Each, without a false move, would take his place beneath a suspended harness in front of the steam engine (a coal burner) or the ladder truck. In a twixt the harness would drop and they would all be hitched up. The firemen would take their places, there would be a certain routine of detail, and, meanwhile, our beloved fire horses would be stomping a solid hoof on the fire station floor, or tossing a lovely maned head, or posing with a noble head held high and flashing bright eyes, and all tense for a getaway. They seemed to say, "All right! All right! What are we waiting for! ! ?" It was all done in a few minutes.

Then the harness would be unclicked and go aloft again and the horses would clop, clop leisurely back to their stalls, usually with one or two nipping at the flank of another peevishly or in play.

But sometimes before they returned to their stalls there would come the greatest thrill of all. The little boys and girls would be permitted inside to pat the broad sides of the huge animals or caress their soft noses. Then, if you were especially fortunate, a kind fireman would raise you onto the broad back of Ned or Dolly, and that would be the most delightful, satisfying part of all!

1898   Rita Derby ("Nanny")   1970

RESCUED
BY
BLESIS SOLE

by Richard Derby Attwill

When I was a boy, I just loved being told "trouble stories." One of the best of these was told me by my grandmother years ago when we were "down to" Baker's Island for the summer. It was early in the season, and there were just the two of us at the cottage. We were out on the piazza, Nanny drifting forward and back in one of the green, straw rockers, and I, to and fro in the canvas hammock, both of us just idling away the offshore quiet of an island afternoon.

All of a sudden Nanny pointed west and fixed me with the tight-lippedest expression I had ever seen. She had just spied the first dark thunderclouds of summer rolling up over Salem and neighboring Beverly and heading our way, and the wisest thing to do, as far as she was con-

cerned, was to get out of sight as quickly as possible. You see, Nanny had a great respect for thunderstorms, and the reason went all the way back to what happened on a holiday outing many years ago.

The way Nanny remembered it, July 4, 1898 was like a good many other Fourth of Julys on the Massachusetts coast. Her home town of Beverly was seeing a very hot and muggy day, and at one point the thermometer went up to 104°. In the afternoon, the weather became squally and threatening, and heavy showers and horizon flickers of lightning were seen in the south and southwest, and north and northeast.

A newspaper photograph showing a diver over the wreck as the search for victims continued.

Courtesy of Peabody Museum, Salem

"Water kept pouring through the open door and windows, and in minutes it was over my head . . ."

But who cared if there were a few rainstorms round about! It was a holiday, the unofficial beginning of summer, and for everyone to celebrate The Fourth for all he was worth was practically a civic duty.

Nanny was 17 years old and known as Rita Derby on that Independence Day and, like a good many of the young folk from Beverly, was spending the holiday at Salem Willows, a picnic park just 15 minutes across Beverly Harbor by excursion steamer. The steamer in question was the *Surf City,* and it made its daily runs from Beverly to Baker's Island to Salem Willows and back to Beverly.

Late in the afternoon, when the boat started its final trip of the day, storm clouds suddenly gathered in the northwest and began chasing the

Surf City to Baker's. When the steamer docked at the island, a wary few decided to stay over rather than chance the five-mile trip to the Willows. The skies were darkening by the minute, and besides, there was always a good time to be had at the Winnie-Egan Hotel.

Shortly after the boat left Baker's Island, the storm seemed to "peter out," as some put it, and before it reached the island, divided.

"What happened," said Nanny, "was that one part went southerly, the other northerly, and the *Surf City* passed between the two just as slick as a whistle. But you know what?"

Above: A drawing from the Salem News *depicting the scene as the* Surf City *lay partially submerged a few hours after she capsized.*

"What?" I asked, giving a dry swallow, but never taking my eyes from her face.

"I heard afterward that the tail end of one of the storms hit the island with terrible high winds, and dumped hailstones as big as hickory nuts!"

When the *Surf City* reached Salem Willows, there were still skeptics who were far from convinced that the elements had no further plans for getting ornery. True, the Willows might still be dry as a chip, it was only a matter of minutes by boat to Beverly, and fret-and-fumers they might be, but they were still taking the electric cars back through Salem and making sure they arrived safe and sound.

Rita Derby and her companions, however, never gave a second

thought to the threatening heavens. After all, what was a little rain on a 15-minute boat ride back to town? So, joining some 60 other passengers, they boarded the *Surf City*.

"No sooner had the boat pulled away from the landing and headed home," continued Nanny, "than the sky began to get as black as your hat. The wind started to rise something frightful, and the sea turned sickly gray with whitecaps frothing everywhere."

What no one had noticed was that the two storms that separated earlier over Salem Harbor, had circled to the northwest, and just joined forces over Beverly and the Willows.

Seeing that most of the passengers, including Nanny, were on the upper deck and in danger of a good drenching, the captain advised everyone to move inside the cabin.

"Gorry!" Nanny exclaimed. "But I hate to think what would've happened if we'd all had the chance to mind Captain Dalby!" For as she started toward the cabin door, Nanny suddenly saw a gigantic water spout lift out of the harbor only a few yards off the bow!

"Seconds later," she said, "a tremendous gust of wind took hold of the boat and shook it from stem to stern! And then over we went!"

Nanny was hurled away from her companions when the *Surf City* capsized and, with a rush of chilling sea water, pitched headlong into the cabin.

"All at once, it seemed as if there were hundreds of people around me," she said, "clutching at each other, screaming, trying to keep from going under. Water kept pouring through the open door and windows, and in minutes it was over my head."

As people tore at each other in panic, Nanny seized a lamp bracket, and hauled herself to the ceiling. Hands pulled at her shoes and dress, and then the shoes, the dress, the hands were gone.

"At last I forced my arm through one of the windows," said Nanny, "and clawed the air for what seemed ages. All of a sudden someone had hold! Was pulling me through! Was dragging me through the window, across edges of broken glass, and free! And there I was in the arms of that colored man—Blesis

Surf City

Sole! There was that kind and gentle colored man in his little skiff—Blesis Sole—smiling and talking to me, saying, 'There, there, missy. There, there now. It's all right. We's got you, and you's all right. Oh, you's just fine! Yes, you's all right!!' "

What had happened was that many people ashore, including Blesis Sole, had seen the *Surf City* in distress, and, in whatever small craft were handy, lost no time in putting to sea to rescue survivors, most of whom were clinging to the sides of the sinking steamer.

It was only chance, however, that brought Blesis Sole alongside the window from which Nanny, Rita Derby (or, as she is known to the rest of the world, Mrs. Nathaniel Thomas Very), reached desperately for life. For her rescue made her the sole survivor of the nine people who were trapped in the submerged

steamer cabin and became the only fatalities in the sinking of the ill-fated *Surf City* on July 4, 1898 in Beverly Harbor.

When Nanny had finished the story, and a hard shower was peppering the pond below the kitchen window, and I had looked at a pitcher of ice-cold, home-made root beer until Nanny finally poured me some, I asked her what had happened to Blesis Sole.

"Blesis who?" she answered.

"Blesis Sole," I repeated around a molasses cookie. "The colored man who saved your life."

Well, for a few minutes I just had to sit there while Nanny laughed and laughed, and kept on saying, "Well, for the land sakes! Did you ever?" But when she finally became serious, she became *very* serious.

"That's what's so strange," she said quietly. "I don't know whatever happened to Blesis Sole. When he'd brought me back to shore, and I finally rejoined my friends, he somehow just vanished into the crowd. Someone said they thought he worked down around the old Jubilee Yacht Club, but later, when I went out there to find him, no one seemed to know of any such person. And to this day, I've not seen Blesis Sole again—nor ever found out that good man's name."

That night, with the storm long gone out to sea, I lay in bed, trying to make a mind picture of the man who saved my grandmother's life. And as I kept on thinking, it occurred to me that it was because of him that I was where I was, and that I could go to sleep on an island that I loved, listening to a bright-night wind run on bird's feet across a cottage roof and a whistling buoy moan its loneliness off Newcomb's Ledge. Whoever that man was, wherever he might be, bless his soul.

THE LAST RUN
of the
RABBIT TRAIN

The "Rabbit" hopped between Spring-field and Athol, a distance of 48.5 miles. It was a cranky, noisy, dirty, stuffy, old train...Why then was it so important to so many people?

by George William Rae

Train No. 582 was a "mixed" train and, according to the timetable, subject to delay on account of freight. There were those who claimed that you could go rabbit hunting during the freight delays and be back in plenty of time to continue your journey! For this reason, people began calling No. 582 the "Rabbit Train."

Distances between stations along this branch railroad line were short: Springfield to Fiberloid, 5.5 miles; .9 from there to Indian Orchard; another 1.2 miles to Ludlow; 2.9 miles to Collins; 1.9 to Red Bridge; 3.3 miles to Three Rivers; 1.4 to Barretts Junction; 1.5 to Bondsville; and so on, in short "hops" up the Swift River Valley. Some folks say that this was how the "Rabbit Train" got its name.

Whatever the origin of the nickname, there is no doubt that this was one of the most-beloved trains in New England. No. 582 traveled the Athol Branch of the Boston & Albany Railroad from Springfield to Athol, Massachusetts, between August 1, 1880 and June 1, 1935.

The Athol Branch, the "Rab-bit," and all or part of ten Swift River Valley towns disappeared shortly thereafter into the Quabbin Reservoir, the huge, man-made lake which now serves as the water supply for many towns and cities of eastern Massachusetts, principally Boston.

Contemporary accounts of two "last runs" of the "Rabbit" reflect the affection with which this slow, ungainly, and sometimes very "mixed" train was held by inhabitants of the area.

"Blossom-decked, verdant Swift River Valley waved farewell to its passenger train yesterday after 220 passengers, including railroad officials, members of the National Association of Railroad Engineers, veteran engineers and just sightseers filled 3 coaches...," said one writer of the May 26, 1935 "special" on its widely advertised, near-last run. In the coaches were many Valley folks who were looking at the bulldozed and denuded sites of their home towns for the last time.

Another writer said: "During its service the line has earned the name of 'Rabbit'—whether or not this is because of the short distances or because of the fact that it was once popular with hunters is not known. Old-time commuters, confirmed excursionists and everyone else with a yen to see the Swift River Valley from the windows of a railroad coach for the last time will have their opportunity Sunday, May 26, when the B & A Railroad will run a special excursion train from Springfield to Athol as a last blaze of glory for the Branch Line which will be abandoned June 1, 1935...."

To those who knew and loved the "Rabbit," a faithful friend—albeit an often cranky, frustrating, noisy, dirty, stuffy friend—was leaving and they gathered all along the line to say so-long—not goodbye—for none of them really believed that the "Rabbit" was dying; rather it was going on to make its short hops along some Heavenly Branch Line.

The technical data concerning the "Rabbit" does not require much space—and little need be said about its fiery heart, the live steam in its pipes, the disdainful snorts of its stack, or the many nuances of its magnificent bell and whistle. Only

The "Rabbit Train" at Athol, Massachusetts, on its last run 35 years ago

those of us who knew and loved trains can recall their individual characteristics.

The "Rabbit" ran—or hopped —between Springfield and Athol, a distance of 48.50 miles. Total trackage of the branch 52.50 miles; gauge, 4 ft. 8½ in. (standard); rail 56 lbs. It was chartered in 1869; opened December 3, 1873; purchased by the B. & A. R.R. Co. July 8, 1880, for the sum of $439,064.92, and operated by that company from August 1, 1880 until June 1, 1935.

Proving nothing, except that technical data does not *breathe;* it flings off no cinders, frightens no cows, delights no small boys, takes no immigrants blueberrying nor hunters hunting, lovers loving, dancers dancing. Neither does it make for itself a place in the hearts of many hundreds of people of all kinds.

But the "Rabbit" train did. And a considerable number of people still feel sentimental about it.

There are photos of the last run hanging on many walls in the vicinity of the Quabbin watershed.

The one used to illustrate this story came off the wall of the Athol Coal Company.

There are those who have preserved the last timetable with its sad notation reading: "Train No. 582 will not run after June 1."

Historical Societies of the area have many photographs of the "Rabbit."

Mrs. Ruth Snow, a beautician of Athol, has a penny run over by the last train.

Anecdotes come pouring from older inhabitants who knew the train: "I recall riding the cowcatcher when the 'Rabbit' went down to the turntable in Athol."

"Rode it to the dance at North Dana every Saturday; met and courted my wife on it."

"One 'Rabbit' engine was named Uncle Willis—after Willis Phelps, who was one of the builders of the road. Had the name right on it in brilliant paint. 'Phelps' turned purple, but then learned to be right proud of it—his descendants were, too."

"Those were the days of woodburning engines. Airbrakes were still a matter of suspicion in the minds of old-timers. Engines had shining brass trimmings, glittering cylinders and gaily painted, cone-shaped stacks, and driving wheels painted a bright red."

"Excess speed was frowned upon by Willis Phelps. It is told that he had heard the engineers were speeding whenever they could, and there were complaints, and fears of accidents were expressed. He decided to check the road in different places. In some way the word leaked out as to when and where Phelps was to watch and check speeds. Engineers slowed down at these places to 15 miles per hour, but ran it up to 40 as soon as Phelps was out of sight. After that he dealt roughly with all complaints about the 'Rabbit!'"

Suddenly it was all going to end —the regular blowing of the whistle to awaken schoolboys; the chuffing trips through the beautiful Valley; the excitement at the turntable; the romance of clacking wheels; the homely, grumbly, companionable assurance that all was well, implicit in the dear old "Rabbit."

But there was to be a second last run—the very last—on June 1, 1935. Ed Kent was to be the engineer, as he had been for a long time, and Joe Dube of Springfield was to fire engine No. 1049, last of the "Rabbit" engines and a perfectly awful, beat-up, clanking monster with an ideal "Rabbit" personality. Ed Brownell rode the rear end as brakeman. When everyone was aboard at the old B. & A. station at Springfield, it was Conductor Joseph Sherman who pronounced the final, benedictional: "B-o-o-o-o-r-r-r-d!"

The "Rabbit" turned away from the Connecticut River for the last time and pointed its blunt nose toward Fiberloid. The day was clear, the sky bright blue. Smoke towered and cinders rattled back over the B. & A. boxcar, the Texaco and Sinclair tank-cars, the RPO, passenger, baggage cars, and caboose.

In the passenger cars, Mike Walsh helped with the ticket collection. He—who was usually full of whip-lash Irish humor—was subdued. There were 145 passengers on the last run, most of them, like Nellie Vaughn, Mrs. Bertha Leary, Dick and Bob Walker, Sophie Towers, Ruth Snow, Walter Spaulding, Daisy Parker, Grace Haskins, Belle Thayer, Stan King, and James Pratt, were there because they loved the train, or wanted the memory of a last ride through their vanishing valley; but some riders were distinguished by their connection with the "Rabbit" or the railroad line.

Among these were Burt Scott, Trainmaster of the B. & A., and R. D. Fuller, District Passenger Agent of Springfield. Men who worked for railroads—or had something to do with the irresistible "Rab-bit"—were not there just because it was part of their job to be there.

The train made its usual short hops up into the Swift River Valley, picking up more passengers on the way, passing through cuts soon to be silent, acknowledging the sad waves, the blinking eyes, the choked cheers, with bright, undaunted blasts from its impertinent whistle.

But most of the people—the "Rabbit's" people—were gone, the farms, the homes, the businesses, the towns themselves; even the dead from the cemeteries had been removed for reburial elsewhere. The whistle echoed a bit more hollowly, its melancholy deepening as it moved into the treeless, houseless basin that was to hold the water supply of the eastern cities—through West Ware, Enfield, Greenwich Village, Morgan Crossing, Soapstone, North Dana...

Standing on the platform at Athol, as the "Rabbit" pulled in there for the last time was John D. Smith, who had been standing there 62 years before when the original "Rabbit" hopped in for the first time.

A contemporary writer described the departure from Athol on the return trip: "The last train on the 'Rabbit Road' so-called, better known as the Athol Branch of the B. & A., pulled out of Athol last Saturday afternoon about 1:40 amid the waving of hands and the blowing of whistles and a goodbye to a road that has given yeoman service to this section for the past 62 years and which started when Athol people subscribed close to $100,000. There were 115 passengers on the 'last ride' and quite a number came all the way from Springfield to make the round trip. There were several aboard who rode on the first train in 1873, among these were E. Hager of North Dana and his brother Arthur of Athol, both of whom were passengers on the very first train in 1873. Station Agent Roseberry autographed B. & A. timetables for over an hour before the departure...."

Now the "Rabbit" was really headed for the last roundhouse. For the last time the Athol crossings and South Athol heard the saucy whistle. Already the tracks curving southward out of Athol were beginning to look abandoned. Those aboard the train gazed out the windows wistfully. North Dana ... Soapstone (usually a flagstop; no more would the flags wave the huffing "Rabbit" to a halt) ... Morgan Crossing ... Greenwich Village and on into the Valley where many of the stations were already gone, along with the residents and the businesses ... Greenwich, where once the "Rabbit" picked up three hundred cars of ice in a single winter ... Enfield, where the massive evidence of the Valley's fate—huge piles of sand and rock—were being assembled for the Quabbin dam ... on through West Ware—and out of the Swift River Valley forever.

If there was anyone at West Ware with a mind at all poetic, he might have watched the "Rabbit" take the curve leading to Gates Siding and thought: The "Rabbit" could have passed Gates and gone on to Bondsville, Barretts Junction, Three Rivers; but then again it might not have. The "Rabbit" might just have taken a last mighty leap to 40-odd miles of invisible track; and when I walk at night down along the edge of Quabbin in the future, I'll hear a long, low whistle, and perhaps see a headlight moving through the wet darkness reflecting on the sky...

CRUISE SHIP WITH A
VENGEANCE

As the Fort Victoria *sank beneath them on December 18, 1929, the author and her friends never dreamed they'd bump into her again!*

by Marion Russell, *as told to Richard M. Hallet*

It was nearly noon, December 18, 1929, when Kay, Kirkie and I boarded the Furness Line ship *Fort Victoria* for our long-dreamed-of Christmas trip to Bermuda.

In our stateroom we opened suitcases and hung up a few "crushables" and then went down to lunch. After that we turned in and slept for a couple of hours. When we came on deck again, the fog was thick, and the ship's whistle kept blaring "NO . . . NO . . . NO" . . . as if she didn't like what she was sticking her nose into.

We three girls didn't share her apprehensions. This was our first ocean voyage, and fog was merely something that spoiled the view.

"She's practically stopped," Kirkie said.

And then it happened.

The crash and lurch were simultaneous. It was as if a donkey had put his hind hoof through a wash-boiler—only a thousand times worse.

We picked ourselves up—people had been thrown every which way—and ran to the port side of our vessel just in time to see a huge black prow backing out of a V-shaped hole in our plating. We had been rammed almost directly amidships by another ship—the Clyde liner *Algonquin,* we learned later. She backed away and got lost in the fog.

Some of the passengers clustered around the hole. It didn't look

very big to my landlubber eyes. I really cheered up at sight of it.

"It doesn't look alarming," I said to Kirkie, "I don't think it goes under water."

When we got home we might begin to say the hole was big enough to drive a coach and four through. I believe that's the usual expression

when a ship is rammed. Just now we were thinking it was no worse than a dent in a fender.

But our optimism was considerably dampened when we heard a seaman say, "Back to New York for us!"

As it turned out, even he was being optimistic.

We fled to our stateroom and began packing our suitcases. People do even stranger things than that when a ship is in trouble. A steward promptly put a stop to this.

"Don't monkey with those pretty dresses," he said sternly. "Just put on your life preservers and come up on deck."

We got into them somehow, but I had the feeling that a lot of time was passing. Finally, I rushed out of that stateroom so fast I left my hat behind. When I realized this, I turned to run back after it. The lights in the corridor were growing dim. Then they went out altogether. It did really seem as if the poor *Fort Victoria* was giving up the ghost, and I lost interest in my hat.

A seaman with a flashlight came pushing at us.

"You know your life-boat?" he cried.

"Number 8," we chorused.

But Number 8 had been crumpled by the bow of the Clyde liner.

"Go back aft and try Number 10," he said.

We ran to Number 10, but it already had its fill of passengers and was half way down to the water.

We rushed for Number 12. This boat, too, was filled and swung out. But there was a hitch in the proceedings. Deck officers were arguing with our luncheon companion—a lady with a beautiful Samoyed dog.

"Put my dog in," she cried.

"No room for dogs, ma'am."

"Then I won't come myself."

Can you imagine it? I did just have a flash of admiration for a woman who would drown with her dog sooner than abandon it. The officer must have shared this feeling. At all events he put the dog across, and then the lady. And then us three girls. The boat hung in the davits about two feet from the side of the ship, as two men swung me across by the elbows. I had a dizzying glimpse of the cold December ocean rolling far below; and then I found myself stuffed into that boatload in a very inelegant way. I was straddled on a man's knees, with my chin jammed against the life preserver of a great burly fellow in front of me.

Now the boat was being lowered; and just to add to the excitement, the seamen failed to coordinate the davits. I know that's not sea language, but you see what I mean. The after part of the boat went down and the forward part didn't. The falls had got jammed somehow.

We really were at a dreadful

angle, and everybody instinctively grabbed what was in front of him— or her. We were stuck together like a swarm of bees on a limb. The man on whose knees I had been deposited hugged me for dear life, and I passed on that hug to the man in front of me.

It was certainly a travesty of any sort of Bermuda socializing we had dreamed of. I looked steeply down over my shoulder, and I must have screamed along with the others. It was all a matter of screaming seconds; and then a seaman in the bow cut the Gordian knot. Quite literally. He swung his ax and cut the jammed rope off clean. Down we came and

The front page of the Boston Post *on the morning of December 19, 1929, only told half the story.*

smacked the water.

That really was a jar—a tooth-pulverizer, Kirkie called it later. And at the same time a shower of blood sprayed my spring coat. The man who had saved us just hadn't been able to stop his ax. It had swung around in a full circle and clipped the scalp of the man below him. He wasn't badly hurt, it turned out, but his blood just seemed to fly everywhere.

I really was quite dazed by all this. What brought me to was an oar handle thumping against my shoul-

der blades. The man back of me was one of the crew, and was trying to row with me on his knees. No wonder the boat went in circles! But he was really a terrible oarsman, and it wasn't all because he had a girl jammed on his knees either. He just lacked experience. I wished I could change places with him because my Maine summers had made me a pretty good oarsman. But there I sat on his knees while he just made futile dabs at the water.

Perhaps because of his bad rowing, we were in at the death of the *Fort Victoria*. The fog lifted just the least bit, and there we saw our poor ship poised, like a drunken slack-rope walker, just ready to take the plunge. She was listed badly. Suddenly she roared and rolled over and sank.

The pilot boat *New Yorker* picked us up, wet and half frozen, and landed us at Staten Island. From here we were taken to the McAlpin Hotel in Manhattan. Reporters thronged around us, first one or two, and then a dozen, and then perfect quantities. Questions instead of waves lashed at our heads. Photographer's bulbs flashed. This was fame's little day with a vengeance. We were survivors, and people whose lives have been saved are naturally important, I suppose. Saints and sinners, we were all survivors. (Actually no lives were lost.)

A reporter called out, "Anyone from Boston?"

Kay, Kirkie and I spoke up eagerly as Boston survivors, and the cameras clicked and flashed again. With the result that my Uncle Fred, in Boston, picking up a paper on his early morning walk, saw my picture on the front page.

A fine suite of rooms had been

reserved for us at the McAlpin. We had breakfast in bed, in nightgowns donated by the Furness Line. Our own clothes, right down to the skin, had been whisked away to be washed, dried and pressed.

Kirkie said, "It's really more exciting than if we had got to Bermuda."

It was indeed! Still, we were dead for sleep. In fact I had got into bed and was already half asleep when the telephone rang. I came broad awake when a man announced that if we wished to continue the voyage to Bermuda, the Furness Line's *Fort St. George* would be ready to board at 11 A.M.

"Is he crazy?" Kirkie yelled.

"We'll be there," I told the Furness Line man, and hung up.

Kay and I went to work on Kirkie. We told her it was so nice of the Furness Line to put another ship at our disposal with such promptness. We could still get to Bermuda before Christmas.

"Christmas!" Kirkie echoed. "And no clothes!"

"The Furness Line has given each of us a brush and comb, don't forget," we urged.

We finally persuaded her; and shortly before noon we boarded the *Fort St. George.* I had had just time to rush out to buy a new hat and a small overnight case. We were going in just the clothes we stood in.

The *Fort St. George* was out of dead storage, I guess. Certainly she didn't have the fresh paint and the fine-lady airs of our dear, departed *Fort Victoria;* but she did have the same officers and crew, although not the same passengers, mostly. I think we three were almost the only survivors to come aboard. I know I didn't see any of the old familiar faces.

We were thoroughly exhausted now, and just dropped into our bunks without undressing.

"Wake me up when we get to Bermuda," Kirkie muttered.

We slept like the dead, and didn't even know when the ship got under way.

And then—IT HAPPENED AGAIN!

What woke us was the horrible grinding, trampling sound of it. Our ship shook and shivered from stem to stern . . . the engines seemed to be going full astern.

We jumped out of our bunks and looked through the porthole. The

From l. to r.: Bertha Kirks, Marion Russell, and Katherine Watson as they arrive back in N.Y. after surviving two *shipwrecks.*

lights of the New Jersey coast were shining brightly. This was proof enough that it wasn't the fog this time that had done us in. Lucky it was that we hadn't undressed! We rushed for the deck, and this time I jammed on my hat.

Things were following much the same pattern as the day before. There were a few minor differences, to be sure. For one thing I was just remembering that I didn't know the number of my lifeboat. I had a death grip on my handbag, and that was all.

Getting on deck I bumped into a stalwart form that looked familiar. He caught me by the elbow to steady me, and then I recognized him. He was the officer who had thrown me into Number 12 lifeboat on the *Fort Victoria.*

"You again," I gasped. "I don't know the number of my lifeboat."

"Go for Number 12 as usual," he laughed. "You had good luck with that one."

"Have we gone aground?"

"We've gone aground on the *Fort Victoria,"* he told me.

We just literally and unbelievably had. The *Victoria* had sunk right in mid-channel, there hadn't been time to buoy the area, and now we had trampled on her corpse. An unkind fate just couldn't leave her alone.

"How big is the hole in us?" I asked my officer.

"Can't tell yet. Maybe no hole at all. You girls get your life preservers on. You know how."

We certainly did. We got them on, and went and stood by Number 12. But as it turned out, the *Fort St. George* had backed off unhurt, and after a little delay we went on to Bermuda.

News of us had gone on ahead, and we were treated all over again as survivors. It was all the more exciting because we were practically the only survivors who had survived as far as Bermuda.

The island gave us a royal reception. We really didn't miss those dresses that had gone to the bottom with the *Fort Victoria.* We had the time of our young lives, and to this day it remains *the* experience of a lifetime.

1902

off to th

In 1902 the writer of this article was the possessor of a steam Locomobile.

At that time there were very few automobiles in this country. A lot of experimental work was underway, particularly in France, with various types of gasoline engines and there were some commercial cars in use. In this country much was being undertaken with gasoline engines but progress had been particularly directed toward what was known as a steam carriage. It was well named for it did look much more like a carriage than like today's automobiles. The steam was produced in a boiler heated by a gasoline flame. Perhaps the best type then produced here was the Locomobile which was manufactured in Bridgeport, Connecticut.

My car was the third one in this part of Massachusetts; the first one was a French car, the second was owned by the local agent for the Locomobile. Of course they were all of much interest to our contemporaries. My car was painted a dark color with bright yellow panels on each side of the wagon body, which quite accurately describes it. There

was a patent leather dashboard just like a horse-drawn vehicle except for a whip socket. I don't know why it was omitted; it would not have looked out of place. The carriage was steered by a jointed contraption which lifted up when you wanted to get out, but which bent down on your lap when you sat down. By moving this forward and back it turned the front wheels, which were connected. The throttle, which governed the speed, was a small lever worked by the right hand, the steering being accomplished by the left hand. A very small movement of the throttle sometimes produced rather sudden and startling results. The carriage could be reversed by using another lever and there was a brake pedal.

Our longest trip during this period was through the White Mountains, then largely virgin territory so far as motors were concerned. Our first stop was Nashua, New Hampshire, a distance of about 125 miles. We were careful to avoid Boston and travelled as much as possible by back roads, as we knew the effect the cloud of steam, which accompanied us, would have on horses. It

was not unusual for them to bolt, leaving the vehicle behind or taking the occupant of the carriage where he had not the slightest desire of going. There were then no garages, and it was only after long and serious argument with the hotel proprietor at Nashua that our carriage was allowed to rest in the hotel stable yard, and then only if covered with blankets which the proprietor provided.

Leaving the next day, our difficulties began in earnest, not so much with our means of locomotion as with other people's. The roads were narrow and rutted with steep grades and when the engine was working hard going up a hill we left behind us more than the usual cloud of steam. Sometimes we were enveloped in it. It was not to be surprised at that almost every horse we met tried to climb the nearest stone wall and leave for parts unknown. The horse was not interested in what happened to the conveyance he was pulling.

On meeting a horse and wagon we always stopped, drew off the road as far as possible and fearfully awaited our fate. Most everyone was

WHITE MOUNTAINS by Frederic H. Taber

A short account, by the first man to drive a car through the White Mountains, describing a few problems and some negative reactions.

a good sport, but pioneering of this kind could not be recommended to anyone with a weak heart.

Our second night was at the Weirs on Lake Winnipesaukee, not a long day's drive today, but then a difficult one. It was now that our troubles really began for the road up to and over the Franconia Notch was frightful. It was especially so going up the Notch itself, no wide, hard-surfaced and well-drained road as now, but one rutted and deep in mud. No grading at all, but first a pitch down and then a steeper climb up the next rise. The only way we made it was for my companion, who was much older than I and who could not operate the machine, to jump out and run alongside pushing as hard as he could on the rises and then when momentum was again secured, leaping back to his seat to repeat the process over and over again.

We finally reached the top of the Notch more or less exhausted and stayed at the hotel there over night. This hotel, the Franconia Inn, burned down years later and the whole area through the Notch is now

a National Forest. Having rested up sufficiently, the next day we continued to Franconia and Lisbon, our destination. The road down the Notch was bad by modern standards, but it was downhill and so much easier to negotiate. Our trip was commented on in the local paper, which mentioned the distance of 240 miles in four days, an average of about 60 miles a day, as quite an accomplishment. From remarks we heard, our Locomobile must have been one of the first, if not the first, horseless carriage to take this route and make it successfully.

After a short stop at Lisbon, we returned over the Crawford Notch then to Intervale, Portland, Portsmouth and home. A rather longer ride and one which took 5 days, but was uneventful except for bad going up the Crawford Notch and exceptionally poor roads in the state of Maine. Altogether it was quite a journey and the predecessor of many others in later years through the same area.

If there had not been such a great development of the automobile by Henry Ford so that the new method of getting around became

commonplace, the early use of the automobile would have ended before it started. The restrictions on when, where and how fast to drive, coupled with the local sheriff's prejudices, nearly put an end to it as it was. A picture at that time of an automobile continuing on its way with the occupant of the horse-drawn carriage, who had been thrown out on the road, aiming a rifle at the motorist, with the caption "The bullet is still faster than the automobile" marked the height of this feeling.

It was not until the Model T Ford was being distributed in volume that this antagonism to the so-called "rich man's carriage" began to abate. With it also started the agitation for better roads and more of them, until the needs of the automobile have become one of the startling economic facts of the present. All this has taken place in a matter of two generations. Probably never has such a fundamental change in habits happened to so many people in so short a time.

FROM PHILLY TO
FALL RIVER

by Allen D. Howland

Today if you want to go from Philadelphia to Westport Point, you throw a couple of suitcases in the car and off you go —but fifty years ago the trip was a tactical undertaking of the first magnitude.

"Please Leave Your Stateroom Keys Here" read the sign at the foot of the red-carpeted staircase. The keys were huge, of dull brass, and felt slightly greasy to the touch. They made a dull "klunk" as you tossed them into the box on your way to the gangplank and the Fall River pier.

I had forgotten about these distinctive keys until recently when I saw a rack of them as part of the decor in a restaurant near Fall River. They, together with other displayed furnishings from the ships of the old Fall River Line brought back memories of the numerous trips I had taken on the *Commonwealth*, *Priscilla*, *Providence* and other Sound steamers. For, from my earliest childhood until I was well into my teens, my family and I used to travel from Philadelphia to New England at least once, and sometimes twice a year—and we never thought of going any other way than on the Fall River boat.

My father, the youngest in a family of five boys and two girls, was born and brought up in the tiny village of Westport Point, located near the mouth of Buzzards Bay between Fall River and New Bedford. Shortly after he was married, Dad was sent to Philadelphia, but his brothers never got any farther away from home than Fall River. Although they lived and worked in the city, they never missed a chance to get back to the "Point" and their sisters kept the old family home open for them all year 'round. My father, too, whenever he took a vacation, headed back home to hunt and fish with his brothers, and they always arranged their vacations to

At the head of Providence River, 3 steamboats are docked for repairs. From left to right: The *Pomham*, the *Monhegan* and the *Warwick*. The *Warwick* (1873) ran a great many years. She was built as the *Day Star*, then in 1899 was partly destroyed by fire. Later, she was rebuilt and renamed.

coincide with his, so that all the Howland "boys" could be together.

Getting the three of us from suburban Philadelphia to Westport Point was a considerable undertaking in those days, one that involved just about every means of transportation then available, including trains, taxis, ferryboats, steamers, and trolley cars—plus a fair amount of walking. Today you throw a couple of suitcases in the car, and off you go; but 50 years ago a trip such as ours required a considerable amount of advance planning and organization. First, the steamer trunk had to be packed (remember, this was in the ante drip-dry days—you had to take *lots* of clothes) and sent off at least a week in advance by Railway Express. Then came the suitcases and hat boxes which had to hold immediate necessities as well as long-range equipment in case the trunk—as often happened—was late in arriving. On our summer trips, several fishing rods, unwieldy even in their disjointed condition, and a large tackle box were added to our impedimenta; in winter we staggered under the additional weight of a couple of shot guns and an extra suitcase full of Christmas presents.

Somehow we managed to get all this stuff by taxi to the station, up two flights of steep steps and aboard the train. The two-hour ride was relaxing and gave us all a chance to rest up for the rigors that lay ahead. At the Jersey City Terminal we lugged everything across the station concourse and aboard the Liberty Street Ferry. Mother quickly found a seat in the cabin; Dad and I piled the luggage around her and then went forward to watch the ferry butt her way across the crowded waters of New York harbor. On disembarking, we faced the customary problem of how to get to the Fall River Line pier. Only a block away, it was too short a distance for a thrifty New Englander to consider taking a

taxi, but a weary haul for three people laden with luggage and sporting equipment. Occasionally an enterprising porter from the Fall River boat would show up at the ferry slip and we would load him up with all our gear, and then feel so sorry for him that his tip was about as much as our taxi fare would have been. Most often, however, we made the trip unaided, dodging in and out of the heavy traffic, skirting mud puddles and holes in the paving, the suitcases banging against our legs and the fishing rods poking into the people ahead of us. Most of the waterfront traffic was still horse-drawn, including the trolley cars, and my father never failed to point out the low steps that had been recently installed so that ladies in hobble-skirts could get aboard without revealing an unseemly stretch of ankle.

Our arrival at the Fall River Line pier brought the answers to two questions that puzzled us ever since we bought our tickets: (1) which steamer would we be sailing on? and (2) would we have an inside or an outside stateroom? With reference to (1), much as we loved the *Priscilla* and the other older ships, we always hoped it would be the *Commonwealth,* for she was newer, roomier, and her dining room was on the upper deck and had windows. On the older ships, you ate in a room which my mother described as "below the water line," and the food always upset her stomach because she couldn't see out. I don't believe the dining saloons were actually that far down in the hold, but they were windowless, and the silver and glassware rattled a good deal because of the proximity of the engine room. As for (2), an outside room was greatly to be preferred because it was cooler and you could lie in the berth and look out at the lights and the passing shore line. The fact that passengers pacing the deck could also look in at you didn't

bother me as much as it did my parents, who were forever closing the sliding shutters just when there was something I wanted to see. If the stateroom was inside, it was always infernally hot, and your only view was through a narrow grating high up in the wall, and you had to prop yourself up in a most uncomfortable position to do even that.

On those lucky voyages when we occupied an outside room on the *Commonwealth,* you would have thought that everyone would have been happy; but such was not the case. My mother hated traveling by boat and I believe she would have gone almost any other way, if it had been the least bit practical—and if Dad would have let her. The basic reason for her feeling this way was her easy tendency to seasickness, even though she maintained that the steamers were stuffy, crowded, and smelled bad as well. As a matter of fact, her stomach began to feel queasy on the brief ferry ride, and it never quite got back to normal until she set foot on the dock at Fall River. The part of the trip which she dreaded most came about 1 A.M., when the steamer left the quiet waters of Long Island Sound and sailed for a short time in the open ocean before rounding Point Judith and entering Narragansett Bay. Mother always told us the next morning how rough it had been and how much she suffered; but Dad insisted that the waters off Point "Jude" were as smooth as a millpond and that mother was the only person he knew who could snore and be seasick at the same time.

It never took us long to get settled in our stateroom, for there just wasn't enough room for any extensive unpacking. Those rooms were marvels of compactness. In addition to the two berths, they held a couple of stools with stiff red upholstery that could be very uncomfortable if you sat on them naked, a towel rack, a medicine chest and

The *Commonwealth*—berthed for the winter

The *Perry* was built for local service

The *Priscilla* going past Bourne Bridge

The *Plymouth* taken from Covell house

The *New Shoreham*—Providence to Newport to Block Island

The *Mount Hope* approaching Newport

a basin with running water; the other facilities were down the corridor—or under the lower berth. Also under the berth were the life preservers, so old and dry they looked as if they would disintegrate as soon as they got wet. I never trusted them—to me a life preserver was a doughnut-shaped thing with a rope attached to it. These so-called life jackets looked much too complicated to be really safe, even though the instructions showed a lady and a gentleman wearing them and standing practically erect in the water.

After settling in, and getting mother safely established in a deck chair on the lee side, Dad and I proceeded with our customary exploration of the ship. This always started with a visit to the top deck, which we made very brief, for it was extremely sooty up there; also because we had once been caught close to the funnel when the steam whistle went off, and we had no desire to repeat that ear-splitting and soul-shattering experience. So, after a reassuring glance at the magnificently moustached Captain in the wheelhouse and checking the time by the clock on the Colgate factory across the river in Jersey City, we descended to the lower decks.

One thing that always impressed me with the Fall River Line management was their prodigality with white paint, surpassed only by the niggardliness with chippers and scrapers. Year after year, the paint had been slapped on, coat upon coat, until it stood a good quarter of an inch thick in places and it was a wonder that any moving parts ever moved at all. The decks were covered with something that looked like sheet lead and the cinders under foot

made walking a noisy business. We went over the ship from bow to stern, carefully inspecting the lifeboats and life rafts which were kept in impeccable condition, so perfect in fact that I used to wonder if the thickly painted davits would work, or if the carefully coiled ropes could even be straightened out.

The call of "All ashore that's going ashore!" brought us to the side of the ship, from where we could watch the visitors scurrying to leave, the hauling in of the gangplank, and finally the casting off of the giant hawsers. Then, hurriedly to the bow to watch as the ship, blowing her whistle repeatedly, nosed out into the North River, turned and headed down towards the Battery. Once we were underway, Dad took me to the lowest deck and a doorway from which we could look down into the brightly lighted engine room. All the Fall River steamers were sidewheelers, and it was an awe-inspiring sight to stand there and watch the huge, powerful cranks making their endless revolutions. Shafts, wheels, belts, and pistons were also in noisy motion, but it was those tremendous cranks, painted a bright red, rising from the pit, heaving over and dropping out of sight again, that dominated the whole scene and made you feel that the ship was tearing through the water at a tremendous rate of speed. In the midst of all this clamorous activity the members of the engine room crew moved with studied nonchalance, squirting oil here, turning a valve there, wiping off the brass work with cotton waste, and seeming to escape being caught and crushed in the machinery by only the narrowest of margins. Of all the crew, though, the one I admired the most

was the one who stood on a little platform jutting out over the engine itself and who, just as the great red crank reached the top of its stroke, stretched out his hand and gave a quarter-turn to one of the grease cups, then stood back to wait until it again came within his reach. There was something so assured, so completely confident, so effortless in his motion as he put out his hand to tend the heaving monster below that I could have watched him all night.

There was always plenty to see as the steamer rounded the Battery and headed into the East River. Most interesting, of course, was the succession of great bridges under which we passed. I had known all about the Brooklyn Bridge for years, but on every trip it came as a surprise to realize how many other bridges there were to Brooklyn. As we approached each span, it seemed utterly impossible that our ship with her tall funnels and flagpole at the bow could ever pass underneath; but we managed it somehow, and each time there was a brief moment when you could look straight up and see the stream of cars, trucks, trains, and pedestrians moving overhead and for just those few seconds hear the roar they made in passing.

As we approached Hell Gate, Dad always took me to the bow where we could watch the sailors taking precautions against this dangerous stretch of water. Actually, about all they did was loosen up the ropes that held the anchors to the deck, after which they lounged around in bored attitudes until it was time to tighten up the lashings again. My father assured me, however, that they couldn't take any chances, for it was no easy job to get a steamer of our size through this tricky channel with its swirling currents and sunken rocks. He loved to tell of the time when he was traveling from Fall River to New York and the fog was so thick that they had to anchor for two days just outside of Hell Gate. It was the steamship company's responsibility to feed the passengers free for as long as they were delayed, and this they did —but at a minimum outlay. The fog proved a bonanza to the boatmen who lived near the Hell Gate channel, for they did a brisk business ferrying the hapless passengers ashore at $10.00 a head. By the beginning of the second day, almost every one was willing to pay this exorbitant fee rather than face another meal of watered-down bean soup.

It was now beginning to get dark, and time to pick up Mother and get our dinner. The food on the Fall River Line was reputed to be excellent, but for some strange reason I can remember little about it, except that the milk toast was exceptionally good. I am sure that I ate many meals of more substance than milk toast, yet none of them sticks in my mind. I do remember that the dining saloons on all steamers were beautifully appointed, that the table linen was spotless, the service excellent, and that on each table were double lamps with fringed red shades (the use of red in its scheme of decoration was practically a trade mark of the Fall River Line).

By the time we came on deck again, it was dark and there was nothing to see but the lights on shore and the occasional blinker of a lighthouse or a channel buoy. In those days people used to drive their cars down to the water's edge to "watch the Fall River boats go by," and they would blink their headlights and blow their horns as we passed. The ship replied to this greeting by sweeping its searchlight back and forth along the shore and by an occasional blast on its whistle. I always hated to go to bed, but when I

did (in the upper berth), I was asleep in no time and all the turbulence, real or fancied, off "Point Jude" never wakened me.

The first thing you realized on getting up the next morning was that most people who took the Fall River boat weren't going to Fall River at all. They got up early, as the boat was docking, and walked across the pier to board the train for Boston, their true destination. We were more leisurely, however, and by the time we came down the stairs and tossed our brass key into the box, the ship was nearly deserted. With all our luggage and gear, which seemed somehow to have become heavier and more cumbersome, we labored across the gangplank to have breakfast in the little railroad restaurant on the pier.

Although Westport Point was only 16 miles distant from Fall River, actually we had come to the most difficult part of our journey, that part which bitterly exasperated my Mother and made her vow each year that she'd never spend her vacation in New England again. For the facts were these: Westport Point lay so far off the beaten track that there was no way to get there unless you had a car; and we had no car. On the other hand, each of Dad's brothers had one and drove back and forth from Fall River two or three times a week. Therefore, the natural supposition would be that one of them would meet us on the dock and drive us the rest of the way. This supposition was strengthened by the fact that all of them were delighted to have Dad come to visit them and, as I have said, all of their vacation arrangements had been made to suit his. Unhappily, by the time we got there all of them were at Westport so busy fishing or making preparations to go fishing that there was just no time left to come to the city and pick us up. To my Father this was perfectly understandable and reasonable—no

doubt he would feel the same way himself—but Mother simply could not understand it, even though she had put up with the same situation year after year. She had plenty to say about men who seemed to think that fishing or cutting up bait was more important than offering a lift to their brother and his luggage-laden family.

After all opinions had been fully expressed, we wound up by doing the only thing possible under the circumstances: we took a taxi to the center of town, where we finally caught the inter-urban trolley to New Bedford, got off at Park Street, and, luggage and all, trudged the last six weary blocks to the home of my Mother's sister. Here my Father lounged about the house all afternoon, while luggage was unpacked and repacked (my Mother and I were staying in New Bedford for a while, which necessitated a redistribution of clothing). Then, that evening, after darkness had made fishing impossible, one of his brothers arrived to drive him on the final leg of the journey that took him at last to Westport Point, his brothers, and the unalloyed joy of fishing.

It is strange, I think, that my recollection of our trips *to* New England in those years are so vivid yet I can recall almost nothing of the details of our journeys home. We used the same means of transportation, we retraced our steps precisely, we hauled the same amount—perhaps even a larger load—of luggage, yet what I remember of trips home is as clouded and indistinct as my memories of the trips away are clear and lasting. The only explanation I have to offer is trite, but true—half the fun and excitement of a vacation is getting there. Going home is no fun at all!

The steam buffs carry on in Section VII. Memorabilia is usually kept in the attic . . .

. . . but storing those giant STEAM ANTIQUES poses special problems.

LIVE STEAMERS

Try building an old-fashioned alarm clock small enough to fit inside a watch case, and you've come close to the problem of miniaturizing a scale-model steam engine.

by Franklynn Peterson

A shrill whistle subdues the birds singing in their new nests, and a hiss of steam paints a new cloud in the fierce blue spring sky. Engine number 8001 (*Left*) of the New York Central liner rattles across the bridge and around a smooth bend in the track. Sprouting corn pokes up green arms in a bare brown field on one side of the right-of-way. Tall weeds dance gracefully in the breezes across the track. Into a long straight-away now, the engine speeds up, hissing with a hotter determination, whistling with renewed vanity.

At the Pioneer Valley depot, only a gentle grinding of brakes brings the engine to a surrender and the engineer hops off the flatcar he was riding behind the tender. Engine 8001 is only five feet long and weighs just a little more than the engineer who guides it around the quarter mile of track at the Pioneer

---

Left: Engine 8001 is five feet long and weighs just a little more than its engineer, who guides it around the track from a perch on a flat car hitched to the engine. Ten m.p.h. in such a position can be quite a thrill.

Below: This photo was taken from one of the engines pulling into the Pioneer Valley depot. Club members can be seen preparing engines for a run.

Valley Live Steam Club in Southwick, Massachusetts. Club members have a dozen Lilliputian locomotives which run on the club's right-of-ways, but on the day of a meet, three or four dozen trains from all over the country will build up traffic problems no modern railroad has ever contended with.

Not an amusement park ride, but not a toy electric train either, the Pioneer Valley rolling stock is steam locomotives built exactly like engines which once hauled passengers and freight on the CM&St.P., the B&O, the Soo Line. Inside and out, the engines are authentic working repro-

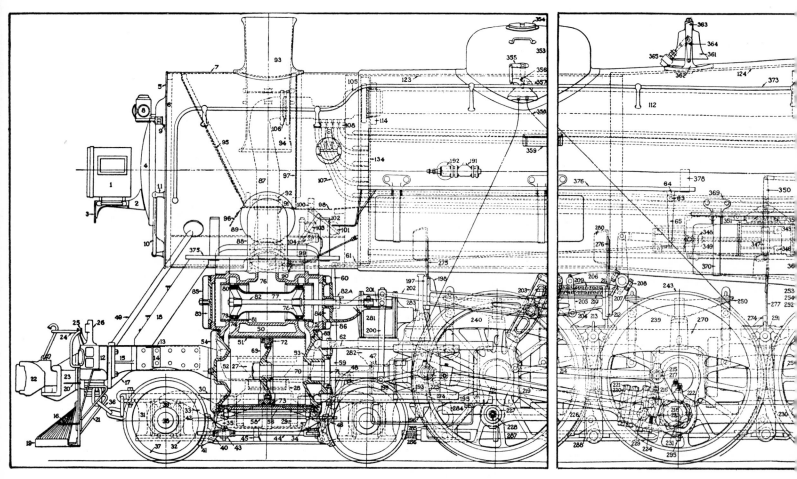

ductions except they are 1/16th the size, 1/12th as big, or 1/8th scale. Engines built to the 1/16th size come as short as a foot long and weigh 25 pounds. The big ones can stretch out to 10 feet and weigh half a ton.

The pokey but faithful old steamers were built with an economy of parts. No chrome, no fancy padding or streamlining, no gadget ever rode a steam engine that wasn't essential to dependable operation of a railroad. And that's how the model steamers are built. Try building an old-fashioned alarm clock small enough to fit inside a watch case, and you've come close to the problem of miniaturizing a scale-model steam engine. But nobody considers that *challenge* to be a *problem* . . . that is what the hobby is all about.

Building and driving small-scale steam locomotives as a hobby

actually got its start in England. A railroad engineer loved his trade so much he adopted the name of his line, L.B.S.C. It seems Mr. L.B.S.C. designed a number of tiny steam-driven engines and published "how-to-do-it" stories in model maker magazines. Carl Purlinton of Boxford, Massachusetts, picked up copies of the model engine blueprints and started his own versions back in 1931. Now Purlinton writes his own stories on model building and is still active in the Pioneer Valley Live Steam Club.

Even though the hobby was launched on Yankee shores in 1931, it never achieved much popularity until the colorful era of steam engine railroading was drawing its last puffs of steam. Model railroad buffs preferred the electric train, and in South wick a club of model train builders had built themselves one of the larg-

est layouts of track in the country—100 feet by 30. Alas, the factory building where the club's right-of-way was nailed to the floor cut off the steam. Winter meetings became endurance contests to see whose hands froze first. Worse yet, the train wheels also froze.

Thanks to the factory's turning off their steam, the electric train buffs decided to switch their attention to live steam trains. In 1952 the Pioneer Valley Live Steamers was incorporated by 11 railroading fanatics who bought 11 acres of land to convert into a model railroad line. All of the charter members still living are active in the club.

Fifteen years of active railroad-

A side elevation of a Baldwin 4–8–2 type locomotive illustrating its 385 parts. Courtesy of Baldwin-Lima Hamilton Corporation.

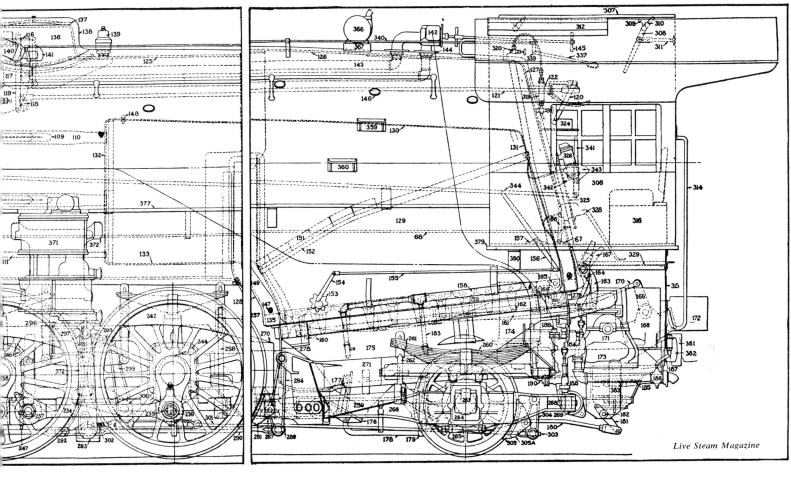

Live Steam Magazine

ing have done wonders for the 11 acres of farm land the club bought. A tobacco drying shed was converted into a club house, or depot as those in the know call it. A genuine pot-bellied stove, of course, heats the depot. And the waiting room is fringed by a lunch counter to one side and a small machine shop to the other. Vintage lanterns, bells, and steam locomotive headlights line the depot.

Over the years the club has laid a quarter mile of track. Since there are three divisions within the model steam engines, there are three sizes of tracks ranging from 3½ to 7 inches. Members keep the gandydancer going almost all the time laying new track or replacing old.

Signal lights line the tracks to control traffic. There is a water tank for refilling the tenders, a sight long-gone from tracks all over our mod-ern countrysides. One bit of nostalgia has to be omitted. There is no coal pile. Getting hold of a good grade of coal is so difficult these days that each member keeps a tight control over his own fuel supply. All except that one infidel who runs his engine on oil!

Since the built-up tracks serve as a dike to contain the spring thaw, a pond graces the Pioneer Valley railroad yard much of the year. And the pond gave the members a good excuse to build their prodigies a bridge. But because the largest engine ever to build up a head of steam on the Pioneer Valley line weighed as much as a modern car, engineering the small bridge was no small job. Fortunately one of the members is a civil engineer with M.I.T. training. His carefully authenticated blueprints were con-verted into a concrete and steel bridge with a generous added portion of jackknife carpentry.

A round house was added recently so the club members' 12 locomotives could be left "in the yard." The M.I.T. engineer struck again when he designed a hydraulic turntable in the round house to lift the heavy engines and head them in the other direction. Borrowing the mechanism from a garage hoist, and building tracks on top of it, the members can now lift their mechanical children six feet in the air for repairs. That's something no modern railroad has accomplished yet.

Even though the hobby of live steam model railroading was given the "high sign" by a railroad man, there are practically no professional trainmen devoted to the hobby. At Pioneer Valley, besides the engineer of a civil nature, there is a dentist,

229

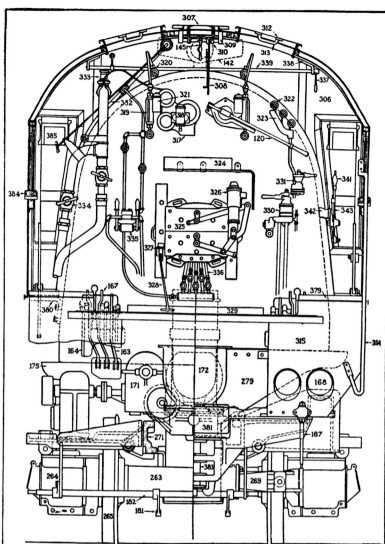

Rear elevation of a Baldwin 4–8–2 type locomotive showing cab fittings.

Robert Hornsby of Beverly Farms, Mass., pulls into the PVLS Station with Frank Dreschler's 1½" 4–4–2 from Whitestone, N.Y.

No. 13 is a passenger train and only 1/16th the size of its real counterpart. The only detail that reveals its true size is the cushion at the rear of the tender.

a photo finisher, a camera store owner, many retired men of all trades except railroading, and a number of chief-cooks-and-bottle-washers.

A Pennsylvania member of the Pioneer Valley Club, however, is a steam engineer by profession, and his home workshop shows it. His impressive collection of power tools may be driven from three sources of energy. He can connect to steam from the factory boiler he's in charge of; his own boiler sits in the family's basement; and if he really wants to abandon tradition, he can flip a switch and run the shop electrically.

The steam engineer, Harry Quick, is busy building his fourth live steam model engine. One of his earlier models could pull a dozen men sitting side-saddle on flatcars. That would seem to be the record for pulling, and a speed of 13 m.p.h. tops the racing category. Since the engine that hit 13 m.p.h. was 1/12 the real size, that would equal about 150 m.p.h. on a real steam locomotive. One limitation on the speed of steam models is nerve. Unlike the electric trains where the "engineer" sits at a remote transformer, a live steam engineer rides right behind his steam boiler and keeps his hand on the throttle. Ten m.p.h. on a two-foot-long steam engine can be quite a thrill. Shades of Casey Jones!

One fascinating aspect of the model steam engine is its total disregard for competition. When the club members get together, they don't race each other or engage in weight-moving contests. They talk shop and swap construction hints. An official meet is nothing but a social get-together where members and visitors come to run their engines. If the engine pulls a lot, that's nice. A fast engine is pretty exciting too. Some newcomers think if the tiny steamer runs at all that's enough of a miracle!

Pioneer Valley Club members seem to get more of a kick building the live steamers than they do running them. After the months and years of painstakingly detailed construction is behind them, the steam buff turns the throttle over to the Mrs. or Junior while he goes back to the basement to get started on a new model engine. Psychologically this is not a bad strategy . . . many "steam-widows" have taken up the hobby themselves after giving up on ever seeing hubby again.

The epitome of steam fanaticism is represented by a Pioneer Valley member who rounded up an old steam whistle and six locomotive bells. This joker's door bell is not wired to a set of melodic chimes or a simple buzzer. An air compressor blows a long blast on the whistle and then the six bells are set in motion. About all that's lacking is a little man to pop out of a box and say "All aboard!"

Live steamers around the Pioneer Valley may have formed the first club of its kind, but they have company now. Close to two dozen live steam model clubs have been organized on the American continent. Plus Hawaii.

There's even a *Live Steam Magazine* to whet the appetites of cult adherents, but the most prized possession of Pioneer Valley Live Steamers is its collection of ancient railroad and model-making journals. There was a time when a model railroad buff could drop a note to any railroad in the country and ask for a copy of blueprints for any engine they owned or once owned. No more. Blueprints and drawings of steam engines have been tossed out to make room for engineering studies of turbines and generators. Nothing is sacred any more!

When a model builder starts a new project now, he first has to read magazines dating back to the 1920s and 1930s. Some of them offer detailed construction information, but the adventurous buff would rather design his own facsimile of a classic steamer. And when he's finished, the mechanism inside the massive steel engine will operate in identical fashion to its big brother. And a photograph of the outside could pass for a photograph of the outside of the real antique locomotive.

There are two factories which will build you a scale model steam engine in return for a good-sized mortgage on your house. Since few hobbyists are willing to spend that kind of cash—and wouldn't spend it even if they had it—the fine art of "scrounging" is essential in completing a model. Copper boilers are snipped out of sheets, and tubes out of scarce brass. Sheet iron is welded for the body, and steel rods bolted or riveted together for a frame. Cast iron wheels and some structural parts are designed in detail and then taken to local foundries for casting. Swapping molds and drawings is one big function that goes on at any gathering of live steamers. Wheels and parts for many different switch engines were interchangeable, so why shouldn't the pint-sized counterparts do the same?

Literally hundreds of tiny bolts and rivets are slipped into position with pliers and tweezers before a live steamer is taken out for its christening. It isn't enough that an engine just runs. The steamer has to run and look like it's big brother used to. Nobody has built a model steam engine in less than a year, and many have taken three, four, and even five years. But what's the rush? There certainly won't be any new steam engines coming out that will make yours any more obsolete.

Above: Left to right are steamers Ascutney, Kearsarge, Weetamoe, *and the* Armenia White.

Right: Frank and Daniel Woodsum on the Ascutney *about 1926. These two men, together with their brother, Elias Woodsum, (not shown) built the* Lady Woodsum *on the shoreline of Sunapee.*

232

ℒADIES of SUNAPEE

Tree roots had grown around and through the old engine. It was rusted and corroded beyond belief, but it was a piece of history: the history of the steamboat on Lake Sunapee, one of the most colorful in the annals of the Granite State.

by James Newton

Seventy-four years ago when Orison Woodward was riding with his father on the *Lady Woodsum* on Lake Sunapee, in New Hampshire, he had no idea that he some day would have the engine of the steamboat in the basement of his home in nearby Sutton Mills.

Today, the 77-year-old great-grandfather relates with deserved pride the story of how he salvaged the engine by literally digging up the precious museum piece from its six-foot grave just 50 feet from the shores of Lake Sunapee, where it had been buried for nearly 42 years.

It all started in October of 1963 when Mr. Woodward—a retired sawmill operator—told his wife that he

was going to drive over to Lake Sunapee and "dig up the engine of the *Lady Woodsum*." Mrs. Woodward recalls, "When he told me that morning that he was going to dig up that engine and repair it, I thought he'd gone insane."

Mr. Woodward drove the 15 miles from Sutton to the Davis Cabins on Sunapee Lake, his shovel in the back of the old pick-up truck. He explained his purpose to the cabin proprietor and secured the necessary permission to dig where he had remembered watching the *Lady Woodsum* engine being buried more than 40 years before.

Mr. Woodward dug that entire day without finding the two-cylinder

engine; but he was not to be denied his pleasure. Then 75 years old, he returned for a second day of digging and within a few hours he struck the "lode" he had been seeking. Tree roots had grown around and through the engine, it was rusted and corroded beyond belief, and sand had caked like near-rock in all of the operating parts.

But the great-grandfather from Sutton—standing not more than five feet tall and small of body—worked throughout the day with a spirit that would have exhausted many men one-half his age. On the third day, he returned with an auto wrecker tow truck and pulled the engine from its sandy grave. Mr. Woodward spent

The owners dug a pit and dumped the heart
of the Lady Woodsum *into a sandy grave.*

thousands of hours during that long cold winter, dismantling the engine, cleaning it up, replacing a few parts, and reassembling the half-ton power machine that is now valued at more than $1,500.

The resurrection of the *Lady Woodsum*'s engine is a story in itself, but the history of the steamboat on Lake Sunapee is one of the most colorful in the annals of the Granite State.

The earliest commercial lake boat on the nine-mile-long lake was propelled by horsepower, some 22 years before the *Lady Woodsum* was built on the shoreline of the beautiful waters. Timothy Hoskins and William Cutler, in 1854, launched a large horseboat capable of transporting as many as 100 passengers.

Five years later, Austin Going of New London, New Hampshire, launched the 65-foot sidewheeler *Surprise,* an auspicious occasion on that Fourth of July. This 300-passenger boat operated until the outbreak of the Civil War, when the captain and crew enlisted in the Union cause, and the *Surprise* was dismantled.

Large boat transportation on the lake remained dormant for some 15 years after that, until 1876 when the little steamer *Penacook* and the *Lady Woodsum* were built. The *Penacook* was launched by N. S. Gardner, who is reported to have bought Little Island on the lake for a silver dollar. Mr. Gardner used the *Penacook* for hauling guests from the mainland to his picturesque island; a piece of property that may have been the real estate bargain of the 19th Century.

In 1876, three brothers moved from Harrison, Maine, to Sunapee and opened an era that was to continue for 50 years. The brothers—Frank Woodsum, Daniel Woodsum and Elias Woodsum—built the *Lady Woodsum* with its wooden keel on the shoreline of Sunapee. Fifty feet long and towing a trailer barge for freight, the single-deck steamer could carry a passenger load of 50 delighted vacationists and a crew of three: captain, fireman and purser.

The *Lady Woodsum*—the first of five steamboats built by the enterprising brothers—was in its second year when disaster struck. The small craft exploded during one of its summer runs and sank on Hay Reef, with only the top of the pilot house extending above the surface of the water. One of the three passengers aboard was blown through a window of the boat, and Elias Woodsum was burned so badly by the explosion that he died two hours after being taken ashore. He was the sole fatality, but his death and the loss of the ship all but marked an end to the Woodsum brothers' business venture on Sunapee Lake.

The Boston and Maine Railroad, fully recognizing the value of the steamboat on the lake in terms of summer tourists from Boston and New York, offered to help the remaining two Woodsum brothers raise the *Lady Woodsum* from its watery grave and finance the cost of replacing the boiler and other repairs. The offer was accepted.

Large wooden barrels, lashed together and full of water, were sunk around the reef-bound ship. When all was ready, the water was pumped from the barrels, and the *Lady Woodsum* was raised and towed ashore. Within the year, the repairs were completed, a second deck was added, and a canopy was erected over the top deck to protect the passengers from the sun.

The "new" steamer plied the lake for more than 40 years, carrying thousands of passengers, until it was dismantled in 1920. During those 40 years, the passengers included Orison Woodward of Sutton Mills, who frequently accompanied his father to the resort area where the elder Woodward conducted fishing trips and sold bait.

The engine of the *Lady Woodsum* continued in service at the lake, providing the power for pulling boats from the boat houses until 1922. Then, with the advent of the automobile and after 36 years of service, the owners dug a pit and dumped the heart of the *Lady Woodsum* into a sandy grave. One of the "mourners" was Orison Woodward, who watched as workmen covered the engine with its blanket of dirt and recalled the many months and years of fun he had enjoyed on the steamboat. Forty-one years later he was to remember the engine and its burial ground.

There were other boats on the lake during this gay period, when the tourist business in the area was to reach its zenith. The *Penacook,* previously mentioned, was purchased by Capt. Nathan Young in 1877 and renamed the *Mountain Maid.* This small steamer offered rides around the lake for 50 cents.

In 1885, the 90-foot *Edmund Burke* was built by a Newport-Sunapee syndicate headed by George A. Manson. This steamer, named for a Claremont, New Hampshire lawyer, could carry 600 passengers and was the most formidable competition of the Woodsum fleet.

But Frank and Daniel Woodsum were not to be out-classed. In 1887, the *Armenia White* was riveted together at the lake, the first of

Left: The steamer Kearsarge *at Lake Sunapee Station. She was 70 feet long and could carry 250 passengers.*

Below: By 1888 tourist traffic mushroomed on the lake. In one year the Edmund Burke, *the* Lady Woodsum, *and the* Armenia White *sold a total of 15,000 tickets.*

Below: Steamer Armenia White *at Sunapee Harbor Regatta about 1914–15. The event was held near the end of August and included canoe and boat races and a few runaway buggy horses.*

Carnival Day,
Lake Sunapee, N. H.

four Woodsum boats to be made of steel plates shipped from Chester, Pennsylvania. The *Armenia White* —the largest to ever sail Sunapee Lake—was 101 feet long and 23 feet in the beam, with a 650-passenger capacity. Built at a cost of $17,-000, it was the flagship of the Woodsum Line and carried a crew of seven: captain, engineer, fireman, ticket seller, ticket taker, baggage man, and candy and paper boy.

The *Kearsarge* became the third sister ship of the Woodsum brothers in 1897, having a 250-passenger capacity and measuring 70 feet long.

The launching of the 50-foot *Weetamoe* followed in 1902, and in 1907 the Woodsum brothers launched the *Ascutney,* a 60-foot steamer. These last two passenger vessels carried a three-man crew and could handle 150 to 200 guests.

Throughout these years, the tourist traffic on the lake was reaching unprecedented figures. In 1888, the *Edmund Burke,* the *Lady Woodsum* and the *Armenia White* sold a total of 15,000 tickets.

The Boston and Maine Railroad was doing a record-breaking business. The Lake Sunapee station was equipped with a 10-car siding, a turntable, a large steamboat wharf, a coaling station, and a special bucket tipcar for coal handling. The trains carried hundreds of passengers each day, as well as loads of mail, fresh meat, and provisions for the hotels around the lake. Published accounts report as many as 100 horses waiting at the station, ready to deliver the passengers from the trains to their hotels.

As many as eight and ten sleeping cars would be pushed to the siding at the Lake Station, on Friday nights, waiting for the first morning trips of the steamers. The *Lady Woodsum* and her whistle was usually the first ship of the season to greet the vacationers, with the larger boats coming into service as the season reached its pinnacle.

The daily runs started before 6:30 in the morning, and the steamers hauled their human cargo throughout the long day and well into the night, ending the happy time with a moonlight excursion for the "love birds" who crowded onto the decks for the three-hour ride in total darkness.

One of the many souvenirs of the Lake Sunapee steamboat era owned by Mr. Woodward includes a September timetable of steamer stops in 1914. The Woodsum fleet that fall made no less than 19 different stops around the lake each day, picking up and delivering passengers as the steamers met all Boston and Maine trains.

But during the next 10 years, the "gas buggies" invaded the lake region and the colorful steamers did a toboggan slide into oblivion. The *Edmund Burke*—after a number of various misfortunes—was sold to Capt. George Blodgett and renamed *Wenonah* about 1891. She operated only a few years before being docked with a leak at Blodgett's Landing. On July 4, 1904, the Woodsum competition was set afire and she burned to the water line; now resting there on the lake bottom.

The *Armenia White* sailed the lake for 30 years, before being "retired" for need of a new boiler in 1917. She was tied up at Georges Mills for 21 years, before being cut up and sold for scrap valued at $100.

The *Kearsarge* was converted to oil in her closing years, and sold twice before being cut up for scrap in the middle of the 1930's. The *Weetamoe* was deliberately sunk in 60 feet of water off Pine Cliff, after operating from 1902 until 1926.

The *Ascutney* served first as a steamer, but later was cut down and converted to gasoline before being used as a work boat. But her fate was the same as her sisters': cut up and sold for scrap.

This was the close of a golden era, when the living was slow and easy.

The Lady Woodsum *after her boiler explosion. Notice her new second deck and canopy.*

Left: The steamers Kearsarge *and* Armenia White *at the Lake Sunapee Station.*

BRADLEY'S BACKYARD RAILROAD

by Raymond A. Young

Jim Bradley (left) of Stonington, Conn., bought six old Pullman cars to preserve for posterity—along with lengths of track to put them on. But how do you get a railroad car into your backyard? And why do you want it there in the first place?

Take four generations of railroad men, then add to the family one of the founders of the reconstructed whaling village at Mystic Seaport. From these men, and in their tradition, comes Jim Bradley of Stonington, Connecticut, who is almost single-handedly trying to preserve part of the history of rail transportation.

Bradley's back yard, on the Connecticut shore, borders the New Haven Railroad's Shore Line tracks. And two hundred feet inland, six old railroad cars sit on tracks laid through an abandoned apple orchard. Those tracks weren't intended to be there when James MacNeill Whistler's father built the first railroad into Stonington. In fact, nowhere do they connect with a rail line. They're the result of Bradley's decision to preserve a few of the old cars that steadily click-clack to the scrap heap.

From sleepy Cheseborough Lane, Bradley's home looks pretty much like any other elm-shaded 200-year-old saltbox stuck on the fringes of Developmentville. But, from the tracks and the boats on the Sound, his cars attract a steady trickle of visitors all through the year. The surprising things, to most people who enter his yard, are that Bradley neither maintains a junkyard nor runs a commercial establishment, and that those cars are not sitting there merely because of eccentricity. Rail buffs, and many ordinary people who have ridden the New Haven, feel more pleasure than surprise when they see the cars and learn why they're only a few feet from Jim's tomato patch.

In the early 1960's, Bradley, from his back yard, watched the trains go by and noticed that many of the once-famous old Pullmans and other cars on the Shore Line run were now being hauled "deadhead" —that is, with a train but not part of it. They bore large "C" markings signifying "condemned." He learned that this didn't mean that the cars were simply going to be stored against the day when rail travel would rise again, but that they would eventually be broken up. Bradley saw them going the way of the whale ship, the biplane and the horse, so he thought things over and bought some. The idea was to preserve some of the plush relics of the age of steam for future generations in the plastic-lined jet age. So, between 1962 and the spring of 1964, he bought enough to make up a short train (minus the engine). Leading off are two ex-Pullmans converted to coaches, followed by an old club car, two more Pullmans and tailed off, appropriately enough, by a 1916 parlor car complete with observation platform.

Getting them in, however, was something of a problem. First, Bradley had to prepare his own sidings. As if that wasn't enough, he had to shift part of his proposed tracks after a neighbor objected to some of the cars being so close. It seems that part of Bradley's land extends beyond the Borough of Stonington and into the Town of Stonington, a separate jurisdiction, especially for zoning. So Jim had to keep everything in the Borough, next to his house rather than out beyond it.

Once the sidings were put in, the only thing left to do was bring in the cars. But how do you get a 60-foot-long Pullman into your back yard when there's no track leading in from the main line? Here Yankee ingenuity triumphed again, and Bradley had them brought in by *truck.*

Jim and the movers decided it would be wiser to bring the cars five miles up Route One from the freight siding in Mystic, even though he lives only about a mile by road from the Stonington spur. To get from the Stonington siding, one has to make two sharp curves and then go over a narrow highway bridge spanning the New Haven tracks.

All went well—if slowly—until the movers neared Bradley's front door, where the road ends. From there, they had to go cross-country.

"Mrs. Ainsworth, next door, said we could go through her stone wall if we put it back up again," Bradley says, "so that's what we did. Through there and right through the fields. If you need any railroad cars carried anywhere, Evans Brothers in West Hartford is just about the best in New England. They've probably got about the most experience at that sort of stuff lately."

Strangely enough, Bradley saw only one of his six cars actually trucked in. Duty called too loudly, for at the time he was a substitute clerk in the local post office. His bad luck was to have the mail come in heavy on each moving day. However, either the fates or the local powers that be in the post office were kind to him in May of 1964, and so he got the day off to watch the Stag Hound come through his wall on a

flatbed trailer behind a straining diesel truck.

For New Englanders, the Bradley collection is more than just a few old cars. One former Pullman, the old Stag Hound, is a relic of the now dead Old Colony passenger service down to the Cape. The Old Colony branch of the New Haven is still there, or at least the tracks are, but it's only used for freight service. But, near the end of its career as a passenger run, the Old Colony used the Stag Hound under a different guise.

Re-named the "South Shore Club," the former Pullman was a private chartered car, in which tired bankers, industrialists and other latter-day Brahmins commiserated on the way back from running New England's finances. Bradley hopes to renovate the car, now stripped down on the inside, into the type of parlor-lounge it was in 1930. This car, by the way, was built especially for the old Yankee Clipper express.

Its companion, the Great Republic, coupled to it, was another former parlor car once always identified with that train and with the bullet-shaped steam streamliners that ran from 1937 to the late 1940's.

Swedes, Australians, Frenchmen, Greeks and other foreigners have all wandered into the back lot to see Bradley's cars, but the crowning touch came with a party of three visitors all named John French. That is, John French Jr., III, and IV: the son, grandson and great-grandson of one of the brakemen on the very first Yankee Clipper. The old Great Republic was now a coach, but she was no stranger at all to John French Jr.

All this leads to the question of why a man would spend $2,000 for an old railway coach or Pullman, especially when he has to build what amounts to his own railroad yard and then pay $700 to have each car trucked in.

"The main idea," says Bradley,

His cars attract a steady trickle of visitors throughout the year. The surprising thing to most of them is that Bradley maintains neither a junk yard nor a commercial establishment.

Below: Jim Bradley seated on the steps of his 1916 parlor car.

"is to preserve these old cars. They may be a thing of the past before too much longer. Today, people go by automobile or plane. Remember when everybody rode the train, and people who went any distance went by Pullman? It probably won't be too much longer before long-distance travel and everything that went with it will be as dead as the old Stonington to New York steamboat line."

Bradley hopes that eventually he can turn his cars over to a non-profit historical foundation, similar to the Mystic Seaport a few miles away which originally was an old shipyard.

"The Seaport began with only three people," he points out. "My grandfather, Edward E. Bradley; Carl Cutler; and a fellow named Stillman." Looking around at his tracks through the meadow, he muses over those earlier men interested in another phase of vanished Americana.

"In those days, back when the Seaport was just getting started in the thirties, it wasn't even a full-time proposition. They left the key with a neighbor, so if they weren't around during the day any visitor who wanted to drop in and look around could do so. Gradually, people got interested in the old ships and marine trophies, and look what's there today."

Bradley eventually hopes to have enough cars to reconstruct a complete train, perhaps including a diner, baggage car, and railway post office car. "Time was when just about every express had an R.P.O.," he recalls. "Now most mail goes by truck and they have fewer and fewer clerks sorting it as it's carried along."

Although Bradley injured his hand on a power saw recently, he is continuing to fix his tracks and is making plans to tackle the insides of the cars needing renovation as time and money permit. And, in what was once a farmer's back lot,

they sit: Breslin Tower . . . Stag Hound . . . Great Republic . . . Forrest Hills . . . Fox Point . . . Phillinda . . . the proud cars with their names again blazoned in authentic New Haven colors, where two centuries of Cheseboroughs never thought a railroad track would go, long after the steel lifeline into Stonington has been abandoned.

"I'd like to see the old Yankee Clipper preserved as something other than just a few pictures, models or a plaque someplace," Bradley says. "It's a lot of work, but I think it's worth it."

Plenty of people in Stonington Village can (and do) brag about their ancestors. But if Jim Bradley's dream comes through and he manages to save his fragment of Railroad Avenue, *posterity* may well brag about *him*.

Behind the wheel, Richard Dickey in his 1900 Locomobile.

Ozzie Woodward and the marine engine of the Lady Woodsum (*see "The Ladies of Sunapee," page 233* .

Clifton Hills brought this boiler to supply steam for all the toy engines.

Richard Mitchell's 23-foot, wood-burning steam launch River Queen.

WELCOME TO ALL STEAM BUFFS
People from all walks of life meet once a year to watch the wheels go round, smell hot oil and hear the whistles blow.

by Richard M. Mitchell

The air was filled with the mellow tone of steam whistles and everyone was busy trying to visit with all the other steam fans that had gathered for the event, "New England Steam Launch And Model Meet."

This is a very informal group who love steam power in every form and the representation includes buffs who like steam automobiles, locomotives, whistles, model engines, and many with a great love for the old-time steam launch.

We have no club and no dues but get together at various places when some of us make the effort to get things started. Over the years we have gathered at such places as Nichols Machine Co. in Waltham, Mass., Bradley Franckum's summer home at Lake Winnipesaukee, Fred Semple's summer home on Lake Kezar in Lovell, Maine; Clark's Trading Post in Lincoln, N.H., Robert W. Merriam's Museum of Wireless in East Greenwich, Rhode Island, Phil and Jim Corbin's waterfront home in Salisbury, Mass., owners of the beautiful old steamboat *Sabino;* Steamtown in Bellows Falls, Vt., and on several occasions at my Connecticut River home in Hinsdale, N.H.

In 1950 the first group gathered at my house in Hinsdale to ride in my first steam launch, the *Lou-*

rick. At this time these pioneers could be counted on both hands and on later occasions we have counted over 200 in attendance.

Everyone goes to considerable effort to bring his favorite toys with him, which range from model steam engines you can hold in the palm of your hand to "toys" weighing 3,000 pounds. These arrive in trunks of cars, in pick-up trucks, on trailers and on occasion a beautiful Stanley Steamer will arrive on its own power.

Clifton Hills of West Swanzey, N.H. from time to time has furnished a portable boiler which was used to supply steam to model engines on a long wooden table built especially

Arthur Hughes making steam with this small boiler.

Phil Taylor and Fred Semple's traction engine.

for the occasion. One year Francis Breen of Wilton, N.H. made tender popcorn by steam power. Frederick Semple of Lovell, Maine and St. Louis brought to one of these meets a half-size steam traction engine that he had shipped out from Missouri. This wood-burning two-cylinder traction engine could either furnish stationary power or motive power. Its gleaming black boiler and shiny red moving parts would make any steam buff want to take it home.

At one meet, from Haverhill, Mass. Bob and Richard Dickey appeared with a 1900 Locomobile steamer which they drove up and down the road all day giving rides to friends. Although they had not had the time to restore it to its original beauty, it certainly was unique with its high wire wheels and leather dash. Attorney Paul Bourdon of Woodstock, Vt. sent a 1909 Stanley driven by Harland Whitcomb of North Springfield, Vt. This immaculate car, with its deep olive finish and white striping, was a showpiece in every sense of the word.

At one of our events Ozzie Woodward of Sutton, N.H. brought and operated the large two-cylinder marine engine that was built in 1876 for the Lake Sunapee steamboat *Lady Woodsum.* During the 1920s when this engine was no longer needed a hole was dug at the site of the old Lake Station and the engine rolled in and covered with dirt. Ozzie was on hand and saw this happen and 40 years later as an old man he dug up this engine and completely restored it to running condition. Over 50 of us steam fans stood and watched the little man nearly 80 years old work the condensation out of the cylinders with the large reversing lever. With the cylinders hot and free of water the engine came to life. A big cheer went up from the crowd and Ozzie was the happiest "kid" in New Hampshire on that day. All of his efforts were finally realized, and I am sure it must have brought back boyhood dreams of his many trips on the *Lady Woodsum.*

We have seen model tugs operated by the owner-builders, Willard Jopson of Glastonbury, Conn. and

Frank C. Fuegeman and his marine compound engine.

Interest centers around the "toys" on the table.

Harry Card of Plastow, N.H. and also a model ocean liner by Paul Huntington of Randolph, Mass. Some were radio controlled.

John Clement's steam launch *Aries* attended our Winnipesaukee meet, Fred Semple and Myron Kimball run their launches for our events in Maine, the Corbin's *Sabino* was crowded every trip at Salisbury, Mass. and the *River Queen* and Percy Stewart's *Gemini II* adds flavor on the Connecticut River. For those who like steam and antique radio the Merriams in Rhode Island is the place to go.

A cross reference of this group of steam buffs would produce a professor, doctor, Mississippi River tug boat engineer, railroad men, chemist, millionaire, businessmen, writers, photographers, a Navy Lieutenant, Mr. and Mrs. Meticulous, and the pop-eyed youngsters all rubbing shoulder to shoulder for the love of watching the wheels go round, smelling the hot oil and smoke, and hearing the whistles blow.

William Litchfield built this model tractor engine.

I COLLECT

To most of us, the idea of collecting steam locomotives is as absurd as an antique shop acquiring used space craft. In fact, when F. Nelson Blount, a Rhode Island Industrialist, started collecting iron horses ten years ago, quite a few of his associates thought he was buying so much scrap metal. Today, with a collection numbering over 70, Nelson has amassed the largest collection of steam locomotives in this country.

Nelson Blount, only 46, has spent the last several years attempting, in his words, "to preserve the steam era of America for future generations." In order to accomplish this objective, Nelson has rescued a narrow-gauge railroad and museum from extinction and created a standard-gauge operation featuring a live-steam railroad and general display of railroad equipment. New England travelers have long been familiar with the two-foot-gauge Edaville Railroad in South Carver, Massachusetts, but few realize that the cranberry bog railway owes its salvation from the junk dealer to Nelson. Steamtown U.S.A., Mr. Blount's other live-steam railroad and museum, is now located in North Walpole, New Hampshire and Bellows Falls, Vermont. Both railroads cater to tourists and feature the trademarks of the steam years: belching, barking steam trains with the whistles, bells, and, of course, the "All Aboard." The Edaville two-foot

The late F. Nelson Blount in the cab of Steamtown No. 127. At one point Mr. Blount considered giving away his valuable collection.

OLD STEAM ENGINES   by John Mason

railroad is made up of equipment from the famous Maine narrow-gauge railways, and the excursions wander along a six-mile trail in the cranberry bogs of Cape Cod. Steamtown U.S.A. features a 26-mile, round-trip excursion through both New Hampshire and Vermont countrysides. Right now, North Walpole, New Hampshire is the steam locomotive capital of the world with 35 steam locos on display.

What happened to the iron horse? Well, in the 1940's steam locomotives numbered in the tens of thousands: in 1963 (according to the American Association of Railroads) there were less than 15 operating steam locomotives. The diesel, with its antiseptic horn and boxcar look, replaced the steamer in one short decade. The iron horse dominated the first 120 years of railroading—then suddenly was delivered to the scrap dealer for dissection. To many enthusiasts, the disappearance of the steam locomotive was the end of romance in railroading. For Nelson Blount and many others, a steam locomotive is almost a living being, a machine with a soul.

Nelson grew up when steam was still king, and his courtship with steam railroading resulted in a book in 1938, *Along the Iron Trail,* which was published when Nelson was only 18. The co-author of the book, Fred Richardson, is now Blount's chief executive. Nelson let his interest in

railroading lie dormant as he attacked the world of business and quickly gained a considerable fortune. It is a good thing he did, for no one could think about preserving the steam locomotives without a source of revenue.

Mr. Blount started in the steam railroad business in 1955 when the builder and founder of the Edaville Railroad, Ellis D. Atwood, died in an oil burner explosion. Nelson came on the scene just as it appeared that the brief reprise given to the Maine two-footers was about to end in the junk yard. In addition to operating the "cranberry belt line," Nelson expanded the museum and the general facilities. Being in the steam preservation business, Nelson quickly became aware of the speed at which steam was disappearing in the country. Saving "big steam" presented a distinct problem at Edaville, which is seven miles from the nearest railroad. Undaunted, Nelson moved a locomotive, the Boston & Maine streamliner "Flying Yankee," and two coaches overland in what must have resulted in one of the largest moving bills in New England in some time. From this costly experience, the concept of a separate standard-gauge operation, Steamtown U.S.A., was born. After considering the various locations, Nelson negotiated the purchase of the abandoned North Walpole, New Hampshire roundhouse from the Boston & Maine Railroad.

Since 1960, the Steamtown U.S.A. project has suffered more changes of fortune than can be enumerated. A few months after arriving in North Walpole and being voted $25,000 by the people of Bellows Falls, Vermont to aid the cross-the-river project, the New Hampshire highway department indicated its intention of placing a road through the museum grounds. Where to now?

Then Nelson decided he would give away his valuable collection of steam locomotives to the State of New Hampshire. But, after two years of haggling, New Hampshire rejected the offer.

That was February 1963. By June, the Steamtown Foundation was born. The trustees of the Foundation include such individuals as former Governor of New Hampshire Lane Dwinell, William B. Murphy, President of the Campbell Soup Company, and E. Spencer Miller, President of the Maine Central Railroad. The nineteen Trustees are responsible for the museum portion of the Steamtown U.S.A. project. Nelson has been slowly turning his collection over to the Foundation.

The publicity concerning the Steamtown U.S.A. project quickly aroused the interest of 50 areas in more than 25 states. As of now, indications are that one portion of the locomotive collection will be in central Florida, and the other portion, hopefully, in the Bellows Falls, Ver-

In June of 1965 YANKEE Magazine ran this story on Nelson Blount and his Steamtown U.S.A. project. Since then, a great deal has happened . . .

247

mont area. Plans for the museum locations should materialize later this year.

Meanwhile, as the negotiations proceeded with the State of New Hampshire and the Foundation became a reality, Nelson finalized agreements with the State of Vermont to operate both freight and steam excursions on the defunct Rutland Railway between Bellows Falls, Vermont and Rutland. The new railroad, the Green Mountain Railroad, recently received its permission to operate from the Interstate Commerce Commission. Through all this confusion of events, Steamtown U.S.A. excursion trains traveled from place to place from 1961 to 1964. Steamtown U.S.A. operated excursions at Lake Sunapee in New Hampshire in 1961, Keene, New Hampshire in 1962, North Walpole, New Hampshire in 1963, and had its terminal in Bellows Falls, Vermont in 1964. For the first time, 1965 operations are planned in the same place in Bellows Falls.

The collection of locomotives in North Walpole, New Hampshire deserves a few comments. There are two "Hollywood" locomotives, and the entire Steamtown U.S.A. train appeared in the recent Otto Preminger production, "The Cardinal." The new addition this year, the Union Pacific "Big Boy," is billed as the "biggest locomotive on earth." It weighs over one million pounds.

What is the man behind the throttle of the Steamtown U.S.A. project like? Nelson Blount describes himself as having shifted from a youthful love of steam, to a love of money, to a love of railroading again, and finally a love of God! Surprised? Well, you are likely to hear Nelson repeat, "For we brought nothing into this world, and it is sure that we can carry nothing out" (I Timothy 6:7). In fact, Nelson will talk about his faith at the drop of his engineer's cap. It

all started, he says, after a near-fatal auto accident several years ago, in which his wife was involved. To those who had known him as a hard-bitten businessman, the change in him has seemed remarkable. Most of his friends laughed outright at his self-proclaimed faith. But Nelson has shifted a life that was centered around hobbies of fishing, stunt flying, and big game hunting, to a life of lay preaching and Christian testimony that crowd even the time spent on business matters. In fact, Nelson recently gave his Dublin, New Hampshire farm for use as a Christian preparatory school.

Nelson recently spoke on Don McNeil's "Breakfast Club" program. After relating the story of Steamtown U.S.A. and his new-found faith, Nelson was asked to sum up in ten seconds what was the most important decision in a man's religious life. He replied in effect: "I would ask that you examine your heart; and if you were to die today and have no assurance of salvation, I would ask you to receive Christ as your saviour, and study the Bible alone, carefully." (Romans 10:9, John 3:3.)

The final story on the Steamtown U.S.A. project and its progenitor, Nelson Blount, has yet to be written. Nelson is now donating a great deal of time to lay preaching and keeps the pace generally ascribed to the whirlwind businessman he once was. Nelson is confident that there is enough interest in steam railroading and the era that has recently passed to support the preservation of its most romantic symbol: the steam locomotive. With over 300,000 visitors expected this year at Steamtown U.S.A. and the Edaville Railroad, few can doubt his hopes.

A Corliss steam engine in action during a final demonstration run at the University of Massachusetts. This engine has subsequently been donated to Steamtown U.S.A.

It was fall,
the yellowing time of the year,
and Steamtown's trustees met with a heavy heart. . .

☐ ON A CLEAR EVENING ON THE LAST day of August 1967, F. Nelson Blount, industrialist, evangelist and railroad hobbyist par excellence, taxied off the abbreviated airstrip at Steamtown, Bellows Falls, Vermont, and was never again seen alive. His new plane was found wrecked in an overgrown meadow near Dublin, New Hampshire next day, and New England lost one of its most dynamic and colorful individuals.

For the remaining Trustees of Steamtown, it meant not only the loss of a dear friend but very probably the demise of Steamtown. Contractors switched off their bulldozers, and carpenters took final sawcuts on the woodwork of an uncompleted vehicle shed. It was fall, the yellowing time of the year, and Steamtown's Trustees met with a heavy heart. Fred Richardson, Nelson's friend since boyhood, summed up the dilemma. Although Blount was a clearly gifted money-maker, his skills were no longer available, and cut off in the prime of life, he had not been able to build up an endowment or provide financially for Steamtown's future. In fact when the accountants were first able to report, the tables were turned: Steamtown owed money to the estate.

By a freak turn of events, Nelson had picked a new chairman for the following year, feeling that he wanted to divide the responsibility and work load which he himself had carried almost singlehandedly. One week before his untimely death, he had persuaded Edgar Mead, a young Wall Street investment officer, to take on the title of Chairman with the duties of publicizing the project among financial cronies, while he, Blount, continued the intricate task of enhancing and operating the collection. The optimistic Blount anxiously scanned reports on ticket and museum patronage, which climbed from a few thousand persons annually to the tens of thousands. Picture then the sudden silence at Steamtown when this busy man's career was interrupted forever.

In accordance with the founder's wishes, Mead was nominated and elected to head up the Board, even though the job description had changed radically with Nelson's death. The new chairman and Fred Richardson, who retained his post as vice-chairman, sat down to contemplate the future. The problems essentially revolved around the fact that the museum was far from completed, and there was no money to move ahead. In fact, there was a real question as to whether Steamtown could pay for itself on a day-to-day basis.

The first objective was to place Steamtown on a businesslike footing, if indeed that were possible or even desirable. Many debts had to be paid off, and meanwhile the aging locomotives shivered under winter snow and had their paint seared by the hot summer sun. There was even a serious question as to whether the steam Green Mountain RR could survive, but it was bought by the employees and subsequently began to prosper. The Trustees considered various approaches, including hiring a full-time manager, leasing the property to outside operators, and trying to get by on a bootstrap basis until another Nelson Blount walked down the pike and rescued the situation. Unfortunately, Mead's firm had gone broke in 1968, wiping out his savings, so there was no hope from that source.

Nevertheless, Steamtown kept going, and it exhibited great will to survive. Small but helpful donations began to trickle in. Attendance began to rise. Old debts were gradually liquidated. And wonder of wonders, the collection continued to grow in size and scope as locomotives, cars and steam machinery were donated and brought in by various admirers. Occasionally cash can be raised by the sale of surplus equipment. "We sometimes don't like to do it," admits Mead, "but like other museums we have a duty to do the best by our really prize exhibits, and therefore we try to dispose of surplus coaches, fire engines and the like for cash or to acquire something we should have."

The second and perhaps more conspicuous objective is to find means to cover the engines. Each of them measures anywhere from 30 to 100 feet long, by about 10 feet wide, so Steamtown is talking of putting quite a bit of real estate under cover. On a tour of the vast Steamtown collection recently, Mead pointed out that numerous approaches are possible, all dependent on how much money can be made available. It could be a circular roundhouse, a simple brick or steel structure, or even a glass-covered trainshed. A professional architect and train fan by the name of Fielding L. Bowman designed a master plan that could be built on a step-by-step basis. Perhaps the dozen or so most valuable engines could be covered at the start.

Chairman Mead, who takes an active interest in all details of the restoration and preservation program, even to donning overalls on holidays, thinks that the collection is in the best condition since the start of Steamtown. The 1970 target is to paint or restore every engine on the active roster, a tall order, but now close to fulfillment. He plans movies, slide shows, working model railroads, and despite a host of complications, steam engines which actually operate for demonstration purposes. "We think that locomotives and steam engines are about as exciting as you can get," says Mead, "and the possibilities are really unlimited."

A Steamtown train attended the 1969 Centennial Golden Spike celebration in Utah.

Index